SYMBOLIC VIOLENCE

SYMBOLIC VIOLENCE
CONVERSATIONS WITH BOURDIEU

Michael Burawoy

DUKE UNIVERSITY PRESS
DURHAM AND LONDON
2019

Printed in the United States of America on acid-free paper ∞
Designed by Drew Sisk
Typeset in Garamond Premier Pro by Westchester Publishing Services

Library of Congress Cataloging-in-Publication Data
Names: Burawoy, Michael, author.
Title: Symbolic violence : conversations with Bourdieu / Michael Burawoy.
Description: Durham : Duke University Press, 2019. | Includes
    bibliographical references and index.
Identifiers: LCCN 2019006364 (print)
LCCN 2019009132 (ebook)
ISBN 9781478007173 (ebook)
ISBN 9781478005803 (hardcover : alk. paper)
ISBN 9781478006473 (pbk. : alk. paper)
Subjects: LCSH: Bourdieu, Pierre, 1930–2002—Criticism and
    interpretation. | Sociology—France—History—20th century. |
    Sociology—Philosophy.
Classification: LCC HM479.B68 (ebook) | LCC HM479.B68 B873 2019
    (print) | DDC 301.01—dc23
LC record available at https://lccn.loc.gov/2019006364

Cover art: Design and illustration by Drew Sisk

For Eriki

Every power to exert symbolic violence, i.e. every power which manages to impose meanings and to impose them as legitimate by concealing the power relations which are the basis of its force, adds its own specifically symbolic force to those power relations.

— PIERRE BOURDIEU AND JEAN-CLAUDE PASSERON,
REPRODUCTION IN EDUCATION, SOCIETY AND CULTURE

For symbolic power is that invisible power which can be exercised only with the complicity of those who do not want to know that they are subject to it or even that they themselves exercise it.

— PIERRE BOURDIEU, "ON SYMBOLIC POWER"

CONTENTS

ACKNOWLEDGMENTS

For many years I was a Bourdieu skeptic. Under pressure from Berkeley graduate students to take Bourdieu seriously, I enrolled in Loïc Wacquant's Bourdieu Boot Camp course in the spring of 2005. It opened my eyes to the ever-expanding panorama of Bourdieu's oeuvre. It was in the memos for that course that I first began imaginary conversations between Bourdieu and Marxism. It took me another four years to develop my own seminar on Bourdieu. Teaching is the greatest teacher of all. I owe an incalculable debt to the students who have passed through those seminars but also to the many audiences who have listened to and commented on the enactment of one or more of the conversations.

Let me mention just a few who have enhanced these conversations with conversations of their own—in Berkeley with Gabe Hetland, Zach Levenson, Mike Levien, Mara Loveman, Fareen Parvez, Gretchen Purser, Raka Ray, Adam Reich, Ofer Sharone, Mary Shi, Shelly Steward, Cihan Tuğal, and Loïc Wacquant; in Madison with Gay Seidman and Matt Nichter; in South Africa with Kate Alexander, Shireen Ally, Andries Bezuidenhout, Jackie Cock, Bridget Kenny, Oupa Lehoulere, Prishani Naidoo, Sonja Narunsky-Laden, Irma du Plessis, Vish Satgar, Jeremy Seekings, Ari Sitas, Tina Uys, Ahmed Veriava, Michelle Williams, Eric Worby, and, of course, Luli Callinicos and Eddie Webster; in France with Quentin Ravelli, Ugo Palheta, Anton Perdoncin, Aurore Koechlin, and Sebastian Carbonell. In addition, I was very fortunate to have two encouraging but anonymous reviewers for Duke University Press.

One friend and colleague, in particular—Jeff Sallaz—has been a source of continual support. When he was a graduate student at Berkeley he put up with my skepticism toward Bourdieu, and then he was generous enough to help me through my conversion. When I first went public with my conversations at the University of Wisconsin–Madison in 2008, he listened to the recordings in Arizona and sent me invaluable comments. When Ruy Braga heard of my Madison conversations he thought they would be important in Brazil for bridging the divide between Marxists and Bourdieusians. So he organized their translation and publication in Portuguese under the title *O marxismo encontra Bourdieu* (Marxism meets Bourdieu).

At the same time, Karl von Holdt, then head of the long-standing Society, Work and Politics Institute (SWOP) at the University of the Witwatersrand in Johannesburg, invited me to give lectures in 2010. He bravely accepted my proposal to extend the six Madison conversations to eight. I faced a stimulating and engaged audience, as there always is at Wits, but I had a problem convincing them of Bourdieu's importance. Karl saved the day, stepping in at the end of every lecture to show the relevance of Bourdieu's ideas for South Africa. His conversations about my conversations were duly published by Wits University Press in 2012 as *Conversations with Bourdieu: The Johannesburg Moment*. Since then there has been a French version in preparation by a group of young French sociologists.

The biggest challenge of all was to produce a US version—one suited to the US world of sociology. When Gisela Fosado of Duke University Press invited me to do just that, I set about revising the lectures once again and included two further conversations: one of Bourdieu with himself based on the book *La misère du monde* (*The Weight of the World*), and a prologue tracing my successive encounters with Bourdieu—from skepticism to conversion to engagement. Finally, I wrote a new conclusion that arose from an ongoing dialogue with my colleague Dylan Riley, in which I redeemed Bourdieu against Dylan's Marxist critique.

This all took much longer than expected, but now it is finished. Each conversation can be read by itself, but there is a cumulative theme that interrogates the underappreciated concept that lies at the heart of Bourdieu's writings—symbolic violence.

My lifelong friend and fellow Marxist Erik Wright had difficulty fathoming my Bourdieusian odyssey. While recognizing the enormous influence of Bourdieu's work, he had little patience for its arbitrary claims, its inconsistencies, and its obscurantist style. His skepticism notwithstanding, it was Erik who invited me to give those experimental Madison lectures in 2008. He helped me through them, commenting on them and orchestrating a lively conversation with the audience. He had a unique capacity to draw out what was salvageable, to separate the wheat from the chaff. For more than forty years I was blessed by his generosity—emotional, intellectual, social, and culinary—as we each took intersecting paths between sociology and Marxism. He left us while I was putting the finishing touches to this book. I miss him badly, as will so many others. He was an extraordinary human being. I dedicate this book to him and to the many adventures we had together.

ENCOUNTERING BOURDIEU

My path to Bourdieu has been long and arduous, strewn with skepticism and irritation. His sentences are long, his paragraphs riddles, his essays perplexing, his knowledge intimidating, his books exhausting, and his oeuvre sprawling. When I thought I understood, I wondered what was novel. Struggling with his texts, I experienced the full force of symbolic violence. Pierre Bourdieu is not only the great analyst of symbolic violence, but he is also the great perpetrator of symbolic violence, cowing us into believing that some great truth is hidden in his work. For many years I was anti-Bourdieu.

Taken individually his works are incomplete, but as the pieces came together I began to see the vision that arose from his theory of symbolic violence—a breathtaking panorama stretched before me. Only by putting symbolic violence and its ramifications into conversation with Marxists, those enemies from whom he borrowed so much, could I begin to grasp and then grapple with the ambition of his theoretical mosaic. The conversations began as a mischievous game, but little by little the pace quickened, turning into a trot and then into a headlong gallop as I became absorbed in my own game, obsessed with Bourdieusian theory. The Bourdieusian lens rose ever more powerful, ever more paradoxical, posing a new challenge to Marxism and giving a new meaning to sociology.

In the United States, as in other countries, sociologists grew increasingly receptive to Bourdieu over time, to the point that he is now one of the discipline's most-cited figures (Sallaz and Zavisca 2007). Critical sociologists of education such as Annette Lareau (1989) were among the first adopters, extending Bourdieu's early research on "schools as reproduction machines." As more of Bourdieu's books became available in English, scholars began discussing and applying his famous troika of interrelated concepts: habitus, capital, and field. The reproduction of class through education continued to be an arena for the fruitful application of these concepts (Lareau 2003; Kahn 2011). Cultural sociologists, in works such as Michèle Lamont's *Money, Morals, and Manners* (1994), considered how cultural capital creates symbolic boundaries in national contexts. Ethnographers began to use the concept of habitus to consider the interplay among structure, situation, and character (Wacquant 2004; Desmond 2007; Sallaz 2009). More recently, political and economic sociologists have adopted the concept of field to map and understand institutional space (Fligstein 2002; Eyal, Szelényi, and Townsley 1998; Medvetz 2012). As Bourdieu-inspired research in the US has developed, researchers increasingly work with multiple dimensions of Bourdieu's theoretical troika.

However, American sociologists rarely elaborate these concepts into a full-fledged account of symbolic violence—a form of domination that works through concealing itself from its agents, or, in Bourdieusian language, a form of domination that works through misrecognition. The central thesis of this book is that behind Bourdieu's ideas of habitus, capital, and field lies the deeper notion of symbolic violence, itself connected to reflexivity and public engagement. My goal is to unravel this underlying structure of Bourdieu's theory by bringing his different works into dialogue with others, especially Marxists, who have also struggled to understand political and cultural domination.

In putting Bourdieu into dialogue with the Marxist tradition, I am following what he demands but rarely undertook, that is, to locate himself in relation to his opponents, to those he repressed or dismissed. He advanced the tools of reflexivity, adept at reducing others to their social position or their place within fields, but he conveniently left himself out of the account. This prologue is my attempt to give some sense of how, as a Marxist, I struggled with Bourdieu and how these imagined conversations emerged from successive encounters with his work, positioning him in relation to an intellectual-political tradition he repudiated.

There are three phases to my encounter. The first was *skepticism*, when I found Bourdieu's work pretentious and unoriginal. The second was *conversion*, when I discovered the depth and scope of his corpus to be seductive and a worthy challenge to Marxism. In the third phase, *engagement*—the chapters of this book—I bring Bourdieu into conversation with the enemies he thought he had slayed: in particular, Marx, Gramsci, Fanon, Freire, and Beauvoir. In putting him into conversation with C. Wright

Mills, I show how the two converge, albeit from different national and historical worlds. I then dare to generate my own conversation with Bourdieu, based on my own ethnography, engaging his idea of the twofold truth of labor. This then leads me to put Bourdieu into conversation with himself, surfacing a fundamental contradiction that threads through his work, between the logic of theory and the logic of practice. In the conclusion I offer a provisional assessment of Bourdieu's oeuvre. But first, here in this prologue, I follow Bourdieu's prescription to reveal my modus operandi behind the opus operatum—the finished product that is the nine conversations.

SKEPTICISM

My first encounter with Pierre Bourdieu's work occurred when finishing my dissertation at the University of Chicago. It was 1976. My teacher, Adam Przeworski, gave me an obscure article to read: "Marriage Strategies as Strategies of Social Reproduction" (Bourdieu [1972] 1976), since reproduced in *The Bachelors' Ball* ([2002] 2008a). Here Bourdieu likens the kinship system in his home in the rural Béarn to a card game in which players are dealt a particular hand (a combination of daughters and sons of different ages) to consolidate or expand their patrimony. Heads of families develop matrimonial strategies in light of the uncertain outcome of fertility strategies. There were rules to be followed—some hard, some soft—but the game was, nonetheless, one of continual improvisation. For Przeworski, Bourdieu's article offered a rare game-theoretic model of social reproduction, analogous to the model he was developing for the strategies of political parties competing in elections under the limits defined by a changing class structure (Przeworski and Sprague 1986).

The reproduction of social structure through strategic action was akin to my own representation of life on the shop floor in south Chicago (Burawoy 1979). I and my fellow machine operators strategized over the deployment of the social and material resources at our command within the confines of the elaborate rules of "making out"—rules that were enforced by all, often against our individual economic interests. Orchestrated by the participants, so I argued, the game of "making out" simultaneously secured and obscured surplus labor, thereby mystifying the underlying class relations, a process that Bourdieu would call misrecognition. While I didn't appreciate it at the time, there was a strange convergence with Bourdieu's notion of symbolic violence—a game that seduces participants into spontaneous consent while concealing the social relations that are the conditions of its existence. Only many years later would I recognize similar arguments at the heart of Bourdieu's account of "double truth" in gift exchange, education, consumption, politics, and more.

Before that moment of epiphany, though, my skepticism toward Bourdieu's work only deepened with each encounter. If the first meeting with Bourdieu didn't leave a deep impression, the second encounter left me puzzled. This was the book that first made Bourdieu famous in the English-speaking world—his collaboration with Jean-Claude Passeron, *Reproduction in Education, Society and Culture* ([1970] 1977). Put off by the abstruse language, I shrugged my shoulders and wondered what the fuss was all about. The elaborate enumeration of propositions and sub-propositions that made up their "Foundations of a Theory of Symbolic Violence" led to the same conclusion as Bowles and Gintis's (1976) in their more accessible *Schooling in Capitalist America*, which had also just appeared: education reproduces class inequality. In their much discussed "correspondence principle," Bowles and Gintis show how working-class children go to working-class schools that lead to working-class jobs.

Yet there was an important difference. Bourdieu and Passeron argued that working-class kids went to "middle-class schools" and couldn't cope because they didn't possess the appropriate cultural capital. They retreated in shame, destined for the lower levels of the labor market. Still, the originality escaped me. Basil Bernstein (1975) had made the same argument far more convincingly—the "restricted" linguistic codes of working-class kids disadvantaged them in schools that favored the "elaborated" linguistic codes of children from the middle and upper classes. Paul Willis's *Learning to Labour* (1977) would make the even more interesting argument that working-class lads rebel against the school's middle-class culture, leading them to embrace working-class culture and to enthusiastically seek working-class jobs. By comparison *Reproduction* appeared formalistic in its exposition, wooden in its abstraction, and mechanical in its understanding of human behavior. It was functionalism at its worst. Or so it appeared.

But I had another axe to grind. As a follower of Louis Althusser (1969), Nicos Poulantzas (1973), Étienne Balibar (1977), Maurice Godelier (1972), and other Marxist structuralists, I found *Reproduction* to be an unacknowledged iteration of their arguments. Thus, Nicos Poulantzas's analysis of politics and the state and Étienne Balibar's analysis of law showed how formally neutral and "relatively autonomous" apparatuses, when placed alongside class inequality, reproduced that inequality and, moreover, did so in the name of universalism. The state and the law may not recognize class but in so doing all the more effectively reproduced class—an argument that Marx had made long ago in *On the Jewish Question*. In the same way, Bourdieu and Passeron showed how the arbitrary culture (presented as universal) of the "relatively autonomous" school reproduces arbitrary (class) domination. Yet they wrote the book as a critique of Marxism even as they appropriated some of its reigning ideas. In short, *Reproduction* was annoyingly pretentious, with few references to other works, while claiming an undeserved novelty.

During the 1980s Bourdieu's US audience widened as translations of his work multiplied and secondary commentaries began to emerge.[1] He was fast becoming a popular figure in Berkeley where I was teaching. So I began by studying what was becoming a canonical text, especially among anthropologists: *Outline of a Theory of Practice* ([1972] 1977)—an analysis of the Kabyle, a major ethnic group in Algeria. Yet I found his theory of practice uncannily similar to the one developed by the Manchester school of social anthropology. Particularly curious was his recapitulation of the work of my teacher in Zambia, Jaap van Velsen—a Dutchman and Oxford-trained lawyer, who became an anthropologist under the influence of Max Gluckman. Van Velsen's monograph, *The Politics of Kinship* (1964), based on fieldwork in Malawi in the 1950s, argued that social action cannot be represented as the execution of prescribed norms but rather should be regarded as the pursuit of interests through the strategic manipulation of competing norms. True to his training, van Velsen regarded legal contestation as a metaphor for society. It was a profound break with classical anthropology, which relied on informants who spun stories of symmetrical kinship patterns—idealized versions of their community in which the anthropologist was treated to what was supposed to happen rather than to what actually happened.

Van Velsen's methodology was to document a succession of contentious cases that showed marriage patterns to be the result of feuding villagers appealing to alternative norms. Dispensing with "informant anthropology," he focused on the discrepancy between how people actually behaved and how they claimed to behave. Bourdieu advanced a parallel theory of strategic action in his study of the Kabyle but without intensive observational material—he was not trained as an anthropologist and, according to Fanny Colonna (2009), he did not even take field notes. For Bourdieu, this body of literature from across the Channel was not worthy of serious engagement, even though his endnotes showed he was not unaware of the Manchester school and, in particular, of the work of van Velsen. If there was anything novel to Bourdieu's approach it was the concept of habitus, which, so it appeared to me, only added obfuscation to the Manchester school's situational analysis.

Outline of a Theory of Practice also suffered from an anthropological romanticism portraying the Kabyle as some isolated, self-reproducing "tribe" untouched by the colonial order, removed from the anticolonial struggle and disconnected from the wider economy. There is but one solitary reference to a migrant returning from France who enters the analysis because he violated the norms of gift exchange. In contrast, the second novelty of van Velsen's (1960) work, and of the Manchester school more generally, was to determine how village life was shaped by wider social, political, and economic "fields" in which it was embedded. Thus, van Velsen (1967) traced anomalous matrimonial strategies among the Lakeside Tonga to the absence of men who had migrated to the South African mines. This was the extended case method that explored microprocesses in their relation to a wider context. Ironically, given Bourdieu's later focus on "fields," *Outline of a Theory of Practice* showed no sign of any wider colonial field embedding the Kabyle. At the time, I was unaware of Bourdieu's other work on Algeria that put colonialism front and center, namely his study of urban working classes as well as the resettlement camps in the rural areas. Indeed, as others have pointed out, there is a certain variance within his Algerian writing (Goodman and Silverstein 2009), divided as it is between upholding the pristine "traditional" ethnic group and embracing a world-historical modernity brought to Algeria through colonialism. He would conceive of social change, as Bronisław Malinowski had done before him, as a clash of cultures. Once again, after reading *Outline of a Theory of Practice* I wondered, why all the fuss? It's been said before and better.

The next step on my Bourdieusian odyssey took me to Bourdieu's magnum opus, *Distinction*, first published in English in 1984. I took this monster of a book with me to Hungary where I was then working in the Lenin Steel Works. Every day, after coming off shift, I would write up my field notes and then turn to *Distinction*. His "correspondence" analysis didn't correspond to my experiences of working-class life in state socialist Hungary. But it was not the best of circumstances to appreciate such a complex, detailed, exhaustive, and exhausting interrogation of the French class structure through the lens of cultural consumption. Still I understood enough—or so I thought—to wonder whether Antonio Gramsci had not said it all before, but more succinctly and with more respect for the working class.

At the time I was not aware of Bourdieu's antipathy to Gramsci, but the idea that the cultural realm had a logic and coherence of its own, partially autonomous from the economic—a culture that emanated from the specific conditions of the dominant class but nonetheless claimed universality, seemed to be none other than a repackaging of Gramsci's notion of hegemonic ideology. Given that *Distinction* was written in 1979, when Gramsci's work was widely read in France, it was especially strange that his name appeared but once in this voluminous book. Moreover, the class structure that framed Bourdieu's analysis—dominant, new and old petty bourgeoisie, working class—seemed to fit Gramsci's class perspective (with the notable absence of the peasantry), as did the division of the dominant class into economic and cultural fractions. It was only a partial replication of Gramsci since the chapter on politics had no conception of civil society or class struggle. I would later consider Gramsci and Bourdieu as antagonists, but at the time *Distinction* did not live up to the claim that it represented some theoretical breakthrough in class analysis; rather it was a subliminal adaptation of Gramscian ideas.

Whether it was the analysis of education, or rural Africa, or cultural consumption in France, there seemed to be little that was original. How was it, then, that I should descend from an adamant skepticism into the madding crowd of Bourdieusian devotees?

CONVERSION

With the erosion of interest in Marxism and feminism in the 1990s, Berkeley graduate students were developing a taste for Bourdieu—especially with what was then called the cultural turn. They could have their materialist cake and eat it with cultural sophistication. Bourdieu was fast becoming the theorist of the moment, replacing Habermas and Foucault. Moreover, unlike these others, he was a sociologist with an enthusiasm for systematic empirical research. Graduate students were knocking on my door, demanding I take him more seriously. At Berkeley, qualifying examinations in sociology include a required field in social theory as well as two substantive fields. Students taking theory with me have to put the classics into conversation with a contemporary theorist of their choice. While the list of acceptable contemporary theorists was substantial, I drew the line at Bourdieu because, so I claimed, he had no theory of history or social change—his was a theory of social reproduction and not very original at that.[2]

As Bourdieu's light shone ever more brightly—especially after Loïc Wacquant joined the department in 1994 and Bourdieu's visit to the campus in 1995—the clamoring only became louder. So in 2003, I received a delegation of four graduate students—Sarah Gilman, Fareen Parvez, Xiuying Cheng, and Gretchen Purser—requesting a reading course on Bourdieu.

I agreed to meet with them every week and they could try to persuade me that my dismissive sentiments were a great mistake. I read their memos and listened to their presentations. Slowly but surely they introduced me to the astonishing breadth of Bourdieu's research. While still skeptical I did begin to realize how little I knew about Bourdieu's work and how limited was my understanding of his theory. The ice was melting but very slowly.

Toward the end of the semester Gretchen Purser, exasperated by my continuing obduracy, came into my office, excitedly pointing to two pages toward the end of *Pascalian Meditations* on the twofold truth of labor. Here Bourdieu appeared to have adopted my theory of the labor process. I say "appeared to" because there was no reference to my book *Manufacturing Consent*—where I had argued that capitalist work was organized to simultaneously secure and obscure surplus labor—although it had been earlier discussed and excerpted in Bourdieu's journal *Actes de la Recherche en Sciences Sociales*. In Bourdieu's rendition this became the "twofold truth of labor"—on the one side there was the experience of the workers and on the other side there was the social scientist's truth, structurally inaccessible to those workers. Bourdieu even invoked the idea of exploitation as being obscure to workers. It was strange to find this Marxist blip in an ocean of anti-Marxism and even more surprising that Bourdieu was writing about labor, never one of his central concerns (except, of course, as I was later to learn, in his Algerian writings).

There was another intriguing convergence in our interpretation of social structure as a game whose uncertainty secures participation while simultaneously obscuring the conditions and consequences of its reproduction. I didn't realize at the time that "securing and obscuring" was the essence of symbolic violence, the key to Bourdieu's approach to all social fields, to the wider society, and, indeed, to all societies throughout history! "Securing and obscuring"—though, of course, he never used those words—defined his methodology as well as his theory; it was the basis of the relation between the logic of practice and the logic of theory. Whereas I had confined the idea to the labor process, for Bourdieu symbolic violence seemed to be ubiquitous, to have no limits—a claim that I shall question in these conversations.

But I'm getting ahead of myself. Let's return to the narrative of my discovery of Bourdieu with those four graduate students. Their memos had piqued my curiosity—it appeared that I was clearly more Bourdieusian than I ever imagined. I clearly needed a remedial course in Bourdieu. I was in luck. In 2005, I asked my colleague Loïc Wacquant for permission to take his graduate seminar on Bourdieu. He agreed, but on the condition that I behave like any other graduate student, doing all the readings and submitting weekly memos. I happily complied. Loïc would deal the death blow to any remaining doubts I might have had about the importance of Bourdieu.

Professor Wacquant is exciting and excitable—a brilliant expositor and merciless critic. He had no compunction about terrorizing the class, including me. Here was an uncompromising defender of all things Bourdieu, as if the master were flawless and the only thing left to do was to put him to work, applying him to the problems of the world. Wacquant had thrust himself on Bourdieu, studied at his feet, and became a close collaborator, coauthor, official interpreter, and propagator-in-chief. In effect he became Bourdieu's adopted son, and he oversaw many of the English translations of Bourdieu's writings, acting as the guardian of Bourdieusian truth. I learned a vast amount from Wacquant, who, as he used to say, knew Bourdieu's works better than Bourdieu. This book is a product of his course.

Wacquant refers to his course on Bourdieu as a boot camp. Indeed, it was—involving a massive amount of reading and the writing of weekly memos. An entirely new vista opened up before me—Bourdieu's early work on Algeria, his enunciation of the craft of sociology, his successive accounts of the peasants of Béarn, his analysis of politics, of the academy, of literature and painting, his brilliant theoretical consummation in *Pascalian Meditations*, his dissection of the ruling class in *State Nobility*, not to mention his public interventions *On Television* and the weighty tome *The Weight of the World*.

It was in that class that I first interrogated Bourdieu's relation to the unmentioned elephant in the room—Marxism. I was struck by Bourdieu's increasing hostility to Marxism, yet his concepts—misrecognition, struggle, capital, field, *illusio*, class domination—exhibited an obvious Marxist provenance. You might say his hostility was the revenge of a habitus cultivated in the anticolonial struggles of Algeria and in the tumult of Paris of the 1960s, and animated by a resentment toward his Marxist colleagues who had dominated the École Normale Supérieure. He was living proof of his own theory that intellectual gladiators cannot escape the ideas of their opponents—they are often part of a common intellectual field with its own shared but unstated principles (*nomos*).

My weekly memos focused on the relation between the assigned Bourdieu reading and a prominent Marxist. Loïc would do a spot-check reading of our memos, randomly humiliating their authors in class. He especially enjoyed ridiculing my memos, and I must confess I enjoyed it too. It was exhilarating to be learning so much, especially from someone who never flinched from defending everything Bourdieu wrote. I became addicted to Bourdieu, treating his works as a field site, taking copious notes, trying to make sense of his corpus and its internal contradictions. It became a giant, moving jigsaw puzzle that I'm still piecing together.

The convergences between my own work and Bourdieu's—his notions of strategic action, symbolic violence, and misrecognition—that had earlier been the grounds for dismissing him as unoriginal, now became the basis of a fascination. Beyond that, I was now drawn to the meta-questions he poses around the meaning and importance of social science. He asks not only the fundamental question of social reproduction but also considered what is distinctive to and the basis of sociological knowledge as opposed to other social sciences. He applies his sociological theory to the world of sociology. He asks if and how it is possible and why it is necessary to transmit such sociological knowledge beyond the academy. These were the questions I had been grappling with for more than a decade.

Inspired by the engaged sociology I had discovered in South Africa and the dissident sociology I had found in Hungary, turned off by the instrumentalization of sociology in Russia, and perturbed by the hyper-professionalism of sociology in the US, I had become an advocate for public sociology. I had made it a theme in my department and then of the meetings of the American Sociological Association in 2004. Public sociology was one of four types—professional, policy, critical, and public—that emerged from posing two questions. First, sociology for whom? For the academic or the extra-academic audience? Second, sociology for what? As a means to an end (instrumental knowledge) or as a discussion of ends in themselves (reflexive knowledge)? The distinction between instrumental and reflexive knowledge ran through sociology from Max Weber to the Frankfurt School and Jürgen Habermas, while the distinction between sociology for an academic audience as opposed to sociology for an extra-academic audience paralleled Bourdieu's distinction between autonomous and heteronomous poles of a field. I identified with Bourdieu's (1975) concept of the scientific field as a terrain of contested domination.

I became especially intrigued by parallels in Bourdieu's thinking when I read his account of the genesis of the literary field in *Rules of Art* ([1992] 1996). In his rendition the literary field begins with an account of "bourgeois art" (i.e., art sponsored by the dominant classes). In the context of sociology, this is what I had called the *policy moment* in which sociology enters the service of various clients. The first rebellion against bourgeois literature comes from writers attentive to the life of subaltern classes—what Bourdieu calls "social art." Within sociology, this corresponds to *public sociology*, that is, a sociology which is accessible and accountable to diverse publics, and enters into a dialogue with such publics. The literary field, however, is only really constituted when writers separate themselves from both the patronage of bourgeois art and the affiliations of social art to constitute "art for art's sake" (i.e., "pure art" following its own autonomous principles). For sociology, too, this is the moment of its true birth, with the arrival of *professional sociology*, a sociology that is accountable to itself—that is, to a community of scholars developing their own research programs. Finally, the dynamism of the literary field comes from challenges to the consecrated artists (i.e., challenges from the avant-garde who seek to further the autonomy of art but also shift the principles upon which its autonomy rests). Today's consecrated art can be found in yesterday's avant-garde. Within sociology, this was the *critical moment* in which the assumptions of professional sociology are interrogated and transformed. New research programs emerge—at least in part—from the critical theorists of yesterday. I was sold.

Still, there are differences in our understanding of field. My notion of the academic field is organized around a division of labor, a division of knowledge-practices, arranged in a contested hierarchy, whereas Bourdieu's field has less of a structure, based as it is on the distribution of academic capital. Most interesting, however, are our divergent views of public sociology.[3] Bourdieu's theoretical writings are hostile to the idea of the "organic intellectual" connected to the dominated class. Instead he embraces what I call, following Gramsci, the "traditional intellectual"—discovering and then spreading truth from on high. Where I am inclined to give credence to the possibility of a direct and immediate connection between the intellectual and lay publics, Bourdieu considers the dominated as incapable of comprehending the conditions of their own subjugation. Whereas I see the dominated as possessing a kernel of "good sense" that can be elaborated in dialogue with intellectuals, Bourdieu regards them as suffering from an irrevocable "bad sense." For Bourdieu there can be no fruitful unmediated dialogue between intellectuals and publics: either intellectuals manipulate the dominated or the dominated deceive the intellectuals.

The sociologist has a privileged access to knowledge, dependent on a certain leisured existence called *skholè* unavailable to those who have to endure their subjugation. That was Bourdieu's theoretical stance, which he regularly deployed against Marxists or feminists who tried to establish connections to oppressed groups. And yet, at the same time, Bourdieu was never reluctant to present his views to different publics. Toward the end of his life, as he became ever more disenchanted with the direction of social and economic policy, he tried to link up with progressive social movements. Indeed, I would say Pierre Bourdieu became the greatest public sociologist of our time. Here then is the paradox: in theory the dominated are unreceptive to sociology; in practice Bourdieu had no compunction in haranguing them with his sociology. There is a curious gap between his theory and his practice that he never managed to close. This went to the heart of the contradiction that threads through Bourdieu's work and the conversations of this book.

ENGAGEMENT

I was hooked. On the one hand, Bourdieu was so close and, on the other hand, so far. This combination of nearness and distance led me to deeper explorations of the relationship between Bourdieu and Marxism. Few Marxists took Bourdieu seriously. My good friend Erik Wright couldn't understand my preoccupation as he considered Bourdieu's work hopelessly confused, imprecise, and contradictory. Still, knowing of my budding obsession, he proposed I visit his department at the University of Wisconsin–Madison to give a seminar on the work of Pierre Bourdieu. This was an offer I couldn't refuse. So, with some trepidation I agreed to give such a seminar in the spring of 2008. I had a year and a half to prepare. As the appointed semester approached it became clear that this would be no ordinary seminar but a series of public lectures, pitting Marxism against Bourdieu.

How to approach the most influential sociologist of our era, whose work ranges over philosophy, methodology, literature, art, education, politics, sport, journalism, colonialism, political economy, education, intellectuals, and much more? A sociologist who is able to encompass such diverse research within an overarching framework? I wanted to engage him critically with the armory of Marxism, developing the memos I had begun in Wacquant's course. What better place to do this than the Havens Center in Madison that had, for twenty-five years, hosted Left intellectuals from all over the world, including Bourdieu himself? Taking a leaf out of Bourdieu's methodology, I claimed that he could only be understood by putting him into conversation with his putative antagonists. I chose a succession of Marxists who were centrally concerned with the question of cultural domination—starting with Marx himself and moving on to Gramsci, Fanon, Beauvoir, and Mills. Bourdieu ignored these theorists, although all of them dealt with the question of cultural domination that lies at the center of his interest in symbolic violence. He repressed the convergences and divergences that made these conversations so interesting.

Without doubt Marx himself was cognizant of the power of ideological and political superstructures to absorb and contain class struggle. But apart from some very concrete analyses of different political conjunctures and a few memorable and tantalizing aphorisms, Marx had little to offer by way of sustained theory. He was, after all, a theorist of capitalism as an economic system whose reproduction brought about its own downfall. It is interesting that *Capital* was the model Bourdieu took as the basis for his own theory of cultural and political fields.

My engagement with Bourdieu, therefore, centered around the Italian Marxist Antonio Gramsci, who took Marx's hints seriously and became a theorist of superstructures. His notion of hegemony is the Marxist counterpart to Bourdieu's symbolic violence, but with a dramatic difference. If symbolic violence was domination not understood as such, hegemony was the opposite—domination understood as such. The one called for misrecognition, the other for consent. I explored these parallel concepts in a conversation between Bourdieu and Gramsci and then, in another conversation, I puzzled over my own research into the labor process and its political regulation, which was inspired by Gramsci's notion of hegemony but actually looked more like Bourdieu's symbolic violence. At least, that was the case for my ethnographic study of work in the US, but not so for my studies of work in socialist Hungary, where exploitation and domination were transparent. I tried, thereby, to put historical and geographical limits on the relevance of symbolic violence.

Frantz Fanon is an especially interesting figure, as he moved from France to Algeria at the same time as Bourdieu. Like Bourdieu he too would contrast colonial violence with racial oppression in France. Written in 1952, *Black Skin, White Masks* describes the symbolic violence French society wrought on immigrants from the colonies, but it was his analysis of colonialism in *The Wretched of the Earth* ([1961] 1963) that made him famous throughout Africa. Bourdieu regarded him as politically irresponsible, not least for his attachment to the National Liberation Front and for inflaming the radical opposition to French colonialism. Similarly, Bourdieu treated Simone de Beauvoir with contempt, as a dutiful woman dominated by her subjection to the despised Sartre. Yet his treatment of masculine domination as symbolic violence proved to be a pale imitation of *The Second Sex* ([1949] 1989). Finally, I took up C. Wright Mills's skeptical outlook on Marxism to make him Bourdieu's counterpart in the US. The extraordinary parallels between these two sociologists, despite living in different eras and different countries, served to underline their common indebtedness to and divergence from Marxism.

In April 2008 I gave the six Havens lectures under the title "Conversations with Bourdieu" to a skeptical but responsive audience. Hearing about these lectures, Ruy Braga proposed to have them translated into Portuguese and published in Brazil. Given the strength, albeit declining, of Marxism and the popularity of Bourdieu's sociology in Brazil, this seemed to be the perfect trial balloon. They were published in 2010 as *O marxismo encontra Bourdieu* (Marxism meets Bourdieu) with a substantial introduction written by Braga himself that pointed to what was novel—a critical dialogue between Marxism and critical sociology. While Marxists saw Bourdieu as an ally, Bourdieusians tended to regard Marxism as the defeated enemy, yet, as reviews suggested, here was a way for Marxists and Bourdieusians to recognize not just their antagonisms but also their complementarities.

That same year, 2010, Karl von Holdt invited me to give lectures at the University of the Witwatersrand. I proposed to revise the lectures for a very different audience, adding an introductory lecture and one on Paulo Freire—a gesture to Brazilian social science and a Marxist response to Bourdieu's bleak vision of education's role in social reproduction.

The South African lectures were clearly going to be more difficult than the ones in Madison. Apart from such notable exceptions as the sociologists Ari Sitas and Jeremy Seekings and researchers in the field of education, Bourdieu was not so well known among South Africans. At the same time, Marxism was far more entrenched in South Africa, so I would have to convince a skeptical audience that this French sociologist was worth taking seriously. Adopting a critical approach might leave the audience baffled as to why they should bother with this northern theorist. It was not enough to point to his importance in the north; I had to show that Bourdieu could shed light on the problems facing South Africa. It was my intention to put Bourdieu to work in the local scene but—for all my long interest in South Africa and its sociology—I quickly realized I was not up to the task. I was saved by Karl von Holdt himself, who was developing a fast-growing taste for Bourdieu. After each lecture he delivered a fascinating commentary on the South African relevance of the debate between Marxism and Bourdieu.

On the face of it Bourdieu's symbolic order does not fit well with South African reality, but Karl artfully posed the question of the relation between symbolic and material violence—how symbolic violence can engender violent protest involving killings, burnings, and destruction of public property; how apartheid inculcated not a habitus of submission but a habitus of defiance that lives on in the new South Africa; how missionary education, far from reproducing the colonial order, instilled aspirations and conferred symbolic resources that fueled the leaders of the anti-apartheid struggles, including Nelson Mandela and Oliver Tambo. Karl showed how northern theory can travel south, but in the process it takes on new meaning and even transforms itself in the new setting. We published my lectures and Karl's responses to them as *Conversations with Bourdieu: The Johannesburg Moment* (2012).

BOURDIEU IN THE UNITED STATES

Karl welcomed Bourdieu back to Africa, where he had begun his sociological sojourn half a century earlier. The African embrace of Bourdieu, therefore, was perhaps less surprising than the appeal of Bourdieu in the US. In his own empirical research and theoretical legacies, Bourdieu barely recognized any other country but France and Algeria. Yet somehow Bourdieu's work has transcended national boundaries to give sociology a new raison d'être in the US as well as in many other corners of the world. How has this been possible?

Undoubtedly, one attraction of Bourdieu is the conceptual toolkit of capital, field, and habitus. This is not a theory but a set of framing concepts that can be applied to almost any problem, giving mundane research an identity and appearance of theoretical sophistication. Deploying this toolkit effectively circumvents the thorny issues that lie at the heart of the theory of symbolic violence. It appeals to the empiricist tendencies in US sociology.

Still, there have been theoretical traditions in the US, and none so strong as the structural functionalism of the 1950s associated with the name of Talcott Parsons, who, in his time, enjoyed a similar reach and influence across disciplines and national boundaries as Bourdieu. Like Bourdieu, Parsons was hard to comprehend; like Bourdieu, he developed his own conceptual apparatus and language; like Bourdieu, his critique of Marx warranted the dismissal of the entire Marxist tradition; like Bourdieu's concept of symbolic violence, Parsons's notion of "value consensus" explained the coherence and endurance of society.

My first conversation for this US edition is, therefore, between Parsons and Bourdieu—how, amid their obvious divergences, they offer some surprising convergences. If the Achilles heel of Parsons's research program is the deepening conflicts in US society, the Achilles heel of Bourdieu's is the capacity of subordinate groups to see through symbolic violence and comprehend their subjugation. In a new conversation written for this edition, I have wrestled with *The Weight of the World*—a rich collection of essays based on in-depth interviews conducted by Bourdieu and his colleagues with men and women who were living in the bowels of French society. The interpretive essays that introduce each interview are curious in that there is little sign of symbolic violence or even the derivative concepts of habitus and capital. So, in this conversation I play Bourdieu against Bourdieu, highlighting contradictions in his own work, exploring the conditions for the disruption of symbolic violence. There are, I suggest, two Bourdieus: the man of theory expounding on the depth of misrecognition and the man of practice giving credence to the perspectives of the dominated.

My colleague Dylan Riley provides an answer to this paradox by rejecting Bourdieu's theory in favor of his practice. Bourdieu's appeal, argues Riley (2017), lies not in its science, a deeply flawed project, but as an ersatz politics for critically minded scholars who are removed from the experiences and struggles of the popular classes. He argues that when it comes to understanding social class, social reproduction, and social change, Bourdieu's work is so riddled with contradictions and anomalies that its appeal must lie elsewhere. Bourdieu's theory, he claims, resonates with the world of privileged academics, pursuing careers in the elite university, competing for distinction and academic recognition. In my conversation with Riley (Burawoy 2018a) I recuperate Bourdieu against Marxist demolition, suggesting that Riley misrecognizes Bourdieu's originality that revolves around the troika of symbolic violence, reflexivity, and public engagement. I resolve the paradox of two Bourdieus, the disjuncture between his science and his politics, by restoring their unity in an ambitious project—intellectuals on the road to class power—a project that can only be sustained, however, by Bourdieu's misrecognition of capitalism.

Riley's contribution may be a polemical overreaching in its demolition of Bourdieu, but he is onto something important, namely the source of Bourdieu's extraordinary appeal in his affirmation of the intellectual. Bourdieu speaks to the helplessness of the critical social scientist in a world that appears to be ineluctably shifting rightward. That is one aspect of his appeal; the other aspect is his compelling refutation of Marxism. Bourdieu denies Marxism's fundamental category, namely, capitalism, while reinventing and generalizing the idea of "capital." He denies Marxism's theory of history and in the same breath denies its theory of the future, marginalizing class struggles in favor of classification struggles. Finally, Bourdieu abandons comparative methodology that allows Marxism to investigate different societies, past, present, and future. It is remarkable that after all this demolition work, there is still something left for sociologists to work with, but there is—his general concepts on the one side and his theory of symbolic violence on the other. Denying subaltern classes any possible understanding of the conditions of subjugation is the ultimate challenge to Marxism, but Bourdieu accomplishes this with a critical eye toward domination. In these conversations I take all these challenges seriously and mount a response from the side of Marxism.

In his article "Passport to Duke" (1997), Bourdieu scolds American literary scholars for misreading his work as embracing postmodern thinking. Their confusion or "allodoxia" arises because Americans fail to recognize the specific (French) academic field in which his work arose, to which it is a response, and which gives it meaning. He warns against the circulation of texts as though they were "isolated asteroids," detached from their origins, which can be deployed at will to support whatever argument is the flavor of the month. It is an open question whether I have avoided this same fate, but in creating these conversations I have tried to resist the temptation of unmediated appropriation and instant application that diminish Bourdieu's contributions to social theory.

1

SOCIOLOGY IS
A COMBAT SPORT
From Parsons to Bourdieu

> I often say sociology is a combat sport, a means of self-defense. Basically, you use it to defend yourself, without having the right to use it for unfair attacks.
> — BOURDIEU

These sentences are taken from *La sociologie est un sport du combat*, a popular film produced by Pierre Carles in 2001 about the life of Pierre Bourdieu, featuring him at demonstrations, in interviews about masculine domination, in humorous banter with his assistants, in an informal research seminar with his colleagues, in the lecture hall, on television debating with Günter Grass, and, in a final dramatic scene, facing the wrath of Beur youth from a Paris banlieu. We see Bourdieu voicing opposition to government policies, especially neoliberalism, but we also see him on the defensive—stumbling to explain sociology in simple terms to a confused interviewer, or sweating under pressure of interrogation, or intensely nervous when he has to speak in English.

Is this sociology as a combat sport? If so, where are the combatants? We see Bourdieu, but where is the opposition? Where are the other contestants? It's like watching a boxing match with only one boxer. No wonder he can talk of sociology as "self-defense"; no wonder he can seem so innocent and charming with the opposition absent. Where is the reviled Bourdieu, "the sociological terrorist of the Left," "the cult leader," "the intellectual dictator"? Even the Spanish feminist interviewing him about masculine domination lets him off the hook when it comes to his own masculinity—at which point he leans on Virginia Woolf—or when he claims to understand masculine domination better than women do. Significantly, the only time he comes under hostile fire is when young Beurs tell him they are not interested in his disquisitions on oppression—after all, they know they are oppressed—whereupon Bourdieu goes on a tirade against their anti-intellectualism. It seems he has nothing to offer them but words. Here, only at the end of the film, are the first signs of combat.

This absent combat with the absent enemy is not peculiar to the film. Throughout Bourdieu's writings, combatants are slain off-stage with no more than a fleeting appearance in front of the readership. Sociologists, economists, and philosophers come and go like puppets, dismissed with barely a sentence or two. What sort of combat sport is this? He says sociology shouldn't be used for unfair attacks, but how fair is it to tie up the enemy in a corner and with one punch knock them out of the ring? What is this combat without combat? I've searched through Bourdieu's writings to find elaborations of "sociology as a combat sport" but to no avail. Minimally, if this is a true combat sport, there should be rules of play that allow all contestants to show their abilities—their strengths as well as their weaknesses. And the rules should apply equally to all. There is not much evidence of fair play either in the film or in his writings.

The purpose of these conversations, then, is to restore at least a small band of combatants who, broadly speaking, are Marxist in orientation. They are there in Bourdieu's "practical sense" beneath consciousness, circulating in the depths of his habitus and only rarely surfacing in an explicit and verbal form. To attempt such a restoration is to counter the symbolic violence of their erasure with a symbolic violence of my own. It involves a certain intellectual combat. Still, I restore these Marxists not so much to issue Bourdieu with a knockout blow (as if that were even possible), but rather to orchestrate a conversation in which each learns about the other to better understand the self. In this opening conversation, however, I will probe the idea of sociology as a combat sport as it applies to Bourdieu's own practice, leading to his contradictory postures in academic and non-academic fields. I will suggest that a better model than combat is the more open and gentle one of conversation—a conversation between Bourdieu the academic theorist and Bourdieu the public intellectual—if we are to unravel the paradoxes of his life's work.

COMBAT VS. CONSENSUS

I am struck by the translation of the film's title into English: *La sociologie est un sport du combat* becomes *Sociology Is a Martial Art*. There is no warrant for translating *combat sport* as *martial art*. Both words exist in French as they do in English, so why this deliberate mistranslation? I can only conjecture that this is a maneuver to attract an English-speaking—and especially an American—audience for whom labeling an academic discipline as a combat sport would discredit both sociology and the film. It does not suit the sensibility of US academics and would have an effect opposite to the one in France, where academics do indeed seem to relish the idea of combat, where struggles are held out in the open, public arena, and where the academic world merges with the public world. In the United States, on the other hand, the academic world is at once more insulated from the public sphere and also more professional. It is dominated by ideologies of consensus formation and peer review. Here, *martial art*, with its connotations of refinement and science, is a more appropriate and appealing metaphor. Academic exchange operates not according to explicit rules of combat but with unspoken understandings based on a specific culture of engagement. Thus, French-trained Michèle Lamont (2009) is fascinated by the "North American" culture of peer assessment based on trust and mutual respect, just as ignominy befalls Loïc Wacquant when he displays French-style combat in the US academy.[1]

We can better understand Bourdieu's milieu and the work he produced by comparing him to Talcott Parsons, who was born and bred American. Both were the most influential world sociologists of their time. Both conquered their national fields of sociology from the summit of their respective academies—Harvard and the Collège de France. Both reshaped the discipline around the world and in their homelands. Both exerted influence on a variety of disciplines beyond their own. Both wrote in difficult prose that only seemed to magnify their appeal. Both generated waves of reaction and critique, dismissal and contempt, as well as ardent disciples.

The parallels extend to the substance of their social theory. Thus, both were primarily interested in the problem of social order, which they tackled with parallel, functionalist schemes. Parsons focuses on the institutionalization and internalization of common values, whereas Bourdieu explores the constitution of habitus, an enduring set of dispositions acquired in early life and then later modified through participation in multiple fields. Thus, socialization figured equally prominently in both their accounts of social order. Both had difficulty developing an adequate theory of social change, and their thin theories of history relied on the idea of spontaneous differentiation—in Parsons the rise of subsystems of action and in Bourdieu the emergence of differentiated fields. Neither saw the future as very different from the present: revolutionary change was not part of their conceptual repertoire.

Moreover, both were deeply committed to sociology as a science. Indeed, both conceived of sociology as the queen of the social sciences— other disciplines were a special case of or subordinate to sociology. At the same time, both drew heavily on the vocabulary and ideas of the discipline of economics, just as both were hostile to its reductionism. Despite their claims to universalism, their theories were distinctively products of the society they theorized, in the one case the pre-1960s United States and in the other post-1960s France. They were both masters of the art of universalizing the particular—the particular being the social structure of their own countries as they saw it—as neither took comparative research seriously.

But here the parallels cease. If Parsons's social order rested on *value consensus* that prevented a brutish Hobbesian war of all against all, then Bourdieu's rested on *symbolic violence* that secured silent and unconscious submission. Where Parsons endorsed value consensus as freedom, Bourdieu condemned symbolic violence as debilitating to both the dominant and the dominated. Accordingly, if Parsons was rather complacent about the world in which he lived, Bourdieu was consistently critical of it. If Parsons stood aloof from society, in the final analysis, Bourdieu was always deeply engaged with it. Where Parsons saw science and society as based on consensus, Bourdieu took an agonistic view, seeing society as a field of contestation. Science in particular was an arena of competition and struggle through which truth emerges. Where Parsons brushed aside intellectual and political antagonisms that divided the academy, Bourdieu made them definitive of the academic field and of scientific progress.

Their divergence is most clear in the way they built their theoretical frameworks. Parsons's (1937) voluntaristic theory of action, which, like Bourdieu, sought to transcend the dichotomy of structure and agency, laid claim to a grand synthesis of four canonical thinkers—Durkheim, Weber, Marshall, and Pareto. Later, he would incorporate Freud. Parsons not only basked in the glory of canonical figures; he actually created the canon himself by examining their writings in meticulous detail. He brought Durkheim and Weber to the center of the US sociological tradition.[2] He is not alone in building on so-called founders: Jürgen Habermas (1984) follows a similar strategy in his two-volume theory of communicative action, building on the work of Marx, Weber, Durkheim, Simmel, Lukács, and the Frankfurt School, as well as Talcott Parsons himself.

Bourdieu, by contrast, took a dismissive stance toward his competitors and forerunners, largely silencing the giants upon whose shoulders he perched. There is rarely a systematic engagement with any sociological work other than his own. Marx, Weber, Durkheim, Lévi-Strauss, Pascal, and others lurk in his writings, but he refers to them only in passing, as if to do otherwise might minimize his own contributions. He presents himself as the author of his own tradition, committing the sin he accuses other intellectuals of, namely their adhesion to the "charismatic ideology" of autonomous "creation," forgetting that the creator too has to be created (Bourdieu [1992] 1996, 167). In re-creating sociology, Bourdieu fashioned himself after Flaubert, whom he regarded as the creator of the French literary field because he had such a subtle command of its elementary forces. If sociology is a combat sport, then Bourdieu was its grand master, so effective that the combat becomes invisible, taking place backstage.

Parsons was the great synthesizer and systematizer, ironing out differences and contradictions, thereby generating his ever more elaborate architecture of structural functionalism with its own concepts and vocabulary, liable to collapse under its own weight. Bourdieu, by contrast, refused all systematization. His works are incomplete, full of fissures and paradoxes, a labyrinth that provides for endless discussion, elaboration, and critique. As a gladiator he was the expert at defensive maneuvers to elude his assailants. Whereas Parsons specialized in grand theory, at home with rarefied abstractions, far removed from the concrete, everyday world, Bourdieu rarely wrote without empirical reference. For all its difficulty—its long and winding sentences that continually double back and qualify themselves—Bourdieu's theorizing is deeply engaged with lived experience and follows rich research agendas. Where Parsons's architectonic scheme disappeared without so much as a whimper once its founder passed away, its brittle foundations having lost touch with the world, Bourdieu's ideas outlive their author and are far more flexible in their wrestling with an ever-changing reality.

Unlike Parsons—and more like Marx, Weber, and Durkheim— Bourdieu was steeped in the history of philosophy and, like them, his works are relentlessly empirical, ranging from the study of photography, painting, literature, and sport to the analysis of contemporary stratification, education, the state, and language. His writings straddle sociology and anthropology, including studies of peasant family strategies in the villages of the Béarn, where he grew up, as well as his books on Algeria that dwelt on the social order of the Kabyle, written during the period of anticolonial struggles and marking the beginning of his research career. His methods range from sophisticated statistical analysis to in-depth interviewing and participant observation. His metatheoretical innovations, relentlessly applied to different historical contexts and different spheres of society, revolve around his notions of field, capital, and habitus. Even though Parsons was well versed in anthropology, economics, and psychology as well as sociology, in the end even he cannot compete with Bourdieu's originality or scope, nor with his influence across a range of disciplines in the social sciences and humanities.

Parsons was like a vacuum cleaner, sucking in everything that came into his sphere of influence, whereas Bourdieu was more like a mop, pushing backward and forward in all directions. The imagery of the one was consensus building; the imagery of the other was combat; their divergence is reflected in the social theories they developed. Let me turn to that link between the substance of Bourdieu's social theory and sociology as a combat sport.

UNMASKING DOMINATION

Symbolic violence is at the center of Bourdieu's sociology. It is a domination that is not recognized as such, either because it is taken for granted (naturalized) or because it is misrecognized—i.e., recognized as something other than domination. The prototype of symbolic violence is masculine domination. According to Bourdieu, it is not generally perceived as such, so deeply is it inscribed in the habitus of both men and women. He defines habitus—a central concept in his thinking—as a "durably installed generative principle of regulated improvisations," producing "practices which tend to reproduce the regularities immanent in the objective conditions of the production of their generative principle" (Bourdieu [1972] 1977, 78). We are thus like fish swimming in water, unaware of the symbolic violence that pervades our lives, except that the water is not just outside us but also inside us. Drawing on his fieldwork among the Kabyle, Bourdieu ([1998] 2001) describes the way gender domination is inscribed in daily practices, in the architecture of houses and in the division of labor, so that it appears as natural as the weather.

In modern society, education provides one of Bourdieu's most important examples of symbolic violence (Bourdieu and Passeron [1970] 1977, [1964] 1979). The school appears as a relatively autonomous institution following universal rules and eliciting the active participation of teachers and students in the acquisition of labor market credentials. This meritocratic order obscures the bias of the school, whose pedagogy favors those middle- and upper-class students endowed with cultural capital (i.e., those already equipped with the capacity to appropriate mental and abstract teaching—the symbolic goods on offer). The school advantages the dominant classes and reproduces their domination through the participation of the dominated, a participation that holds out the possibility of upward mobility, thereby obscuring the class domination that it reproduces as its basis.

More generally, the dominant classes obscure their domination behind the distinction they display in the cultural sphere (Bourdieu [1979] 1984). Their familiarity with high culture—what Bourdieu calls legitimate culture—is conventionally viewed as a gift of the individual rather than an attribute of their class, acquired through socialization. The dominated are ashamed of their inadequate appreciation of legitimate culture, sometimes pretending to claim knowledge of it that they don't have and endowing it with a prestige that obscures its basis in class-determined cultural capital. Dominated cultures are just that—dominated by material necessity, on the one hand, and by the distinction of legitimate culture, on the other.

We will have reason to interrogate these claims in later conversations, but for now I am concerned with the implications of symbolic violence for Bourdieu's conception of sociology as a combat sport. If society is held together by symbolic violence that misrecognizes the grounds of class domination or gives it false legitimacy, then the task of the sociologist is to unmask the true function of the symbolic world and reveal the domination it hides. This, however, proves to be a most difficult task—symbolic violence is rooted in the habitus, that is, in dispositions that lie deep in the unconscious, inculcated from childhood onward. Even leaving aside the question of habitus, Bourdieu maintained that the dominant classes have no interest in unmasking domination, whereas the dominated do not have the capacity—the instruments of sociological knowledge—to see through domination:

> The sociologist's misfortune is that, most of the time, the people who have the technical means of appropriating what he says have no wish to appropriate it, no *interest* in appropriating it, and even have powerful interests in refusing it (so that some people who are very competent in other respects may reveal themselves to be quite obtuse as regards sociology), whereas those who would have an interest in appropriating it do not have the instruments for appro-

priation (theoretical culture etc.). Sociological discourse arouses *resistances* that are quite analogous in their logic and their manifestations to those encountered by psychoanalytical discourse. (Bourdieu [1984] 1993a, 23)

From a theoretical point of view, therefore, dislodging symbolic violence would seem to be virtually impossible, requiring "a thoroughgoing process of countertraining, involving repeated exercises" (Bourdieu [1997] 2000, 172), but this never deterred Bourdieu from combating it wherever and whenever he could.

COMBAT IN THE PUBLIC SPHERE

From early on, Bourdieu's scholarly career went hand in hand with public engagement. Formative of his outlook on sociology and politics was his immersion from 1955 to 1960 in the Algerian war, first enlisted in the army and then as an assistant professor at the University of Algiers. It was here that he turned from philosophy, which seemed so remote from the Algerian experience, to ethnology, or what we might call a sociology of everyday life. His earliest writings displayed a fascination with the diverse traditions of the Algerian people, but it was not long before he broached the question of the day—the question of liberation—and how colonialism was creating struggles that were transforming the cultural and political aspirations of the colonized.

On his return to France, he would write blistering articles on the violence of colonialism. Soon, however, his sociological research led him away from brutal colonial violence to an analysis of symbolic violence, in particular the way education reproduced class domination. His two books on education, both written with Jean-Claude Passeron, especially the second and better known, *Reproduction in Education, Society and Culture* ([1970] 1977), became controversial for their uncompromising refusal to entertain the view that education can reform society. In the 1970s, rather than write of burgeoning social movements from below, as other sociologists, such as Alain Touraine, were doing, Bourdieu examined the way language and political science conspired to dispossess the dominated, effectively making them voiceless in the political arena. Opinion polls, with their artificial construction of public opinion, served as an archetypal instrument of disempowerment. For Bourdieu, democracy concealed competition among elites within the field of power—elites whose appeal for popular support was driven not so much by a concern for the dominated but by maneuvers within this field of the dominant.

As he ascended the academic staircase, Bourdieu converted his academic capital into political capital, engaging directly in the public sphere. He used his position as professor at the Collège de France, which he assumed in 1981, to draw attention to the limits of educational policy and to begin his attacks on the academy. Still, at the same time, he placed his hope in the potential universality of the state and the creation of an "international" of intellectuals. In the 1990s he deliberately gave voice to the downtrodden in the bestseller *The Weight of the World* (Bourdieu et al. [1993] 1999), a collaborative work of interviewing immigrants, blue-collar workers, and low-level civil servants—in short, the dominated. He joined social struggles, most famously the French general strikes of 1995 that opposed the dismemberment of the welfare state. He spoke out against the socialist government that was socialist in name but neoliberal in content. As he aged, his assaults on neoliberalism and the distortions of the media, especially television, took a popular turn in the book series Liber-Raisons d'Agir. Gone were the long and tortured sentences; in their place he delivered uncompromising attacks written in an apocalyptic tone. Neoliberalism, he warned, meant the subjugation of education, art, politics, and culture to the remorseless logic of the market, not to mention the "flexploitation" of workers and their ever more precarious existence.

His combative spirit in the public sphere, however, collided with his theoretical claims. For a long time Bourdieu had been contemptuous of sociological interventions in politics—social movement sociology or "charitable sociology," as he once called it (Bourdieu, Passeron, and Chamboredon [1968] 1991, 251). He insisted that sociology had to be a science with its own autonomy, its own language, and its own methods inaccessible to all but the initiated. He had dismissed the idea of the organic intellectual as a projection of the habitus and life conditions of intellectuals onto the benighted, yet here he was on the picket lines, leading the condemnation of the socialist government. Having insisted on the depth of symbolic violence, how could he work together with the subaltern? Was he just manipulating them for his own ends, as he accused others of doing? If the social struggles of the subaltern are misguided, rooted in a misrecognition of their own position, was Bourdieu being led astray by joining workers in their protests? We don't know—his practice was at odds with his theory, and he never seemed to interrogate the contradiction. This is what he writes in *Acts of Resistance*:

I do not have much inclination for prophetic interventions and I have always been wary of occasions in which the situation or sense of solidarity could lead me to overstep the limits of my competence. So I would not have engaged in public position-taking if I had not, each time, had the—perhaps illusory—sense of being forced into it by a kind of legitimate rage, sometimes close to something like a sense of duty. . . . And if, to be effective, I have sometimes had to commit myself in my own person and my own name, I have always done it in the hope—if not of triggering mobilization, or even one of those debates without object or subject which arise periodically in the world of the media—at least of breaking the appearance of unanimity which is the greater part of the symbolic force of the dominant discourse. (Bourdieu 1998, vii–viii)

Here, Bourdieu is attributing a certain rationality—you might say "good sense"—to the publics he is addressing, a "good sense" such publics don't have in his earlier writings.

This is the first paradox, the *paradox of public engagement*—the simultaneous claim of its impossibility and its necessity. It leads to the second paradox, the *paradox of relative autonomy*. In fighting neoliberalism, Bourdieu finds himself defending the very autonomy of educational, cultural, and scientific fields that earlier he had claimed were responsible for the reproduction of domination. In the end, he finds himself defending the great institutions of French culture, notwithstanding their role in reproducing domination. A child of the French Enlightenment, Bourdieu claims that the institutions he condemns—the state, the university, literature, and art—do have a universal validity and do represent a rich cultural heritage that should be accessible to all.

You might say Bourdieu is defending not the status quo ante (i.e., the relative autonomy of these institutions) but their full autonomy, so that they become the privilege of all. Yet if this is the case, then it is an entirely utopian project, so that the paradox remains: defending the relative autonomy of cultural fields against market invasion is the defense of the very thing he denounces—symbolic violence. But there is a political project here. In calling for the defense of the cultural, bureaucratic, and educational fields, he aims to rally the interests of intellectuals, artists, and academics—fractions of both the dominant classes and the new middle classes—against market tyranny.

COMBAT IN THE ACADEMIC FIELD

It is easier for intellectuals and academics to attack the excesses of the market than to see themselves exercising symbolic violence over society by virtue of the autonomy they so stoutly defend. While intellectuals denounce physical violence throughout the world, they are reluctant to recognize that they, too, are the perpetrators of violence, that is, a symbolic violence that ensures a taken-for-granted—what Bourdieu calls "doxic"—submission to domination incorporated in bodies and language. Thus, although they may see themselves as autonomous, intellectuals are implicated in the state through its monopoly of the legitimate use of symbolic violence, through consecrated classifications and categories.

But intellectuals, academics, and social scientists are not all of a piece. While most do not recognize their contribution to symbolic violence, some, like Bourdieu, spell out the truth of symbolic violence. This division of intellectuals into those who have good sense and those who have bad sense calls for an analysis of academic fields that reveals what we are up to behind our screens of objectivity, pointing to the ways we deceive both ourselves and others. In short, the sociology that we apply to others must be applied equally to ourselves. The purpose of such reflexivity, however, is not to denounce our fellow scientists but to liberate them from the illusions—scholastic fallacies—that spring from the conditions under which they produce knowledge, namely their freedom from material necessity. Bourdieu criticizes his fellow academics for not recognizing how their material conditions shape their knowledge production, and so they mistakenly foist their theories onto the subjects whose actions they theorize. For Bourdieu, to better understand the conditions of the production of knowledge is a condition for producing better knowledge.

This sounds very fine in principle, but in practice the scientific field, no less than any other field, is a combat zone in which actors struggle to enforce their view of the world—their theories, methodologies, and philosophies. Indeed, Bourdieu ([1997] 2000, 116) refers to the scientific field as one of "armed competition" in which some actors manage to accumulate capital at the expense of others. He assumes, however, that the rules of such combat ensure the production of truth—or, more accurately, the reduction of falsehood—even though, as he says in his article on the scientific field, there is an ever-increasing concentration of capital with its own conservative tendencies. What happens to that open competition for truth when the scientific field is monopolized by a few powerful actors? What ensures the ascendancy of good sense over bad sense, Bourdieusian sociologists over neoliberal economists? Are there rules of combat, or does anything go?

In his own practice of science Bourdieu can be quite ruthless in establishing his domination. As already mentioned, he devotes little time to recognizing the contributions of others, tending to constitute himself as the soul originator of his ideas. He may be standing on the shoulders of giants, but they are invisible, repressed below the surface. He seems to deploy the recognition of others in footnotes and acknowledgments to maximize the recognition that he receives. His very writing is a form of symbolic violence, trying to impress upon the readers his own distinction through esoteric references, appeals to Greek and Latin, and long-winded sentences, all of which have an intimidating effect. Those who dare to openly disagree with him—if they are sufficiently important—are deemed to suffer from irrationality, weak-mindedness, or even psychological disorders manifested in repression and defense mechanisms. Or, more simply, they express the interests that they have by virtue of their place in the academic field. He exercises symbolic violence within the field of science against these infidels, all in the name of the realpolitik of reason and to unmask symbolic violence in wider society. Throughout, he is so sure that he is right that any stratagem to vanquish the opposition seems justified. Here, combat often appears not as self-defense but as "unfair attacks" on enemy combatants.

While content to locate others in the academic field and explain their perspectives in terms of that position, he fails to apply the same principle to himself. The nearest we get to such a self-analysis are his claims to outsider status, coming as he did from peasant background with a "cleft habitus," which allows him greater insight into the workings of the academy and, indeed, of the world. His *Sketch for a Self-Analysis* (Bourdieu [2004] 2007) is just that—a sketch that describes his sufferings in boarding school and as an outsider in the École Normale Supérieure but tells us next to nothing of Bourdieu as a combatant in the scientific field. Indeed, Bourdieu never undertook a systematic sociological investigation of the French field of sociology, in which he became a, if not the, central player. The nearest he gets is *Homo Academicus* (Bourdieu [1984] 1988), which is an incomplete examination of the French academic field as a whole—an examination of the relations among disciplines but not of the disciplinary field itself.

Here, then, we come to the third paradox, *the paradox of reflexivity.* On the one hand, he argues that an analysis of the academic field in which one operates is a precondition of scientific knowledge. On the other hand, he himself undertakes neither an analysis of his own place in the field of sociology nor even an analysis of the field of French sociology itself, as if none of his competitors is worthy of serious examination. Bourdieu's interest in reflexivity—i.e., in scientifically assessing the field of sociology and his position in it—clashes with his interests as an actor, namely to accumulate academic capital, which means to elevate the status of sociology and his position within it. To accomplish these ends, Bourdieu mobilizes the cultural capital that derives from a philosophy degree at the École Normale Supérieure and builds a school of sociology with its own vocabulary, methodology, theory, journal, etc. It involves dis-recognizing others and exercising symbolic violence over them, which, if successful, is at odds with the project of reflexivity and endangers the very project of science.

In these three paradoxes—the public engagement of sociologists, the relative autonomy of fields, and the reflexivity of scientific analysis—we see the contradiction between theory and practice. But according to Bourdieu's own theory, this is to be expected—there is always a gap between theory and practice. We find this argument in all his metatheoretical writings, from *Outline of a Theory of Practice* ([1972] 1977) to *The Logic of Practice* ([1980] 1990) to *Pascalian Meditations* ([1997] 2000). He shows the necessity of the rupture between sociological understanding and common sense, between theory and practice, and how practice reproduces this separation. If people truly understood what they do, if they understood how their practices reproduce their subordination, then the social order would crumble. But for all his interest in reflexivity, Bourdieu does not turn this analysis back onto *himself* and examine the ways in which *his* theory and practice are at odds with each other. There is no internal conversation between Bourdieu and Bourdieu, between his theory and practice, although we will attempt such a conversation in deciphering *The Weight of the World* (Bourdieu et al. [1993] 1999).

The following engagements with Bourdieu, therefore, will study the paradoxical relations among and within the three nodes of Bourdieu's meta-framework: how he condemns symbolic violence but defends the very institutions that reproduce that domination; how he advocates reflexivity by locating intellectuals within their fields of production but fails to do the same for himself; and finally, how he is critical of public engagement and yet this becomes so central to his own identity.

CONVERSATIONS WITH BOURDIEU

Bourdieu's model of sociology as a combat sport certainly casts doubt on the conventional collective self-understanding of scientists as building science through consensus. In his celebrated model, Robert Merton ([1942]

1973) defines the ethos of science as made up of four elements: universalism, communism, disinterestedness, and organized skepticism. Competition is there, but it does not take the form of a combat sport in which the goal is to annihilate adversaries in "armed struggle." Yet, of course, inasmuch as science is a field in the Bourdieusian sense, it must have relations of domination and subjugation that play themselves out as combat. On the one hand, to deny those relations of domination, as is the wont of the dominant, is itself a strategy of domination. It is not surprising, therefore, that Parsons and Merton, who dominated US sociology in the 1950s, should have a consensus view of science. On the other hand, to endorse the idea of sociology as a combat sport without any further elaboration of the rules of that combat excuses opportunistic strategies of dis-recognition, expropriation, and distortion that are inimical to science.

Here, therefore, I want to consider a third model of science, one based on dialogue. The idea is not to suppress difference in the name of consensus but to recognize difference as a challenge to existing assumptions and frameworks. Here one challenges not in order to vanquish but rather to converse in order to better understand others and, through others, to learn the limits and possibilities of one's own assumptions and frameworks. A model of dialogue is not exclusive of the other two models. In order to converse, there must be some common ground to make conversation possible. An inner circle of agreement is necessary for an outer circle of disagreement. Equally, in order to converse within a scientific field, it may be necessary to give voice to subaltern perspectives that are repressed, and that usually requires combat. In a field of domination, conversation cannot be taken for granted; it has to be advanced and defended.

In the conversations that follow, we will bring to life some of the combatants Bourdieu has repressed. I will follow Bourdieu's prescription that to read an author it is necessary to first place him or her in the context of the field of production—competitors, allies, and antagonists who are taken for granted by the author and invisibly shape his or her practice. I cannot re-create all the academic fields within which Bourdieu was embedded. That would be a task far beyond my capabilities, covering as it would philosophy, linguistics, literature, painting, and photography, as well as sociology and anthropology—indeed, the entire French intellectual field. So I have chosen a distinctive group of social theorists who wander like ghosts through Bourdieu's opus, because, unlike Bourdieu, they believe the dominated, or some fraction thereof, can indeed under certain conditions perceive and appreciate the nature of their own subordination. I am, of course, thinking of the Marxist tradition that Bourdieu engages, usually without recognizing it and even to the point of denying it a place in his intellectual field. This is ironic indeed, but perhaps not surprising, since these social theorists were all powerful combatants, both Bourdieu's equals and tackling the same issues that obsessed him.

Like Parsons, Bourdieu considered it sufficient to discredit Marx's ideas as belonging to the nineteenth century to dismiss the Marxist tradition. Effectively, they deny the possibility that those who follow in the path of Marx may have made distinctive contributions through reconstructing the founder's theories. Both Parsons and Bourdieu reduced all Marxists to the same obsolete theory, rather than recognizing the originality of the Marxists who followed Marx, an originality prompted by the internal contradictions and external anomalies in Marxian theory, highlighted by the challenges they faced in their different places and their different times. The original contributions of Gramsci, Fanon, Freire, and Beauvoir (to mention just four who concern us here) are repressed even though, as we will see, they focus on questions parallel to those posed by Bourdieu—questions of cultural domination, colonialism, education, gender, and common sense.

The growth of Marxism has always benefited from an engagement with sociology as its alter ego, and in our era the preeminent representative of sociology is undoubtedly Pierre Bourdieu. He provides an important impetus for reconstructing Marxism for the twenty-first century. That is the ultimate purpose of these conversations. But there is an important lesson here for the followers of Bourdieu. Will they regard themselves as disciples and view the master's work as a finished product with neither internal contradictions nor external anomalies? Will they do to Bourdieu what Bourdieu does to Marxism, deny its historicity? If so, the chance to build a Bourdieusian tradition will be lost, and Bourdieu's work will die on the vine just like that of Talcott Parsons. One can pick grapes only so many times before they perish if the vine itself is not replenished. So will Bourdieu's apostles see a virtue in dialogue with other parallel traditions and thereby recognize the limitations of their founder and build on his ideas?

THE POVERTY
OF PHILOSOPHY
Marx Meets Bourdieu

Economic conditions first transformed the mass of the
people of the country into workers. The combination of
capital has created for this mass a common situation, common interests. This mass is thus already a class as against
capital, but not yet for itself. In the struggle, of which we
have noted only a few phases, this mass becomes united,
and constitutes itself as a class for itself. The interests it
defends become class interests. But the struggle of class
against class is a political struggle.

    — MARX, *THE POVERTY OF PHILOSOPHY*

The historical success of Marxist theory, the first social
theory to claim scientific status that has so completely
realized its potential in the social world, thus contributes
to ensuring that the theory of the social world which is the
least capable of integrating the *theory effect*—that it, more
than any other, has created—is doubtless, today, the most
powerful obstacle to the progress of the adequate theory
of the social world to which it has, in times gone by, more
than any other contributed.

    — BOURDIEU, "SOCIAL SPACE AND THE GENESIS OF 'CLASSES'"

What is Bourdieu saying here? The historical success of Marxism is to have constituted the *idea* of class out of a bundle of attributes shared by an arbitrary assemblage of people, what he calls "class on paper." Aided by parties, trade unions, the media, and propaganda—an "immense historical labor of theoretical and practical invention, starting with Marx himself" (Bourdieu [1984] 1991b, 251)—Marxism effectively called forth the representation and, through representation, the belief in the existence of the "working class" as a real "social fiction" that otherwise would have had only potential existence.

However, this social fiction, this belief in the existence of the working class, is a far cry from "class as action, a real and really mobilized group" (Bourdieu [1984] 1991b, 251), let alone a revolutionary actor as imagined by the Marxist tradition—a tradition that suffers from a self-misunderstanding. The Marxist tradition does not see itself as *constituting* the idea and representation of the working class. It sees itself as a scientific theory *discovering* and then *expressing* the historical emergence of an objective "class-in-itself" that was destined to become a "class-for-itself" making history in its own image. Marx's claim is summarized in the quotation above from *The Poverty of Philosophy*, where Marx excoriates Pierre-Joseph Proudhon for confusing reality and economic categories, for making the intellectualist error of seeing history as the emanation of ideas rather than ideas as the expression of reality. Bourdieu is now joining Proudhon in turning the tables against Marxism, accusing Marx of being a crude materialist, overlooking the importance of the symbolic.

I will now give Marx the chance to respond to Bourdieu by putting the two theorists into dialogue around their divergent theories of history, social transformation, symbolic violence, and contentious politics. To construct such an imaginary conversation, I set out from what they share, namely a contempt for the illusory nature of philosophy. In following their divergent attempts to come to terms with the conundrum of intellectuals repudiating intellectualism, I trace a succession of parallel steps which reveal the internal tensions and contradictions of each body of theory. But first, we must comprehend Bourdieu's complex critique of *Marxism*, which he erroneously reduces to the shortcomings of *Marx's* own theory.

BOURDIEU MEETS MARXISM

Bourdieu acknowledges the immense influence of Marxism. But, Bourdieu argued, Marxism did not have the tools to understand its influence, its own effect—its "theory effect"—without which, according to Bourdieu, there would have been no "working class." As a powerful symbolic system, Marxism gave life and meaning to the category "working class" that then had a significant impact on history.[1] But Marxism could not comprehend its own power—the power of its symbols and its political interventions—because it did not possess and incorporate a theory of symbolic violence. When Marx was writing, this lacuna did not matter, as the economy still constituted the only autonomous field in mid-nineteenth-century Europe and the symbolic world was still underdeveloped. However, with the elaboration of separate cultural, scientific, educational, legal, and bureaucratic fields in the late nineteenth century, and without an understanding of these fields, Marxism lost its grip on reality and its theory became retrograde, becoming a "powerful obstacle to the progress of the adequate theory of the social world" (Bourdieu [1984] 1991b, 251). These fields of symbolic production engendered their own domination effects, overriding and countering Marxism's symbolic power, which had depended on the overriding predominance of the economy.

Disarmed both as science and as ideology, Marxism is unable to compete with other theories that place symbolic power at the center of analysis. As *science* Marxism does not understand that a classification or representational struggle has to precede class struggle (i.e., classes have to be constituted symbolically before they can engage in struggle). This requires a theory of cultural production that it fails to elaborate. As *ideology*, without such a theory of cultural production, Marxism can no longer compete in the classification struggle over the visions and divisions of society. Marxism loses its symbolic power and the working class retreats back to a class on paper— merely an analytical category of an academic theory. Marxism becomes regressive, an obstacle to the development of social theory.[2]

Bourdieu mounts a powerful indictment of Marx but pointedly ignores the significance of Western Marxism—from Korsch to Lukács, from the Frankfurt School to Gramsci—whose raison d'être was to wrestle with the problem of cultural domination and the meaning of Marxism in a world of bourgeois ideological hegemony. Many of their ideas are congruent with Bourdieu's theory of symbolic violence.[3] To understand what the Marxist tradition has accomplished in this regard it is necessary, as a first step, to concentrate on the real limitations of Marx. Against Bourdieu's sweeping dismissal I restore the voice of Marx, repressed or contorted in Bourdieu's writings, to create a more balanced exchange. The imaginary conversation that follows, therefore, is neither a combat sport nor a higher synthesis; rather, it aims at mutual clarification. Following Bourdieu's own call for relational analysis—although he rarely applies this to himself—we cannot appreciate the field of intellectual contest without representing both players, Marx and Bourdieu. By posing each theory as a challenge to the other, we can better appreciate their distinctiveness—their defining anomalies and contradictions as well as their divergent *problematiques*.

Since Marx predates Bourdieu, it is he who sets the terms of the conversation, but my framing will be one that is favorable to Bourdieu's critique, namely Marx's four postulates of historical materialism. First, *history* is seen as a succession of modes of production, arranged in ascending order according to the development of the forces of production. Second, each mode of production has a *dynamics* of its own within which reproduction gives rise to transformation and finally self-destruction. Third, *ideological domination* is secured through the superstructures of society as well as through the mystifying powers of economic activity, both in production and in exchange. Fourth, *class struggle* arches forward, dissolving mystification and the "muck of ages" to usher in the era of communism. As I will show, each postulate raises as many questions for Bourdieu's counter-theory as it does for Marx's historical materialism.

To begin a conversation, there needs to be a point of departure that is also a point of agreement. That point of agreement is their common critique of philosophy that Marx[4] calls "ideology" and Bourdieu calls "scholastic reason." They both repudiate the illusory ideas of intellectuals and turn to the logic of practice—labor in the case of Marx, bodily practice in the case of Bourdieu. This leads Marx to the working class and its revolutionary potential, while Bourdieu moves in the opposite direction—from the dominated back to the dominant classes who exercise symbolic violence. I show how Marx ends up in a materialist cul-de-sac while Bourdieu ends up in an idealist cul-de-sac. No less than Marx, but for different reasons, Bourdieu cannot grasp his own "theory effect." They each break out of their respective dead ends in ad hoc ways that contradict the premises of their theories—paradoxes that lay the foundations for the elaboration of two opposed traditions.

DIVERGENT PATHS FROM THE CRITIQUE OF PHILOSOPHY: LABOR VS. HABITUS

Uncanny parallels join Marx and Engels's ([1845–46] 1978) critique of the "German Ideology" and Bourdieu's ([1997] 2000) critique of "scholastic reason." In *The German Ideology*, Marx and Engels settle accounts with Hegel and the Young Hegelians, just as Bourdieu in *The Logic of Practice* and, later, in *Pascalian Meditations* settles his scores with his own philosophical rivals, especially Sartre and Althusser. Both Marx and Bourdieu condemn philosophy's disposition to dismiss practical engagement with the world. As Marx writes in the first thesis on Feuerbach, the German philosophers elevate the theoretical attitude as the "only genuinely human attitude," while practice is only conceived in "its dirty-judaical manifestation" ([1845] 1978, 143–5). Bourdieu's immersion in the Algerian war of independence and his experience of the raw violence of colonialism called into question the relevance of his philosophical training at the École Normale Supérieure just as, for Marx, the horrors of the Industrial Revolution in Britain made nonsense of the lofty pretensions of German idealism.[5]

Still, *Pascalian Meditations* is Bourdieu's culminating theoretical work in which Pascal is presented as an inspirational philosophical break with philosophy, centering the importance of the practice of ordinary people, emphasizing symbolic power exercised over the body, and refusing the emanation of pure philosophy from the heads of philosophers. *The German Ideology*, on the other hand, is not a culminating work but an originating work that clears the foundations for Marx's theory of historical materialism and materialist history. Although they appear at different stages in their authors' careers, their arguments against philosophy are, nonetheless, surprisingly convergent.

Let us begin with Marx and Engels scoffing at the Young Hegelians, who think they are making history when they are but counterpoising one phrase to another:

> As we hear from German ideologists, Germany has in the last few years gone through an unparalleled revolution. The decomposition of the Hegelian philosophy . . . has developed into a universal ferment into which all the "powers of the past" are swept. . . . It was a revolution beside which the French Revolution was child's play, a world struggle beside which the struggles of the Diadochi appear insignificant. Principles ousted one another, heroes of the mind overthrew each other with unheard-of rapidity and in the three years 1842–45 more of the past was swept away in Germany than at other times in three centuries. All this is supposed to have taken place in the realm of pure thought. (Marx and Engels [1845–46] 1978, 147)

Here is Bourdieu's parallel attack on modern and postmodern philosophers:

> Now, if there is one thing that our "modern" or "postmodern" philosophers have in common, beyond the conflicts that divide them,

> it is this excessive confidence in the powers of language. It is the
> typical illusion of the *lector*, who can regard an academic commen-
> tary as a political act or the critique of texts as a feat of resistance,
> and experience revolutions in the order of words as radical revolu-
> tions in the order of things. (Bourdieu [1997] 2000, 2)

The argument is the same: we must not confuse a war of words with the transformation of the real world, the power of language with the power of practice, things of logic with the logic of things.

But how is it that philosophers mistake their own world for the real world? The answer lies in their oblivion to the social and economic conditions under which they produce knowledge. For Marx and Engels, it is simply the division between mental and manual labor that encourages the illusion that ideas or consciousness drives history:

> Division of labour only becomes truly such from the moment when
> a division of material and mental labour appears. *From this mo-*
> *ment onwards consciousness can really flatter itself that it is some-*
> *thing other than consciousness of existing practice*, that it *really*
> represents something without representing something real; from
> now on consciousness is in a position to emancipate itself from
> the world and to proceed to the formation of "pure" theory, theol-
> ogy, philosophy, ethics, etc. (Marx and Engels [1845–46] 1978, 159;
> emphasis added)

Emancipated from manual labor, upon which their existence nevertheless rests, philosophers imagine that history is moved by their thought. "It has not occurred to any one of these philosophers," Marx and Engels write, "to inquire into the connection of German philosophy with German reality, the relation of their criticism to their own material surroundings" (149).

In identical fashion, Bourdieu argues that philosophers fail to understand the peculiarity of the conditions that make it possible to produce "pure" theory:

> But there is no doubt nothing more difficult to apprehend, for those
> who are immersed in universes in which it goes without saying,
> than the scholastic disposition demanded by those universes. There
> is nothing that "pure" thought finds it harder to think than *skholè*,
> the first and most determinant of all the social conditions of pos-

sibility of "pure" thought, and also the scholastic disposition which inclines its possessors to suspend the demands of the situation, the constraints of economic and social necessity. (Bourdieu [1997] 2000, 12)

The scholastic disposition calls forth the illusion that knowledge is freely produced and that it is not the product of specific conditions—unlike the knowledge of the dominated classes, which is driven by material necessity. Bourdieu does not limit his critique of the scholastic fallacy—i.e., repression of the conditions peculiar to intellectual life—to philosophers; he broadens it to other disciplines. He criticizes anthropologists, such as Lévi-Strauss, and economists for universalizing their own particular experience, foisting their abstract models onto the recalcitrant practice of ordinary mortals. Much as Marx is contemptuous of the Young Hegelians, Bourdieu satirizes Sartre's existentialist renditions of everyday life—the waiter who contemplates the heavy decision of whether to get up in the morning. For most people most of the time, argues Bourdieu, mundane tasks are accomplished without reflection. Only *sociologists*—reflexively applying sociology to themselves and, more generally, to the production of knowledge—can potentially appreciate the limitations of scholastic reason and the necessary distinction between the logic of theory and the logic of practice.

If both Marx and Bourdieu are critical of intellectuals who think ideas drive history, their corresponding turns to practice are very different. For Marx, it is a turn to the *labor* that produces the means of existence.

The premises from which we begin are not arbitrary ones, not dogmas, but real premises from which abstraction can only be made in the imagination. They are the real individuals, their activity and the material conditions under which they live, both those which they find already existing and those produced by their activity. (Marx and Engels [1845–46] 1978, 149)

It is from these material conditions of production that Marx derives the dynamics of capitalism and deepening class struggle: as capitalists compete, so they innovate in ways that lead to the polarization of wealth and poverty, giving rise to crises of overproduction on the one side and intensifying class struggles on the other.

For Bourdieu this theory of capitalism is an (unexamined) mythology—albeit a powerful one at certain points in history—created by intellectuals unable to comprehend the inurement of workers to their conditions of existence because, as intellectuals, they misrecognize the peculiarity of their own conditions of existence. Or as he pithily puts it, "Populism is never anything other than an inverted ethnocentrism" (Bourdieu [1979] 1984, 374). Instead of the transformative power of labor, Bourdieu turns to the generative power of *habitus* implanted in a socialized body.

> In other words, one has to construct a materialist theory which (in accordance with the wish that Marx expressed in the *Theses on Feuerbach*) is capable of taking from idealism the "active side" of practical knowledge that the materialist tradition has abandoned to it. This is precisely the notion of the function of habitus, which restores to the agent a generating, unifying, constructing, classifying power, while recalling that this capacity to construct social reality, itself socially constructed, is not that of a transcendental subject but of a socialized body, investing in its practice socially constructed organizing principles that are acquired in the course of a situated and dated social experience. (Bourdieu [1997] 2000, 136–37)

As the unconscious incorporation of social structure, habitus leads Bourdieu not only to abandon the working class as "transcendental subject" but also to deny the very possibility that the dominated can grasp the conditions of their subjugation, something only the sociologist can apprehend. The sociologist, and more broadly the "Internationale of intellectuals," thereby becomes Bourdieu's putative "transcendental subject."

In short, after breaking with ideology/scholastic reason and arriving at the logic of practice, Marx and Bourdieu then take diametrically opposed paths—the one focuses on the laboring activity of the exploited embedded in production relations, whereas the other turns his back on the dominated in order to return to the dominant class producing symbolic relations. The remainder of this conversation explores these two roads—how they diverge and create their own distinctive sets of paradoxes and dilemmas.

HISTORY: MODES OF PRODUCTIONS VS. DIFFERENTIATED FIELDS

Out of their common critiques of philosophy arise divergent conceptions of history. For Marx the logic of practice is embedded in the concrete social relations into which men and women enter as they labor, that is, as they transform nature. These social relations form the mode of production with two components: the forces of production (relations through which men and women collaborate in producing the means of existence, including the mode of cooperation and the technology it deploys) and the relations of production (the relations of exploitation and ownership through which surplus is produced by a class of direct producers and appropriated by a dominant class). Modes of production succeed each other—ancient, feudal, and capitalist—in a sequence measured by the expansion of the forces of production. As the final mode of production, capitalism gives way to communism, which, being without classes and thus without exploitation, allows for the realization of human talents and needs. It is only with capitalism that the direct producers (i.e., the working class), through their struggles against capital, come to recognize their role as agents of human emancipation.

In his rejection of Marx's teleology as an intellectual fantasy, one might expect Bourdieu to offer an alternative theory of history and a conception of the future. But neither are forthcoming. Instead his work *describes* a movement from traditional to modern marked, first and foremost, by different conceptions of time—the one in which the future is the repetition of the past, cyclical time, and the other in which the future is indefinite, full of possibilities, and susceptible to rational planning. Additionally, along Durkheimian ([1893] 1984) lines, Bourdieu ([1963] 1979) distinguishes traditional society in Algeria from modern society in France by the emergence and differentiation of *fields* (autonomous spheres of action) and by the pluralization of *"capitals"*—resources accumulated within fields and partially convertible across fields.

Where Marx has a succession of modes of production that govern human behavior, Bourdieu has multiple coexisting "fields." They appear as elaborations of Marx's "superstructures," which, as Marx writes in the preface to *A Contribution to the Critique of Political Economy*, are the "legal, political, religious, aesthetic or philosophical forms in which men become conscious of this [class] conflict and fight it out" (Marx [1859] 1978, 5). Thus, Bourdieu has written extended essays on the legal, the political, the bureaucratic, the religious, the philosophical, the journalistic, the scientific, the artistic, and the educational fields. The notion of field draws on and generalizes certain features of Marx's concept of the capitalist mode of production. Indeed, underlining that association, Bourdieu refers to cultural fields as the *political economy* of symbolic goods.

As with the capitalist mode of production, so with the notion of field: individuals enter into relations of competition to accumulate field-specific capital according to field-specific rules. Competition among actors takes place alongside struggles for domination of the field—struggles whose objects are the very rules and stakes that define the field and its capital. In his analysis of the scientific field (Bourdieu 1975), for example, competition leads to the concentration of academic capital, so that challenges from below can either follow a pattern of succession (holding onto the coattails of a powerful figure) or use the more risky subversive strategies that change the rules of the game and, if successful, can generate far more capital in the long run. When capital is diffused and competition intense, dominant groups can be overthrown in a "revolution," but when capital is more heavily concentrated, then change is more continuous, what Bourdieu calls a "permanent revolution."

The analogy to Marx's analysis of the capitalist mode of production is clear, except that in Bourdieu's notion of field there is no mention of exploitation. It is as if capitalism were confined to competition and domination among capitalists, with workers removed from the field. As Mathieu Desan (2013) has argued at length, Bourdieu's conception of field rests on a notion of capital that is far from Marx's—the accumulation of resources rather than a relation of exploitation.[6] Indeed, Bourdieu's only book devoted to the economy as such, *The Social Structures of the Economy* (2005), concerns the social underpinning of the housing market. Here Bourdieu focuses on the role of habitus and taste in the matching of supply and demand for different types of housing. There is no attempt to study housing from the standpoint of its production process—from the standpoint of construction workers, for example. When he turns to the firm as a field again, he focuses on the managers and directors who make decisions rather than on the workers who produce the goods, without whom there would be no decisions. Fields are confined to the dominant classes, whereas the dominated classes only inhabit the structures of social space.

Bourdieu replaces Marx's *diachronic* succession of modes of production, which pays little attention to the superstructures, with a *synchronic* account of the functioning and coexistence of fields. This poses the question of the relations among fields, marked by the recognition of autonomous and heteronomous poles within each field. In *Rules of Art* ([1992] 1996), Bourdieu describes the genesis of the literary field in nineteenth-century France. At its core was Flaubert's drive for literature for literature's sake, which required a break, on the one hand, from art sponsored by the bourgeoisie and, on the other hand, from social realism connected to everyday life. Bourdieu builds into each field a struggle for autonomy against the heteronomous influence of external fields—a struggle that is complicated by challenges to the consecrated elites from the avant-garde.

In his later writings he was particularly concerned with the economic field's subversion of the autonomy of other fields. Thus, in his book *On Television*, Bourdieu ([1996] 1999) describes the subjugation of the journalistic field to the economic field through advertising revenue that demands the widest appeal through the propagation of banalities, sensationalism, and fabrication. This, in turn, distorted the dissemination of knowledge and accomplishments of other fields, not least the field of social science, through amateurish intermediaries he calls "doxosophers," who neutralize any critical message. No less than other fields, the political field is also subject to controlling intervention from economic actors. Although he alludes to the domination of the economic field over other fields, Bourdieu has no theory of the economy and its expansive tendencies.

In addition to the domination of the economic field, Bourdieu describes a field of power that traverses different fields, bringing together their elites into a shared competition for power. This rather amorphous arrangement reminds one of Weber's separate value spheres with a realm of power that oversees society, but again there is no analysis of its dynamics. What is notably missing is any theory of the relations of interdependence and domination *among* fields. As Gil Eyal (2013) has noted, it is curious that someone so concerned about relations *within* fields pays so little attention to the relations *among* fields. Just as there is no theory of history, there is no theory of the totality, just an arbitrary assemblage of supposedly "homologous" fields.[7]

SOCIAL CHANGE: SYSTEMIC TRANSFORMATION VS. HYSTERESIS

We have seen the contrast between Marx's history as the succession of modes of production and Bourdieu's vision of coexisting fields, but Marx also has a notion of history as the dynamics of a mode of production, namely the way the reproduction of capitalism is simultaneously its transformation. Indeed, the capitalist mode of production distinguishes itself by reproducing itself; that is, through a mechanism that operates without recourse to external forces, very different from the feudal mode of production whose reproduction requires extra-economic coercion. Under capitalism the worker arrives at work each day to produce value that contributes to her wage on the one side and to capitalist profit on the other. Needing to survive, she comes to work and does the same the next day. But as capitalism reproduces itself in this way, so it also transforms itself. As capitalists compete with one another they innovate by reducing the proportion of the worker's day contributing to the wage (necessary labor) and increasing the proportion contributing to profit (surplus labor)—through the intensification of work, deskilling, new technology, etc.—which leads to class polarization and crises of overproduction. Is there an equivalent in Bourdieu whereby reproduction becomes the basis of social change?

Just as labor is at the heart of Marx's theory of reproduction, so the very different notion of habitus is at the heart of Bourdieu's theory of reproduction, a concept first developed in relation to the traditional Kabyle society.

> The habitus, the durably installed generative principle of regulated improvisations, produces practices which tend to reproduce the regularities immanent in the objective conditions of the production of their generative principle, while adjusting to the demands inscribed as objective potentialities in the situation, as defined by the cognitive and motivating structures making up the habitus. (Bourdieu [1972] 1977, 78)

Structures generate practices that reproduce structures through the mediation of habitus, which is itself the product of structures, but such reproduction allows room for improvisation within limits defined by structures. It is parallel to Marx's formula: "Men make their own history, but they do not make it just as they please; they do not make it under circumstances chosen by themselves, but under circumstances directly found, given and transmitted from the past" (Marx [1852] 1978, 595). From Bourdieu's point of view what is missing here is the way not just circumstances but individuals carry the past within themselves so that their innovative power is limited as well as facilitated by external *and* internal structures.

> Through the *habitus*, the structure of which it is the product governs practice, not along the paths of a mechanical determinism, but within the constraints and limits initially set on its inventions. . . . Because the *habitus* is an infinite capacity for generating products—thoughts, perceptions, expressions and actions—whose limits are set by the historically and socially situated conditions of its production, the conditioned and conditional freedom it provides is as remote from creation of unpredictable novelty as it is from simple mechanical reproduction of the original conditioning. (Bourdieu [1980] 1990, 55)

Just as moves in a game are improvisations limited by and, thereby, reproducing the rules of the game, so habitus is the generative principle of practices that are innovative but only within limits defined by the social structures they reproduce. Bourdieu often uses the game metaphor to illustrate the spontaneous and unthinking responses of players. He is thinking of tennis or rugby, where players develop a sense of the game and there's no time to reflect, but of course there are games like American football where self-conscious reflection plays its part or games like chess where it is key. Still, the point stands, habitus is the development of skills to improvise within limits defined by the rules. The social order inscribes itself in the largely unconscious habitus through regularized participation in successive social structures. The development of habitus proceeds in phases, with each phase the basis of subsequent formations. Thus, the primary habitus formed in childhood through parenting lays the foundation for the secondary habitus formed in school, which in turn lays the foundations for a tertiary habitus formed at work, so that habitus is subject to continual revision but within limits defined by its past, largely repressed and unconscious.[8]

Armed with habitus, Bourdieu's individual has much greater weight and depth than Marx's individual, who is the effect and support of the social relations into which they enter. For Bourdieu social relations become lodged in a durable, transposable, and largely irreversible habitus, which has an autonomous effect on participation in different social structures. Marx, on the other hand, gives priority to social relations that impose themselves on individuals as "indispensable and independent of their will" (Marx [1859] 1978, 4) without leaving any permanent psychic trace. Capitalist relations impose themselves on laborers inexorably, irrespective of their experience in different institutions in society. Marx does not consider the effects of schools or family on the way people work or invest—he is solely interested in the logic of social relations independent of the distinctive features of the capitalists and the workers who support them. Bourdieu, by contrast, makes spheres beyond the economy key to understanding a given social order, and here lies the secret of both continuity and social change, or social change through continuity.

Habitus is durable; it has a tendency to persist when it confronts new social structures, a phenomenon Bourdieu calls "hysteresis." The resulting clash between habitus and structure can come about in many ways. First, it arises from the mobility of individuals, who carry a habitus cultivated in one set of structures and come up against the imperatives of another. Students from lower classes who enter a middle-class school find it difficult to adapt and either withdraw or rebel.[9] When Algerian peasants with a traditional habitus migrate to an urban context, they suffer from anomie, leading to resignation or revolt (Bourdieu [1963] 1979).

The disjuncture of structure and habitus can also come about through the superimposition of social structures. Bourdieu ([1963] 1979) describes the imposition of a colonial order on a traditional Kabyle society, disrupting accepted patterns of behavior and leading to anticolonial revolution. In that revolution, however, Algerians develop a habitus more in keeping with modernity, a habitus that embraces nationalist aspirations, what Bourdieu calls the "revolution in the revolution" (Bourdieu [1961] 1962, chap. 7). Or back in Southern France in the Béarn where Bourdieu grew up, modernization of agriculture disinherits the peasant farmer, who can no longer find a marriage partner with whom to produce the next generation of inheritors (Bourdieu [2002] 2008a). The farmer retreats into morose resignation while young women, who are no longer prepared to put up with the drudgery of rural life, exit for the city—the one exhibiting an enduring habitus unable to adapt, the other endowed with a more flexible habitus generative of innovative response. The divergent responses of men and women are captured in the "bachelors' ball," where the degradation of the inheritors expresses itself in bodily discomfort and embarrassment as they ring the dance floor, watching the young women freely dancing with men from the town.

Bourdieu's most often cited example of hysteresis is the devaluation of educational credentials that, in his view, explains the student protests in France of May 1968. In *Homo Academicus*, Bourdieu ([1984] 1988) describes how the expansion of higher education created an oversupply of assistant lecturers whose upward mobility was consequently blocked. The ensuing tension between aspirations and opportunities affected not only the young assistants but students more generally, who found that their degrees did not translate into expected jobs. The discordance between class habitus and the labor market appeared simultaneously in a number of fields so that their normally disparate temporal rhythms merged into a general crisis conducted in a singular public time and producing a historical drama that suspended common sense. In this view we might say that history is a succession of unanticipated "conjunctures," unpredictable clashes that punctuate equilibria.

Bourdieu's account of the dynamics of higher education is analogous to Marx's account of the expansion of capitalism through capitalist competition leading to the degradation of the working class, with two provisos. First, where Bourdieu takes the expansion of education as an unexplained given, an exogenous variable, Marx shows how the internal dynamics of capitalism lead to the concentration of capital and the immiseration of the working class. He has a theory of the rise and fall of capitalism. Second, where Bourdieu explains student revolt in terms of the mismatch of expectation and opportunity, disposition and position, Marx stresses the formation of a revolutionary working class as a response to changing social relations.

The fact that people move among a plurality of structures implies the ever-present *possibility* of social change. But this is not a *theory* of social change, which would require a far deeper understanding of the durability of the habitus—how it develops, how new layers of the habitus affect existing layers—leading to a dynamic psychology. But equally, it would require a theory of the resilience of social structures in the face of collective challenge from enduring habiti. In other words, we need to theorize the consequences as well as the origins of the inevitable clashes between habitus and structure: when it leads to rebellion or revolution, when it leads to resignation or innovation, when it leads to exit or voice. Change is ubiquitous but why and how is very unclear.

While the idea of habitus can be deployed to interpret social change and social protest, its main purpose is to explain continuity and underline how difficult social change is to accomplish. Like the French Marxism of the 1960s and 1970s—Althusser, Balibar, Godelier, Poulantzas, with whom he shares so much, leading him to stage exaggerated critiques—Bourdieu's functionalism was not necessarily an expression of conservatism that all is well in society but an attempt to understand the resilience of social structures in the face of contestation, which brings us to the heart of his theory—symbolic violence.

SYMBOLIC VIOLENCE: MYSTIFICATION VS. MISRECOGNITION

Bourdieu developed a set of generative concepts—habitus, capital, and field—but without a theory of history, totality, or even collective action. What he does have, however, is a theory of symbolic violence. Once again we would do well to begin with Marx and Engels, who famously write of the way ideology both appeals and obscures.

> The ideas of the ruling class are in every epoch the ruling ideas: i.e. the class which is the ruling material force of society, is at the same time its ruling intellectual force. The class which has the means of material production at its disposal, has control at the same time

over the means of mental production, so that thereby, generally speaking, *the ideas of those who lack the means of mental production are subject to it.* (Marx and Engels [1845–46] 1978, 172; emphasis added)

Having broken with ideology in order to make material relations the foundation of history, here Marx and Engels temporarily revert to ideology, namely to the power of illusory ideas in sustaining the domination of the dominant class. We should note that, like Bourdieu, Marx and Engels privilege intellectuals in the production of representations of society.

There is ambiguity in Marx and Engels's notion of ideological subjugation. What does it mean to "subject" the dominated to the ideas of the ruling class? Bourdieu might be said to be elaborating Marx and Engels's ideological subjection when he writes,

Symbolic violence is the coercion which is set up only through the consent that the dominated cannot fail to give to the dominator (and therefore to the domination) when their understanding of the situation and relation can only use instruments of knowledge that they have in common with the dominator, which, being merely the incorporated form of the structure of the relation of domination, make this relation appear as natural; or, in other words, when the schemes they implement in order to perceive and evaluate themselves or to perceive and evaluate the dominators (high/low, male/female, white/black, etc.) are the product of the incorporation of the (thus neutralized) classifications of which their social being is the product. (Bourdieu [1997] 2000, 170)

Bourdieu's symbolic violence is irrevocable. Subjugation inhabits the *habitus*, deep in the unconscious. Bourdieu invokes the notion of *misrecognition* to convey the depth of subjugation. There is "recognition" but it is false inasmuch as it is based on the repression of the conditions of its production. We are like fish in water, unable to see the classifications we take for granted, arbitrary classifications that are the basis of an arbitrary domination.

Marx takes the idea of subjugation to ruling ideas in a different direction, arguing that the effectiveness of the ruling ideology depends on its resonance with the *lived experience* of economic relations. Instead of misrecognition, with its roots buried in the unconscious layers of habitus, Marx writes of *mystification* that affects anyone who enters capitalist relations, irrespective of their socialization. *It is an attribute of relations rather than of the individual habitus.* Thus, under capitalism, exploitation is not experienced as such because it is hidden by the very character of production, which obscures the distinction between necessary and surplus labor, since workers appear to be paid for the entire workday. Similarly, participation in market exchange leads to "commodity fetishism" whereby objects, which are bought and sold, are disconnected from their production—the social relations and human labor necessary to produce them. Again, capitalist relations of production are obscured not through an incorporated habitus but through the relations of exchange.

For Marx, however, such mystification is dissolved through class struggle, leading the working class to see the truth of capitalism, on the one hand, and their role in transforming it, on the other:

> It is not a matter of what this or that proletarian or even the proletariat as a whole *pictures* at present as its goal. It is a matter of *what the proletariat is in actuality*, and what in accordance with this *being*, it will historically be compelled to do. Its goal and its historical action are prefigured in the most clear and ineluctable way in its own life-situation as well as in the whole organization of contemporary bourgeois society. There is no need to harp on the fact that a large part of the English and French proletariat is already *conscious* of its historic task and is continually working to bring this consciousness to full clarity. (Marx [1845] 1978, 134–35)

Yet, as Bourdieu insists, for the proletariat to rid itself of the "the muck of ages," as Marx and Engels put it in *The Germany Ideology* ([1845–46] 1978, 193), is not easy. Only under unusual circumstances—and to some extent they pertained in nineteenth-century Europe—does class struggle assume an ascendant path, intensifying itself as it expands, demystifying relations of exploitation as described in *The Manifesto of the Communist Party*. There Marx and Engels ([1848] 1978, 478–83) support their claim by reference to class formation in nineteenth-century England—from scattered struggles to the advance of trade unions and finally to the formation of a national party that would seize state power. In *Class Struggles in France*, Marx ([1850] 1964, 54) argues that the extension of suffrage would "unchain class struggle," although Engels (some fifty years later and fifty years wiser) would be more cautious in proclaiming the immanent victory of the German working class.

This period of history corresponds to Bourdieu's positive assessment of Marxism when it realized its potential in the social world. Subsequently, through its victories, through the concessions the working class wins, its revolutionary temper weakens and its struggles come to be organized increasingly *within* the framework of capitalism. From then on Bourdieu can say that the symbolic violence incorporated in the lived experience prevails over the cathartic effect of struggle.

Having tarred the whole Marxist tradition with Marx's revolutionary optimism, Bourdieu, by labeling it a scholastic illusion, then bends the stick in the opposite direction:

> And another effect of the scholastic illusion is seen when people describe resistance to domination in the language of consciousness—as does the whole Marxist tradition and also the feminist theorists who, giving way to habits of thought, expect political liberation to come from the "raising of consciousness"—ignoring the extraordinary inertia which results from the inscription of social structures in bodies, for lack of a dispositional theory of practices. While making things explicit can help, only a thoroughgoing process of countertraining, involving repeated exercises, can, like an athlete's training, durably transform habitus. (Bourdieu [1997] 2000, 172)

What this "countertraining" might look like is never elaborated, but it has to dislodge the embedded and embodied habitus. Whether class struggle might be a form of "countertraining" is especially unclear as Bourdieu never entertains the idea of class struggle. Symbolic revolutions, if and when they occur, always emanate from above. The working classes are driven by the exigencies of material necessity, leading them to make a virtue out of necessity. They embrace their functional lifestyle rather than reject the dominant culture. An alternative culture remains beyond their grasp because they have neither the tools nor the leisure to create it (Bourdieu [1979] 1984, chap. 7).[10]

Still, Bourdieu does say that "making things explicit" (i.e., critical reflection) "can help" (i.e., can foster some insight into the conditions of subjugation). Yet we know little about the relationship between the conscious and the unconscious. Can critical reflection change the habitus and if so how? There is no theory of habitus to even make sense of the question. Indeed, Bourdieu sometimes seems to dismiss the very vocabulary of consciousness and with it the idea of ideology:

In the notion of "false consciousness" which some Marxists invoke to explain the effect of symbolic domination, it is the word "consciousness" which is excessive; and to speak of "ideology" is to place in the order of *representations*, capable of being transformed by the intellectual conversion that is called the "awakening of consciousness," what belongs to the order of *beliefs*, that is, at the deepest level of bodily dispositions. (Bourdieu [1997] 2000, 177; emphasis original)

Here Bourdieu misunderstands Marx, who does try to grapple with the relationship between ideology as representation and ideology as belief—representations are only effective insofar as they resonate with beliefs. The issue between Marx and Bourdieu is not the distinction between ideology and bodily knowledge but the character of beliefs themselves, whether they are immanent to particular social relations or whether they inhabit the habitus, the cumulative effect of embodied biography.

Having written off the working classes as incapable of grasping the conditions of their oppression, Bourdieu is compelled to look elsewhere for ways of contesting symbolic violence. Having broken from scholastic reason to the logic of practice and having discovered that the logic of practice is impervious to truth, he reverts to the logic of theory, this time to the emancipatory science of sociology and to symbolic struggles within the dominant class. Let us follow his argument.

CONTENTIOUS POLITICS: CLASS STRUGGLE VS. CLASSIFICATION STRUGGLE

While Marx does indeed endow the working class with a historic mission of securing emancipation for all, it is also true that he pays as much if not more historical attention to the driving force of capitalism: the dominant class and its fractions. His crowning achievement—the theory of capitalism elaborated in *Capital*—focuses on the economic activities of the dominant class, the competition and interdependence among capitalists as well as their creative destruction. When writing of politics in mid-nineteenth-century France, he dissects the relationships among different elites; when writing of the factory acts in England, he recognizes the different interests of fractions of capital as well as the landed classes; and when writing of colonialism it is the interests of the bourgeoisie that concern him. His correspondence about politics was almost solely devoted to the strategies of different national ruling classes and their states. Throughout he was acutely aware of the relationship between the bourgeoisie and its ideologists. As he and Engels write in *The German Ideology*,

> The division of labour . . . manifests itself also in the ruling class as the division of mental and manual labour, so that inside this class one part appears as thinkers of the class (its active conceptive ideologists, who make the perfecting of the illusion of the class about itself their chief source of livelihood), while the others' attitude to these ideas and illusions is more passive and receptive, because they are in reality the active members of the class and have less time to make up the illusions and ideas about themselves. Within this class this cleavage can even develop into a certain opposition and hostility between the two parts. (Marx and Engels [1845–46] 1978, 173)

Here Marx and Engels prefigure Bourdieu's division of the dominant class into those high in economic capital (and lower in cultural capital) and those high in cultural capital (and lower in economic capital). Bourdieu, too, recognizes the conflict between these two fractions and casts that conflict in terms of struggles over categories of representation—so-called classification struggles.

The classifications generated through struggles within the dominant class between its dominant and dominated fractions shape the way of life of different classes. *Distinction* works with a simple Marxian schema of class: dominant class, petty bourgeoisie, and working class. Each class has a distinctive set of patterns of consumption: the working class is driven by necessity, extending legitimacy to the dominant class's sense of taste even if that appears remote; the old "petite bourgeoisie" takes up a defensive posture while the new "petite bourgeoisie" seeks to become part of the grande bourgeoisie by adopting its standards and imitating its style of life; the dominant class, with refined self-assurance, is located in different fields, within which they compete among themselves to impose their vision and division on society.

This is a sophisticated elaboration of Marx's idea of the ruling ideology being the ideology of the ruling classes in which a system of classifications creates standards through which individuals from different classes evaluate themselves. The taste of the dominant class—as seen by itself and others—is an attribute of innate refinement rather than a function of a cultivated habitus that derives from access to wealth and leisure, just as the dominated classes regard their own culture as a product of their own inferiority rather than a derivative of necessity. The result is a belief in the legitimacy of the hierarchy of tastes and an enactment that obscures the class conditioning of the hierarchy.

Seemingly voluntary choices—the food we eat, the music we listen to, the films we watch, the sports we play, the photographs we take, and so on—draw us into a relatively autonomous hierarchy of consumption that obscures its underlying class determinants. The same goes for education, which, again, by virtue of its relative autonomy appears neutral vis-à-vis class, drawing students from dominated classes into the pursuit of performances that would lead to upward mobility (Bourdieu and Passeron [1970] 1977). Failure to excel is blamed on inadequacies of the self rather than the class character of the school, which privileges those with cultural capital. Education has, therefore, two functions: a technical function of slotting people into the labor market and a social function of masking the class determinants of educational outcomes. In *State Nobility* Bourdieu ([1989] 1996) describes the struggles within the dominant class that determine the relative importance of educational credentials, as well as the structure of access to and content of education, thereby ensuring, once again, the misrecognition of class domination.

Having closed off the dominated as a source of social change, Bourdieu regards the classification struggles within the dominant class as potential instigators of "symbolic" revolutions capable of shaking the "deepest structures of the social order":

> Likewise, the arts and literature can no doubt offer the dominant agents some very powerful instruments of legitimation, either directly, through the celebration they confer, or indirectly, especially through the cult they enjoy, which also consecrates its celebrants. But it can also happen that artists or writers are, directly or indirectly, at the origin of large-scale symbolic revolutions (like the bohemian lifestyle in the nineteenth century, or, nowadays, the subversive provocations of the feminist or homosexual movements), capable of shaking the deepest structures of the social order, such as family structures, through transformation of the fundamental principles of division of the vision of the world (such as the male/female opposition) and the corresponding challenges to the self-evidences of common sense. (Bourdieu [1997] 2000, 105)

How does this "shaking" affect the sturdy structures of society, let alone threaten the symbolic violence of the dominant class? At one point he acknowledges the possibility that authors of such symbolic revolutions, through the transfer of cultural capital and in certain moments, can instigate subversive action from the dominated.

> The symbolic work needed in order to break out of the silent self-evidence of doxa and to state and denounce the arbitrariness that it conceals presupposes instruments of expression and criticism which, like other forms of capital, are unequally distributed. As a consequence, there is every reason to think that it would not be possible without the intervention of professional practitioners of the work of making explicit, who, in certain historical conjunctures, may make themselves the *spokespersons* of the dominated on the basis of partial solidarities and *de facto* alliances springing from the homology between a dominated position in this or that field of cultural production and the position of the dominated in the social space. A solidarity of this kind, which is not without ambiguity, can bring about . . . the *transfer of cultural capital* which enables the dominated to achieve a collective mobilization and subversive action against the established order; with, in return, the risk of hijacking which is contained in the imperfect correspondence between the interests of the dominated and those of the dominated-dominant who make themselves the spokespersons of their demands or their revolts, on the basis of a partial analogy between different experiences of domination. (188)

This is one of the rare places where Bourdieu allows for the possibility of collective mobilization of the dominated through their recognition rather than misrecognition of domination. Still the initiatives always come from above, from the dominated fractions of the dominant class whose experience of domination allows for a fragile alliance with the dominated classes.

More typically, Bourdieu relies on the inner logic of fields to move society toward a greater universalism, what he calls the realpolitik of reason that is wired into the character of the state:

> Those who, like Marx, reverse the official image that the State bureaucracy seeks to give of itself and describe the bureaucrats as usurpers of the universal, acting like private proprietors of public resources, are not wrong. But they ignore the very real effects of the obligatory reference to the values of neutrality and disinterested devotion to the public good which becomes more and more incumbent on state functionaries in the successive stages of the

long labor of symbolic construction which leads to the invention and imposition of the official representation of the State as the site of universality and the service of the general interest. (124)

This remarkable passage, in which Bourdieu is appealing to the state's "disinterested devotion to the public good" (that will eventually assert itself against the state's usurpers), is written at the very time he is also attacking the French state for continuing to violate its public function, in which the coercive right hand of the state is displacing its welfarist left hand, and when the state is openly assaulting the working class. In the long run, Bourdieu claims, the state will become the carrier of the general interest. But how?

The idea of universality will not prevail simply because it is an attractive ideal—that would be the worst form of idealism—but because certain fields by their very functioning, by virtue of their internal struggles, give rise to a commitment to the universal:

In reality, if one is not, at best, to indulge in an irresponsible utopianism, which often has no other effect than to procure the short-lived euphoria of humanist hopes, almost always as brief as adolescence, and which produces effects quite as malign in the life of research as in political life, it is necessary I think to return to a "realistic" vision of the universes in which the universal is generated. To be content, as one might be tempted, with giving the universal the status of a "regulatory idea," capable of suggesting principles of action, would be to forget that there are universes in which it becomes a "constitutive" immanent principle of regulation, such as the scientific field, and to a lesser extent the bureaucratic field and the judicial field; and that, more generally, as soon as the principles claiming universal validity (those of democracy, for example) are stated and officially professed, there is no longer any social situation in which they cannot serve at least as symbolic weapons in struggles of interests or as instruments of critique for those who have a self-interest in truth and virtue (like, nowadays, all those, especially in the minor state nobility, whose interests are bound up with universal advances associated with the State and with law). (127)

Let us recall that Bourdieu sets out on his Pascalian journey with a critique of scholastic reason for overlooking the way theoretical models, such as those of "rational choice" or "deliberative democracy," are but projections of the very specific conditions under which knowledge is produced. After turning from this fallacious logic of theory to the logic of practice and finding there only misrecognition, Bourdieu returns to the same universalities produced in the scientific, legal, and bureaucratic fields, universalities that he had earlier called into question as scholastic fallacies—the product of the peculiar circumstances of their production. But now he turns to them as the source of hope for humanity.

We are back to the Enlightenment, to Hegel's view of the state, so trenchantly criticized not just by Marx but *also* by Bourdieu (in his earlier writings). Both define the state as having a monopoly of symbolic as well as material violence. Both see the state as presenting the interests of the dominant class as the general interest. But where Marx sees the state as only serving the "common interests of the whole bourgeoisie" (with all the concessions this might entail), Bourdieu sees the state's universalist claims as grounds for an imminent critique, demanding that the state live up to its pretensions. We can see a similar Enlightenment faith in Bourdieu's proposals for an Internationale of intellectuals—the organic intellectual of humanity—recognizing that they are a corporate body with their own interests, but regarding those interests as the carriers of universalism and, thus, forming a corporatism of the universal.[11]

Toward the end of his life, Bourdieu was not only organizing intellectuals. He was to be found on the picket lines of striking workers, haranguing them about the evils of neoliberalism—even as his sociology claimed they could not understand the conditions of their own oppression. His two short volumes, *Acts of Resistance* (1998) and *Firing Back* ([2001] 2003), justify the public engagement of the intellectual in not just exposing the mythologies of neoliberalism but endorsing and even rousing social movements. Yet there is little in his theoretical corpus to see social movements as anything but the manipulation of its leaders—a far cry from his description of the spontaneous movements of unemployed workers and others against neoliberal policies. From a *theoretical standpoint* Bourdieu can explain neither his enthusiasm for nor the source of the social movements he addressed. No different from the people he criticized, he too succumbed to a gap between his theory and his practice, especially when his theory led him into a political cul-de-sac.

CONCLUSION

Marx and Bourdieu set out from similar positions, but they end up in divergent places. They both start out as critics of intellectualist illusions or scholastic fallacies that privilege the role of ideas in the making of history. They both move to the logic of practice. Marx remains wedded to this logic, turning from ideas to labor. Propelled by the concrete form of labor under capitalism, Marx sees a future emancipation realized through working-class revolution. When the working class lets him down, he sets about theoretical work to demonstrate the inevitable collapse of capitalism. Bourdieu, by contrast, sees the logic of practice as deeply mired in domination inculcated in the habitus. So he breaks from the logic of practice and reverts to the practice of logic and to a faith in reason, whether through symbolic revolutions organized by intellectuals or via the immanent logic of the state. Just as Marx revealed and relied on the inner contradictions of the economy, Bourdieu relied on the inner contradictions of the symbolic order. Where Bourdieu starts out as a critic of philosophy and ends up a Hegelian, believing in the universality of reason, Marx starts out as a critic of philosophy but ends up with material production, putting his faith in the universality of the working class through its realization of communism. Each would criticize the other as delusional.

We are on the horns of a dilemma: intellectuals without the subaltern or the subaltern without intellectuals. Each recognizes the dilemma, and in their practice each breaks with his theory. Bourdieu devotes the last years of his life to appealing to social movements, challenging the turn to neoliberalism. However, for his theory to catch up with his practice, Bourdieu needs a far better account of the dynamics of the habitus, the way it changes, and, in particular, how it can be reshaped by critical reflection—how the habitus of consent becomes a habitus of defiance. Without such a move forward, we are left wondering how intellectuals can penetrate their own habitus, how they can escape symbolic violence. How is the habitus of intellectuals different from the habitus of the dominated? Bourdieu suffers from a duality: an optimistic faith in reason and critical reflection and a pessimistic account of durable bodily knowledge unaware of itself. After distinguishing between the logic of theory and the logic of practice, he needs to bring them into a dynamic relation.

Equally, Marx, despairing of the working class that carries the burden of revolution, throws himself into the world of theory and devotes himself to demonstrating that capitalism must inherently destroy itself. Like the Young Hegelians he had earlier criticized, Marx battles with intellectuals as though the fate of the world depended on it. As Bourdieu says in the opening epigraph, Marx failed to grasp the power of his own theory as an ideology that could galvanize a collective will, but, in the final analysis, Bourdieu equally failed to explore how critical reflection or symbolic revolutions can have real effects.

It would take another Marxist, Antonio Gramsci, to transcend the separation of theory and practice. In a world defined by cultural domination, what he called hegemony, Gramsci develops a more balanced conception of class struggle, organized on the terrain of dominant ideology. In so doing he distinguishes between traditional intellectuals like Bourdieu, who protected their autonomy in order to project themselves as carrying some universal truth, and organic intellectuals like Marx, who sought a closer alliance with the dominated, elaborating their kernel of good sense—good sense acquired in the collective transformation of nature.

As we shall see, Gramsci is just one of a succession of Marxists who have dealt with questions that Marx failed to address adequately. This is what we might call the Marxist tradition or the Marxist research program. The question is whether a Bourdieusian research program will develop, tackling the abiding anomalies and contradictions of his corpus, or whether his followers will be content to apply the lexicon of "capital," "habitus," and "field" to different situations and allow his body of theory to be defined as a final and incontrovertible truth. The question, in other words, is whether Bourdieu's disciples will do to Bourdieu what he erroneously tries to do to Marxism, to reduce everything to the founding figure as if there could never be any further advances. If Bourdieu is to live on and be a worthy competitor to Marx, it will be necessary to think with Bourdieu against Bourdieu.

3

CULTURAL DOMINATION
Gramsci Meets Bourdieu

It would be easy to enumerate the features of the life-style
of the dominated classes which, through the sense of their
incompetence, failure or cultural unworthiness, imply a
form of recognition of the dominant values. It was Antonio
Gramsci who said somewhere that the worker tends to
bring his executant dispositions with him into every area
of life.

— BOURDIEU, *DISTINCTION: A SOCIAL CRITIQUE
OF THE JUDGMENT OF TASTE*

It's like when these days people wonder about my relations
with Gramsci—in whom they discover, probably because
they have [not] read me, a great number of things that
I was able to find in his work only *because* I hadn't read
him. . . . (The most interesting thing about Gramsci, who
in fact, I did only read quite recently, is the way he provides
us with the basis for a sociology of the party apparatchik
and the Communist leaders of this period—all of which
is far from the ideology of the "organic intellectual" for
which he is best known.)

— BOURDIEU, "FIELDWORK IN PHILOSOPHY"

This is an additional reason to ground the corporatism
of the universal in a corporatism geared to the defense
of well-understood common interests. One of the major

obstacles is (or was) the myth of the "organic intellectual," so dear to Gramsci. By reducing intellectuals to the role of the proletariat's "fellow travelers," this myth prevents them from taking up the defense of their own interests and from exploiting their most effective means of struggle on behalf of universal causes.

— BOURDIEU, "THE CORPORATISM OF THE UNIVERSAL"

If there is a single Marxist whom Pierre Bourdieu should have taken seriously, it would have to be Antonio Gramsci. The theorist of symbolic violence must surely engage the theorist of hegemony. Yet I can only find passing references to Gramsci in Bourdieu's writings. In the first epigraph to this chapter, Bourdieu appropriates Gramsci to his own thinking about cultural domination, in the second he deploys Gramsci to support his own theory of politics, and in the third he ridicules Gramsci's ideas about organic intellectuals.[1]

Given the widespread interest in Gramsci's writings during the 1960s and 1970s, when Bourdieu was developing his ideas of cultural domination, one can only surmise that the omission was deliberate. Bourdieu's allergy to Marxism here expresses itself in his refusal to entertain the ideas of the Marxist closest to his own perspective. He openly declares that he has never read Gramsci and that, if he had, he would have made his criticisms abundantly clear. Of all the Marxists, Gramsci was simply too close for comfort.

Indeed, the parallels are remarkable. Both repudiated Marxian laws of history to develop notions of class struggle in which culture played a key role, and both focused on what Gramsci called the superstructures and what Bourdieu called fields of culture, education, and politics. Both pushed aside the analysis of the economy itself to focus on its effects—the limits and opportunities it created for social change. Their interest in cultural domination led both to study intellectuals in relation to classes and politics. Both sought to transcend what they considered to be the false opposition of voluntarism and determinism, and of subjectivism and objectivism. They both openly rejected materialism and teleology and instead emphasized how theory and theorist are inescapably part of the world they study.

If one is looking for reasons for their extraordinary theoretical convergence, their parallel biographies are a good place to begin. Unique among the great Marxist theoreticians, Gramsci—like Bourdieu—came from a poor rural background. They were similarly uncomfortable in the university setting, although for Gramsci this meant leaving the university for a life of journalism and politics, before being unceremoniously cast into prison by the fascist state. Bourdieu, by contrast, would make the academy his home, climbing to its very peak and becoming a professor at the Collège de France. It was from there that he made his sorties into political life. No matter how far removed they became from the rural world into which they were born, neither ever lost touch with that world. They both made the experience of the dominated or subaltern an abiding preoccupation.

Given the similarities of their social trajectories and their common theoretical interests, their fundamental divergences are all the more interesting—closely tied, one might conjecture, to the very different historical contexts or political fields within which they acted. Gramsci, after all, remained a Marxist and engaged with questions of socialism at a time when it was still very much part of the wider political agenda, whereas Bourdieu distanced himself from Marxism, prefiguring what would become a post-socialist world. A conversation between Bourdieu and Gramsci built on their common interest in cultural domination promises to clarify their divergent politics. I begin such an imaginary conversation by tracing the intersection of their biographies with history, and then I draw out the parallels in their frameworks, before examining their divergent theories of cultural domination—hegemony versus symbolic violence—and their opposed theories of intellectuals.

PARALLEL LIVES OF PRACTICE

In seeking to comprehend human political interventions, Bourdieu's concept of habitus—the embedded and embodied dispositions acquired through life trajectories—invites us to examine the intersection of biography and history. The political lives of Gramsci and Bourdieu are the cumulative effects of four sets of experiences: (1) early childhood and schooling that saw each migrate from village to city in pursuit of education; (2) formative political experiences—i.e., Bourdieu's immersion in the Algerian revolution and Gramsci's participation in the politics leading up to the factory council movement; (3) theoretical development—for Bourdieu in the academy, for Gramsci in the communist movement; and (4) final redirections, in which Bourdieu moves from the university into public sphere, while Gramsci is forced to retreat from party to prison. At each successive moment, Bourdieu and Gramsci carry with them a habitus or, as Gramsci (1971, 353) calls it, the précis of their past, which guides their interventions in new fields.

Both Gramsci and Bourdieu grew up in peasant societies. Gramsci was born in Sardinia in 1891; Bourdieu was born in 1930 in the Béarn in the Pyrenees. Both were children of local public employees: Bourdieu the son of a postman who became a clerk in the village post office; Gramsci the son of a clerk in the local land registry who was imprisoned on charges of malfeasance. Bourdieu was an only child, but Gramsci was one of seven children, all of whom played a major role in his early life. Both were very attached to their mothers—in both instances women from higher-status backgrounds than their husbands. They both shone at school and by dint of willpower advanced from their poor villages to metropolitan centers, each with the support of devoted schoolmasters.

Undoubtedly, Gramsci's life was more difficult. Not only was his family far poorer, but he also suffered from the physical and psychological pain of being a hunchback. Only with his deep reserves of determination and with support from his elder brother could Gramsci in 1911 make his way to the mainland of northern Italy, on a scholarship to study philosophy and linguistics at the University of Turin. In similar fashion, Bourdieu would make his way to the preparatory lycée and then enter the École Normale Supérieure, where he studied philosophy, then the apex of the French intellectual pyramid.

Coming from a rural background to the urban metropolis, whether Turin or Paris, was daunting—both were fish out of water in the new middle- and upper-class milieu of the university. Bourdieu writes of his disjointed habitus: "the durable effect of a very strong discrepancy between high academic consecration and low social origin, in other words a *cleft habitus*, inhabited by tensions and contradictions" ([2004] 2007, 100). Although they both became brilliant intellectuals and political figures, neither lost touch with the sources of his marginality, his village and his family. Gramsci's devotion to his family and rural mores is captured in his letters from prison, just as Bourdieu remained similarly close to his parents, returning home periodically to conduct field research. Their rural upbringing is deeply embedded in their dispositions and thought, whether by way of an obdurate inheritance or a vehement reaction.[2]

Gramsci never finished university but dived into Turin's working-class politics, which was heating up during the First World War. He began writing for the socialist newspaper *Avanti!* and also for *Il Grido*. After the war he became the editor of *L'Ordine Nuovo*, the magazine of Turin's working class, designed to articulate its new culture and destined to become the mouthpiece of the factory council movement and the occupation of the factories of 1919–20. Bourdieu, on the other hand, left university and after a year teaching in a lycée was drafted for national service in Algeria in 1955. He would remain in this war-torn country for five years, conducting fieldwork when his military service was over, teaching at the university, and through his writing representing the culture and struggles of the colonized, both in town and village. With the political clampdown after the temporary setback to the anticolonial movement in the 1957 Battle of Algiers, Bourdieu's position became untenable and he was eventually forced to leave in 1960. Thus, in their formative years after university, both Gramsci and Bourdieu were fundamentally transformed by struggles far from their homes.

Even during these years, however, Gramsci was politically much closer to his allies than was Bourdieu, whose political engagement manifested itself at a scientific distance. The bifurcated world of colonialism removed Bourdieu from the colonized, just as the class order of Italy thrust Gramsci, although an émigré from the semi-feudal Sardinia, into working-class politics. Accordingly, at this point the two men took very different roads. Following the defeat of the factory councils, Gramsci became a leader of the working-class movement, a founding member of the Communist Party in 1921, and its general secretary in 1924, precisely when fascism was consolidated. He spent time in Moscow with the Comintern and in exile in Vienna, but traveled throughout Italy after 1923 at a time when being an elected deputy gave him political immunity. This ended in 1926 when he was arrested under a new set of laws, and in 1928 he was brought to trial. The judge declared that Gramsci's brain must be stopped for twenty years. He was sent to prison where, despite contracting numerous and ultimately fatal diseases, he produced the most creative Marxist thinking of the twentieth century—the famous *Prison Notebooks*. Ironically, it was the fascist prison that kept Stalin's predators at bay. Gramsci's health deteriorated continuously, until he died in 1937 of tuberculosis, Pott's disease (which eats away at the vertebrae), and arteriosclerosis, just as an international campaign for his release was gaining momentum.

Bourdieu's trajectory could not have been more different. After Algeria, he passed into the academy, taking up positions in France's leading research centers and writing about the place of education in reproducing the class relations of French society. Bourdieu was to be elected to the prestigious chair of sociology at the Collège de France in 1981, which made him a preeminent public intellectual and an inheritor of the mantle of Sartre and Foucault. From the beginning, his writings had political import and bearing, but they took on a more activist and urgent mission in the mid-1990s, especially with the return to power of the socialists in 1997. He publicly defended the dispossessed, attacked the ascendant technocracy of neoliberalism, and above all assailed the mass media and journalists in his book *On Television*. He undertook various publishing ventures, from the more academic *Actes de la Recherches en Sciences Sociales* to the more radical Liber-Raisons d'Agir book series. In his last years he would try to forge a "collective intellectual" that transcended national and disciplinary boundaries, bringing together progressive minds to shape public debate.

If Gramsci moved from party political engagement to a more scholastic life in prison, where he reflected on the failed socialist revolution in the West, Bourdieu took the opposite path, from the scholastic life to a more public opposition to the growing tide of market fundamentalism, even addressing striking workers and supporting their struggles. Gramsci's organic connection to the working class through the Communist Party exaggerated the revolutionary potential of the working class. Thus, in prison he devoted himself to understanding how the elaborate superstructures of advanced capitalism, which included an expanded state as well as the state's relation to the emergent trenches of civil society, "not only justifies and maintains its domination but manages to win the active consent of those over whom it rules" (Gramsci 1971, 245).

By contrast, Bourdieu's adoption of a more overt political posture toward the end of his life came with an already elaborated theory of cultural domination, one based on an analysis of strategic action within fields and its allied concept, habitus. In the late 1990s, finding the public sphere increasingly distorted by the media, Bourdieu assumed a more offensive posture, even to the extent of openly supporting protest movements. His spirited defense of intellectual and academic autonomy and his aggressive attacks on neoliberalism made him one of the most prominent public figures in France.

Gramsci's prison writings reflected on and advanced beyond his political practice. He wrote about the ideal Communist Party—the "Modern Prince"—but he could never find one in reality. If Gramsci's theory advanced beyond his practice, the reverse was true for Bourdieu in his last years. He burst onto the political scene without any warrant from his theorizing, which pointed to actors lost in a cloud of misrecognition. Here, practice moved ahead of theory. To examine the respective disjunctures of theory and practice, we need to put their theories into dialogue with each other.

CLASS, POLITICS, AND CULTURE

It is difficult to slice up these two bodies of theory into parallel and comparable segments, since each segment achieves meaning only in relation to the whole. Still, I will make parallel cuts into each body of theory, even at the cost of overlap and repetition. I begin with their broad frameworks for the study of class, politics, and culture that can be found in *The Modern Prince* (Gramsci 1971, 123–205) and *Distinction* (Bourdieu [1979] 1984). In these writings, both Gramsci and Bourdieu divide a social formation into parallel homologous realms—the economic, which gives us classes; the political-cultural, which gives us domination and struggle; and, for Gramsci, the military, which sets limits on struggle.

For Gramsci, the economy serves to provide the basis of class formation—working class, peasantry, petty bourgeoisie, and capitalist class. The economy determines the objective strength of each class, while setting limits on the relations among those classes. But the struggles and alliances among classes are organized on the terrain of politics and ideology, a terrain that has its own logic. The political structure, for example, organizes the forms of representation of classes, in particular political parties. Each political order also has a hegemonic ideology, that is, a hegemonic system of ideologies that provide a common language, discourse, and normative visions shared by the contestants in struggle. Class struggle is not a struggle between ideologies but a struggle on the terrain of ideology over the articulation of the different elements of a single ideological system. Alternative hegemonies can emerge in moments of organic crisis, but otherwise they have little support. Finally, there is a military order that, in relation to class struggle, for the most part is invisible, entering only to discipline the illegalities of groups and individuals or to restore order in times of fundamental crisis. Gramsci is as concerned about its political moment (i.e., the subjective state of military personnel) as about the technical preparedness of the coercive forces.

Similarly, Bourdieu has homologous realms, with the major division between the economic and the cultural realm. Again, there is no analysis of the economic as such, and classes, as in Gramsci, are taken as given: dominant classes, petite bourgeoisie, and working class. But classes cannot be reduced to the purely economic; they contain a combination of economic and cultural capital, so that the dominant class has a chiastic structure divided between a dominant fraction strong in economic and weak in cultural capital and a dominated fraction strong in cultural and relatively weak in economic capital. Equally, the middle classes are also divided between the old petite bourgeoisie (emphasizing economic capital) and the new petite bourgeoisie (emphasizing cultural capital). Finally, the working class has a minimal amount of both types of capital, and so its members are forced into a life governed by material necessity.

Gramsci wheels his classes into the political arena, where their interests are forged and organized. Here we find political parties, trade unions, chambers of commerce, and so forth representing the interests of given classes in relation to other classes, each class battling to advance its own narrow corporate interests. Two classes—specifically capital and labor—also seek to reach the hegemonic level and represent their own interests as the interests of all. In parallel fashion, Bourdieu focuses on the way the cultural realm masks the class stratification upon which it is founded. Absorption in the practices of the dominant—"legitimate"—culture hides the class-based cultural resources that make these practices possible. The appreciation of art, music, and literature is possible only with a leisured existence and inherited cultural wealth, but it is presented as an attribute of gifted individuals. In their self-representation, individuals are in the dominant class because they are gifted; they are not gifted because they are in the dominant class. All cultural practices—from art to sport, from literature to food, from music to holidays—are ranged in a hierarchy that is homologous to the class hierarchy. The middle classes seek to imitate the cultural practices of the dominant class, while the working class grants legitimacy by abstention—high culture is not for them. They are driven by functional exigencies adapted to material necessity.

If for Gramsci the cultural realm is a realm of class struggle, for Bourdieu it dissipates class struggle. Struggle takes place within separate cultural fields or within the dominant classes, but it is not a class struggle. It is a classification struggle—a struggle over terms and forms of representation. Bourdieu rarely goes beyond classification struggles within classes to class struggle between classes, which perhaps explains why military force never appears in his theoretical accounts.[3] These divergences between Gramsci's and Bourdieu's notions of politics require us to attend to the differences between two very different terrains of contestation—civil society and the field of power.

CIVIL SOCIETY VS. FIELD OF POWER

Gramsci's innovation was to periodize capitalism not in terms of the transformation of the economic base (competitive to monopoly capitalism, or laissez-faire to organized capitalism, etc.), but in terms of the rise of civil society—the associations, movements, and organizations that are separate from the economy and the state. Thus, he was referring to the appearance of trade unions, religious organizations, media, schools, voluntary associations, and political parties that were relatively autonomous from but nevertheless guaranteed and organized by the state. The "trenches of civil society" effectively organized consent to domination by absorbing the participation of the subaltern classes, giving space to political activity but within limits defined by capitalism. Participating in elections, working in trades, attending school, going to church, and reading newspapers had the effect of channeling dissent into activities within organizations that would compete for the attention of the state.

This had dramatic consequences, Gramsci argued, for the very idea of social transformation. Attempts to seize state power would be repulsed so long as civil society was left intact. Rather, it was first necessary to carry out the long and arduous march through the trenches of civil society. Such a *war of position* required the reconstruction of civil society, breaking the thousand threads that connected it to the state and bringing it (civil society) under the direction of the revolutionary movement, in particular its party, which Gramsci calls the "Modern Prince." The seizure of state power (i.e., the *war of movement*) was but the culminating act in a long, drawn-out conflict. The century-long struggle against South African apartheid, especially in the 1980s, the advance of Solidarity in Poland during 1980–81, and even the civil rights movement in the United States—all are examples, more or less partial, of a war of position. The point is simple: assault on the state might work where civil society was "primordial and gelatinous" (e.g., the French Revolution or the Russian Revolution) but not in advanced capitalism. Lenin's theory of revolution, which prioritized assault on the state, as formulated in *State and Revolution*, is not a general theory but reflected the specific circumstances of Russia.

Although it does contain elements of a classification struggle, the idea of a war of position on the terrain of civil society, forging a popular challenge to the social order, finds little resonance in Bourdieu's theory. Strangely for a sociologist, Bourdieu has no notion of civil society. What we find instead are leaders of the organizations of civil society—party leaders, trade union leaders, intellectual leaders, religious leaders—competing with one another in the *field of power* above civil society, employing their representative function to advance their own interests, more or less unaccountable to their followers (Bourdieu 1991, part 3). Where Gramsci emphasizes class struggle—although by no means to the exclusion of struggle within classes, especially within the dominant class—Bourdieu, as we have seen, focuses on classification struggles, that is, struggles within the dominant class about dominant classifications. Just as in Gramsci's analysis the state coordinates the elements of civil society, so in Bourdieu's the state regulates the classification struggles through its ultimate monopoly of the legitimate means of symbolic violence.

Classification struggles have consequences for, but are not affected by, the dominated. Bourdieu makes no reference to civil society—for him there is no effective politics except in the field of power, confined to the dominant classes. As for Weber, the majority are steeped in the stupor of subjugation, manipulated by their spokespeople.

HEGEMONY VS. SYMBOLIC VIOLENCE

At first blush, hegemony and symbolic violence appear very similar, ensuring the maintenance of the social order not through coercion but through cultural domination. Indeed, there are places where they appear to be saying the same thing, but that would be to obscure fundamental differences—differences that ultimately reside in the capacity of the dominated to understand and contest the conditions of their existence.

Hegemony is a form of domination that Gramsci famously defined as "the combination of force and consent, which balance each other reciprocally, without force predominating excessively over consent. Indeed, the attempt is always made to ensure that force will appear to be based on the consent of the majority" (Gramsci 1971, 80). Hegemony has to be distinguished from dictatorship or despotism, where coercion prevails and is applied arbitrarily without regulatory norms. Hegemony is organized in civil society, but it embraces the state too: "The State is the entire complex of practical and theoretical activities with which the ruling class not only justifies and maintains its dominance, but manages to win the active consent of those over whom it rules" (244). A lot rests on the idea of consent, of a knowing and willing participation of the dominated in their subjugation.

Bourdieu sometimes uses the word *consent* to describe symbolic violence, but it has a connotation of much greater psychological depth than hegemony. In *Distinction*, Bourdieu writes of habitus as the "internalized form of class condition and of the conditioning it entails" ([1979] 1984, 101). "The schemes of the habitus, the primary forms of classification, owe their specific efficacy to the fact that they function below the level of the consciousness and language, beyond the reach of introspective scrutiny or control by the will" (466). In *Pascalian Meditations*, Bourdieu writes,

The agent engaged in practice knows the world but with a knowledge which . . . is not set up in the relation of externality of a knowing consciousness. He knows it in a sense, too well, without objectifying distance, takes it for granted, precisely because he is caught up in it, bound up with it; he inhabits it like a garment [*un habit*]. He feels at home in the world because the world is also in him, in the form of habitus, a virtue made of necessity which implies a form of love of necessity, *amor fati*. ([1997] 2000, 142–43)

Thus, symbolic violence does not depend on physical force or even on legitimacy. Indeed, it makes both unnecessary:

The state does not necessarily need to give orders and to exert physical coercion, or disciplinary constraint, to produce an ordered social world, so long as it is able to produce incorporated cognitive structures attuned to the objective structures and secure doxic submission to the established order. (178; see also 176)

Symbolic violence is defined in opposition to the notion of legitimacy, which is skin deep, but also to hegemony, which is based on an awareness of domination, a practical sense that is also conscious. In a telling passage, Bourdieu dismisses the notion of false consciousness, not by questioning the notion of falseness (as is usually the case) but by questioning the notion of consciousness:

In the notion of "false consciousness" which some Marxists invoke to explain the effect of symbolic domination, it is the word "consciousness" which is excessive; and to speak of "ideology" is to place in the order of representations, capable of being transformed by the intellectual conversion that is called the "awakening of consciousness," what belongs to the order of beliefs, that is, at the deepest level of bodily dispositions. (177)

Instead of false consciousness, Bourdieu talks of "misrecognition": the way in which people spontaneously recognize the world as a *mis*recognition that is deeply rooted in the habitus and seemingly inaccessible to reflection.

Gramsci couldn't be more different. Instead of misrecognition, we have a knowing, rational consent to domination, and instead of habitus, he develops the notion of "common sense" that contains a kernel of "good sense"—practical activity that can lead to genuine understanding—as well as inherited folk wisdom and invading ideologies:

> The active man-in-the-mass has a practical activity, but has no clear theoretical consciousness of his practical activity, which nonetheless involves understanding the world in so far as it transforms it. His theoretical consciousness can indeed be historically in opposition to his activity. One might almost say he has two theoretical consciousnesses (or one contradictory consciousness): one which is implicit in his activity and which in reality unites him with his fellow-workers in the practical transformation of the real world: and one, superficially explicit or verbal, which he has inherited from the past and uncritically absorbed. But this verbal conception is not without its consequences. It holds together a specific social group, it influences moral conduct and the direction of the will, with varying efficacity, but often powerfully enough to produce a situation in which the contradictory state of consciousness does not permit of any action, any decision or any choice, and produces a condition of moral passivity. Critical understanding of self takes place therefore through a struggle of political "hegemonies" and of opposing directions, first in the ethical field and then in that of politics proper, in order to arrive at the working out at a higher level of one's own conception of reality. (Gramsci 1971, 333)

Here we enter the crux of the difference between Gramsci and Bourdieu. Whereas Gramsci looks upon the practical activity of collectively transforming the world as the basis of good sense and potentially leading to class consciousness, Bourdieu sees in practical activity the opposite: it leads to a class *un*consciousness and acceptance of the world as it is. Compare the astonishingly parallel passage in Bourdieu:

> To point out that perception of the social world implies an act of construction is not in the least to accept an intellectualist theory of knowledge: the essential part of one's experience of the social world and of the labour of construction it implies takes place in *practice*, without reaching the level of *explicit* representation and *verbal* expression. Closer to a class unconsciousness than to a "class consciousness" in the Marxist sense, the sense of position

one occupies in the social space (what Goffman calls the "sense of one's place") is the practical mastery of the social structure as a whole which reveals itself through the sense of the position occupied in that structure. The categories of perception of the social world are essentially the product of the incorporation of the objective structures of the social space. Consequently, they incline agents to accept the social world as it is, to take it for granted, rather than to rebel against it, to put forward opposed and even antagonistic possibilities. (Bourdieu [1984] 1991b, 235; emphasis added to underline the parallels with Gramsci)

In other words, for Bourdieu, common sense is simply a blanket of bad sense, seemingly for everyone, except for a few sociologists in the scientific field, who miraculously see through the fog, whereas for Gramsci different classes have different potentials for developing insight into the world they inhabit, differently endowed with good sense depending on their relation to production. The working class in particular is favored through its collective transformation of nature, whereas production among the peasantry and petty bourgeoisie is too individualized, and the dominant class does not engage directly in production.

The contrast with Lenin is illuminating. Like Bourdieu, Lenin considered the working class by itself to be incapable of reaching more than trade union consciousness. Lenin concluded that truth—carried by the collective intellectual—has to be brought to the working class from without ([1902] 1975, [1917] 1975). From this, Bourdieu recoils with horror—the working class is too deeply mired in submission to be altered by such presumptuous vanguardism, which endangers both intellectuals and workers. Gramsci, on the other hand, argues against Lenin's notion of "falseness," and instead emphasizes the duality of consciousness. He grants the working class its kernel of truth that opens the door to intellectuals, who can then elaborate that truth through dialogue. From these profound differences emerge contrary views not only of class struggle but also of the role of intellectuals.

INTELLECTUALS: TRADITIONAL VS. ORGANIC

Unique among classical Marxists, Gramsci devotes much attention to intellectuals and their relation to themselves, to the working class, and to the dominant classes. We saw how Marx was not able to explain himself to himself—first, how a bourgeois intellectual could be fighting with the working class against the bourgeoisie and, second, how and why all his literary efforts mattered for class formation and class struggle. He simply had nothing systematic to say about intellectuals. Gramsci's interest in cultural domination and working-class consciousness led him to take seriously the role and place of intellectuals.

He begins with the important assumption that everyone operates with theories of the world, but there are those who specialize in producing such theories, whom we call intellectuals or philosophers. Of these, there are two types: organic and traditional intellectuals. The first is organically connected to the class it represents, while the second is relatively autonomous from the class it represents. Under capitalism, subordinate classes rely on the first, while dominant classes are advantaged by the second. Let us explore the distinction further.

For the working class to become a revolutionary force, it requires intellectuals to elaborate its good sense within common sense. Such an elaboration takes place through dialogue between the working class and a collective intellectual—the Communist Party that Gramsci refers to as the "Modern Prince" as permanent persuader. This is a matter not of bringing consciousness to the working class from without, which marks Gramsci off from Lenin, but of building on what already lies within it. The organic intellectual can only be effective through an intimate relation with the working class, sharing its life, which, in some readings of Gramsci, means coming from the working class.

We can see why Bourdieu dismisses the idea of "organic intellectual" as mythological. Since the common sense of the working class is all bad sense, there is therefore no good sense, no kernel of genuine understanding within the practical experience of the working class, and thus nothing for intellectuals to elaborate. There is no basis for dialogue, which therefore degenerates into populism—an identification with the working class, which is none other than a projection of their own desires and imaginations onto the working class, a class that intellectuals mistakenly claim to understand:

> It is not a question of the truth or falsity of the unsupportable image of the working class world that the intellectual produces when, putting himself in the place of a worker without having the habitus of a worker, he apprehends the working-class condition through schemes of perception and appreciation which are not those that the members of the working class themselves use to apprehend it. It is truly the experience that an intellectual can obtain of the

working-class world by putting himself provisionally and deliberately into the working-class condition, and it may become less and
less improbable if, as is beginning to happen, an increasing number of individuals are thrown into the working-class condition without having the habitus that is the product of the conditionings "normally" imposed on those who are condemned to this condition.
Populism is never anything other than an inverted ethnocentrism.
(Bourdieu [1979] 1984, 372–74)

In other words, the intellectual, whose habitus is formed by *skholè* (a world
that is free of material necessity), cannot appreciate the condition of the
members of the working class, whose habitus is shaped by the endless and
precarious pursuit of their material livelihood. Temporary immersion into
factory life generates in the intellectual an abhorrence for the conditions of
working-class life, while the working class itself, inured to its subjugation,
looks at the intellectual with incomprehension.

Intellectuals, being part of the dominated fraction of the dominant
class, experience their lives as subjugation, leading some to identify with
the dominated classes. But this identification is illusory. They have little in
common with the working class. Intellectuals are much better off explicitly
defending their own interests as the interests of all—the universal interests
of humanity:

Cultural producers will not find again a place of their own in the
social world unless, sacrificing once and for all the myth of the
"organic intellectual" (without falling into the complementary mythology of the mandarin withdrawn from everything), they agree to
work collectively for the defense of their interests. This should lead
them to assert themselves as an international power of criticism
and watchfulness, or even of proposals, in the face of the technocrats, or—with an ambition both more lofty and more realistic, and
hence limited to their own sphere—to get involved in rational action to defend the economic and social conditions of the autonomy
of these socially privileged universes in which the material and intellectual instruments of what we call Reason are produced and reproduced. This *Realpolitik of reason* will undoubtedly be suspected
of corporatism. But it will be part of its task to prove, by the ends to
which it puts the sorely won means of autonomy, that it is a corporatism of the universal. (Bourdieu [1992] 1996, 348)

We are back with the realpolitik of reason—a claim that in protecting their own autonomy, intellectuals can at the same time defend the interests of humanity. Bourdieu proposes the formation of an Internationale of intellectuals, but why should we have any more confidence in his "Modern Prince" than in Gramsci's? What ends—what visions and divisions—has Bourdieu in mind for this "organic intellectual of humanity"?[4] Why should we trust intellectuals—the historic bearers of neoliberalism, fascism, racism, Bolshevism, and so forth—to be the saviors of humanity? In dissecting the scholastic fallacies committed by others, is Bourdieu not committing the greatest fallacy of all, the self-misrecognition of the intellectual as (potential) bearer of a deceptive universality? Bourdieu has replaced the universality of the working class based in production and carried by the political party with the universality of the intellectual based in the academy.

In Gramsci's eyes, Bourdieu's universalistic defense of intellectuals is the ideology of the traditional intellectual, who, through defending autonomy, becomes all the more effective in securing the hegemony of the dominant classes. The latter seek to present their interests as the interests of all, and for that they require relatively autonomous intellectuals who genuinely believe in their universality. Intellectuals who are closely connected to the dominant class cannot represent the latter as a universal class. Thus, a thoroughgoing critical stance toward the dominant class for pursuing its own corporate interest—to wit, its uncompromising and short-sighted pursuit of profit—can still advance bourgeois hegemony. Can intellectuals represent their autonomy in opposition to bourgeois hegemony without being accountable to another class? Bourdieu says yes: intellectuals can represent interests above class. Gramsci says no: in the final analysis, there are no interests above class. Gramsci's organic intellectual not only elaborates the good sense of the working class but also attacks the claims of traditional intellectuals to represent some true universality independent of class.

CONCLUSION

Gramsci and Bourdieu may appear convergent at one level, but at a deeper level they are mirror opposites: Bourdieu attacks Gramsci's organic intellectual as mythical, while Gramsci attacks Bourdieu's traditional intellectual as self-deluding. At bottom, the divergence rests on claims about the (in)ability of the dominated to understand the world and the (in)ability of intellectuals to transcend their corporate or class interests. To these two questions, Gramsci and Bourdieu have opposite answers: Gramsci claims the dominated can have a partial insight into their worlds and organic intellectuals exist to elaborate that insight; Bourdieu, by contrast, claims the dominated cannot comprehend their subjugation, while intellectuals, so long as they are autonomous from classes, can see and represent the truth through the fog of cultural domination.

Their opposition does not mean that conversation is futile. Throughout his prison writings, Gramsci shows how aware he is of the Bourdieusian critique by returning time and again to the difficulties of sustaining a reciprocal dialogue between the party and its followers, between leaders and led. As we know, in his own critique of the organic intellectual, Bourdieu drew on Gramsci's reflections on the alienation of politics from the rank and file. On the other hand, Bourdieu knows only too well the limitations of intellectuals' claims to universality and the danger of scholastic fallacies that trap them into a parochial corporatism. In other words, each recognizes the partial truth of the other; so they can provide each other with important correctives.

More than that, as we shall see, there are surprising crossovers. In the argument between Freire and Bourdieu, Gramsci will side with Bourdieu, defending conventional schooling for all. Even more surprising is Bourdieu's embrace of the organic intellectual in *The Weight of the World* (Bourdieu et al. [1993] 1999), an ethnography of suffering in French society that I discuss in chapter 9. In the next conversation, with Fanon, Bourdieu will reproduce the Gramscian position, claiming good sense for the Algerian working class and bad sense for the peasantry. Caught in the contradictions between theory and practice, different historical conjunctures led him to adopt different positions.

COLONIALISM AND REVOLUTION
Fanon Meets Bourdieu

But above all I wanted to get away from speculation—at that time [1960s], the works of Frantz Fanon, especially *The Wretched of the Earth*, were the latest fashion, and they struck me as being false and dangerous.

— BOURDIEU, "FIELDWORK IN PHILOSOPHY"

What Fanon says corresponds to nothing. It is even dangerous to make the Algerians believe the things he says. This would bring them to a utopia. And I think these men [Sartre and Fanon] contributed to what Algeria became because they told stories to Algerians who often did not know their own country any more than the French who spoke about it, and, therefore, the Algerians retained a completely unrealistic utopian illusion of Algeria. . . . The texts of Fanon and Sartre are frightening for their irresponsibility. You would have to be a megalomaniac to think you could say just any such nonsense.

— BOURDIEU, INTERVIEW IN LE SUEUR, *UNCIVIL WAR*

Bourdieu's stance toward Marxism becomes more hostile as we move from Marx to Gramsci and now to Fanon. Bourdieu is prepared to acknowledge the insights of Karl Marx and, indeed, so many of his ideas find an echo in the writings of Marx. As I have already suggested, his theory of cultural domination can be seen as an extension of Marx's political economy from material to symbolic goods. While Bourdieu wants to distance himself from his counterpart in the Marxist tradition, he nonetheless shows a grudging respect by turning Gramsci against Gramsci.

When it comes to Frantz Fanon, the gloves are off, as we see in the rare quotations above, taken from two interviews. I have found no other explicit commentary on Fanon in Bourdieu's works. As with other Marxists, once we allow Fanon to respond, we see both astonishing parallels and glaring divergences. Bourdieu's enmity toward Fanon—there is no evidence that Fanon even knew Bourdieu—is perhaps all the deeper because their lives in Algeria overlapped. But they were worlds apart: the one a scientific observer from the metropolis sympathetic to the plight of the colonized, attempting to give them dignity by recognizing their distinctive traditions; the other a psychiatrist from Martinique trained in France and dealing directly with victims of violence on both sides of the colonial divide. The one was attached to the university and ventured into communities as research sites, while the other worked in a psychiatric hospital before committing himself to the liberation movement (the FLN).

Still, the enmity is especially interesting, given how similar are their accounts of colonialism and its effects, namely those found in Fanon's *The Wretched of the Earth* ([1961] 1963) and Bourdieu's less-well-known works written while he was in Algeria or soon thereafter—*The Sociology of Algeria* (1958), *Travail et travailleurs en Algérie* (*Work and Workers in Algeria*, 1963, written with Alain Darbel, Jean-Pierre Rivet, and Claude Seibel), and *Le déracinement* (*The Uprooting*, 1964, written with Abdelmalek Sayad).[1] Certainly, the two writers refract their writings through different theoretical lenses—modernization theory and Third World Marxism—which reflect serious disagreements, but it surely cannot account for Bourdieu's venomous hostility, especially as within his modernization theory there is more than a whiff of Marxism.

We need to look elsewhere for the source of Bourdieu's contempt for Fanon, namely their places in the French political and intellectual scene. The two men were not only located on different sides of the color line within the political field of war-torn Algeria, but, just as significantly, they occupied opposed positions within the French political field—overlapping with, but distinct from, the Algerian political field. When Bourdieu moved back to France, he entered a very different intellectual world—that of the metropolis rather than the colony. There, despite his sympathies for the colonized, he positioned himself in opposition to the Third Worldism associated with

Sartre and expressed most vividly in the writings of Fanon. We must not forget that the Algerian question created a near civil war within France itself, with positions ranging all the way from fervent defense of the anticolonial revolution to uncompromising support for the settler regime. Indeed, the extremes were organized militarily within France. Bourdieu vacillated in the middle. As soon as he was associated with Sartre's antagonist, Raymond Aron, he did not take the side of Fanon and Sartre.

It is significant, then, that with immersion in the French political field, Bourdieu breaks with his own apocalyptic writings on Algeria to offer a completely different rendering of Algerian society. His best-known Algerian writings are not the early ones but the heavily theorized treatises *An Outline of a Theory of Practice* ([1972] 1977) and the subsequent version, *The Logic of Practice* ([1980] 1990). Based on a timeless, context-free construction of the rural Kabyle[2]—an anthropological mythology if ever there were one—it is here that Bourdieu develops the concepts of symbolic capital, habitus, doxa, and misrecognition, which are then used to paint France in functionalist colors. Here lies Bourdieu's brilliance (and, one might say, his limitations)—to take the elementary forms of a fabricated Kabyle social life as the building blocks for studying advanced capitalism. What differentiates the latter from the former is the coexistence of differentiated fields—a notion notably absent in his writings on the Kabyle.

Physical violence is, thereby, relegated to the colony, while *symbolic* violence is pinned to the metropolis—but, ironically, through the extrapolation of a self-reproducing, harmonious, autochthonous Kabyle society. At the same time, Bourdieu's analysis of France exhibits uncanny parallels with Fanon's first book, *Black Skin, White Masks* ([1952] 1967), which describes the symbolic violence of the French racial order. But where Fanon stresses the *psychoanalysis* of internalized oppression in the context of the French racial order, Bourdieu undertakes the *socio-analysis* of "distinction," supported by the undeveloped psychology of habitus. Equally important, however, is their inverse trajectory: Fanon moves from symbolic violence to social revolution, whereas Bourdieu moves in the opposite direction, from social revolution to symbolic violence.

This, then, is how I will construct Fanon's calm response to Bourdieu's violent denunciations. I begin with their early careers—from margin to center to margin—and from there explore their parallel accounts of colonialism, showing how they inflect those accounts with different theories, before finally comparing their reverse trajectories that culminate in Bourdieu's *critical pessimism* with regard to symbolic violence in France and Fanon's *revolutionary optimism* with regard to colonial violence in Algeria.

CONVERGENT BIOGRAPHIES:
FROM MARGIN TO CENTER TO MARGIN

Bourdieu and Fanon overlapped in Algeria, during the period of intensive struggles for national liberation (1954–62). Bourdieu arrived in 1955 to do his military service, whereupon he became absorbed by the fate of the Algerian people. He stayed on, taking a position at the University of Algiers, turned from philosophy to ethnology and sociology, and dived into research on all facets of the life of the colonized. Wading into war zones with his research assistants, he became a chronicler and witness to colonial subjugation and the evolving struggles. By 1960 his presence had become politically untenable and he left Algeria for France, where he embarked on his illustrious career as a sociologist, indelibly marked by his Algerian experiences.

Fanon arrived in Algeria in 1953, two years before Bourdieu, also from France, where he had recently completed a degree in medicine and psychiatry. In Algeria, he was appointed head of the Blida-Joinville Psychiatric Hospital and through his patients he vicariously experienced the traumas of colonial violence. He concluded that psychiatry was no solution to the suffering and so he became involved in the liberation struggle, leading to his expulsion from Algeria in 1956. He went to Tunis, where he continued his psychiatric work, and then to Accra, where he became a roving ambassador for the FLN in different parts of North and West Africa. He died of leukemia in 1961, just before Algeria achieved independence but not before he had finished *The Wretched of the Earth*, the bible of liberation movements across the world.

In their different ways, both Bourdieu and Fanon were well prepared to develop original interpretations of their Algerian experiences. They both made the uncomfortable journey from periphery to center. Bourdieu grew up in a small village in the Béarn, where his father graduated from sharecropper to postal employee. Only Bourdieu's brilliance and the support of his teachers took him all the way to the École Normale Supérieure. Fanon grew up in Martinique in a Creole family with middle-class aspirations, before entering the Free French Army in 1943. He served in North Africa, witnessing colonial oppression of a sort he had never seen before, and then in eastern France, where he discovered the meaning of metropolitan racism. He was back in France in 1946, studying to be a doctor in Lyon. Both Bourdieu and Fanon had bitter experiences of marginalization in France: the one based on class, which Bourdieu describes in *Sketch for a Self-Analysis*, and the other based on race, which Fanon exposed in *Black Skin, White Masks*. Both were well equipped to be horrified by the abominations of settler colonialism, although their race and political propensities would position them differently within the colonial order.

The reverse transition from center to periphery, from France to Algeria, demanded a wholesale reorientation of the schemes of understanding they had acquired in their formal training in France. They both converged on a sociology of colonialism—Bourdieu from philosophy that he found too removed from the brutality of French colonialism and Fanon from psychiatry that couldn't grasp the structural features of colonial domination. Their accounts of colonialism are remarkably similar.

SEVEN THESES ON COLONIALISM: BOURDIEU EQUALS FANON

Notwithstanding their convergent trajectories from periphery to center and then from center back to periphery, given their divergent positions and dispositions, one would expect Bourdieu the French *normalien* philosopher and Fanon the Martiniquan psychiatrist to have clashing understandings of the colonial condition. Such an expectation of divergence is only intensified if one takes into account Bourdieu's later denunciation of Fanon's writings as "speculative," "irresponsible," and "dangerous." It is all the more interesting, therefore, to discover striking parallels in their analyses of colonial domination, anticolonial struggles, and the supersession of colonialism. As evidence, let me draw on two texts, both written in 1961, one year before Algeria's independence—Bourdieu's "Revolution Within the Revolution"[3] and Fanon's *The Wretched of the Earth*.

I

Colonialism is a system of domination held together by violence. In his familiar evocative way, Fanon writes,

> Their first encounter was marked by violence and their existence
> together—that is to say the exploitation of the native by the settler—
> was carried on by dint of a great array of bayonets and cannons.
> ([1961] 1963, 36)

Bourdieu is equally clear:

> Indeed, the war plainly revealed the true basis for the colonial order: the relation, backed by force, which allows the dominant caste to keep the dominated caste in a position of inferiority. ([1961] 1962, 146)

Bourdieu avoids the concept of race, reluctant to use it in his analysis not only of colonialism but also of French society, where he is far more comfortable deploying class as his critical concept.

2

The colonial situation is fundamentally one of segregation of colonizers from colonized. In Fanon's terms, colonialism follows the principle of "reciprocal exclusivity," admitting of no compromise:

> The zone where the natives live is not complementary to the zone inhabited by the settlers. The two zones are opposed, but not in the service of a higher unity. Obedient to the rules of pure Aristotelian logic, they both follow the principle of reciprocal exclusivity. No conciliation is possible, for of the two terms, one is superfluous. ([1961] 1963, 38–39)

For Bourdieu, too, segregation defines colonialism:

> In short, when carried along by its own internal logic, the colonial system tends to develop all the consequences implied at the time of its founding—the complete separation of the social castes. ([1961] 1962, 146)

Bourdieu continues to use the term *caste* rather than *race* to grasp the structural character of colonialism, missing thereby the specificity of race that remains central in Fanon's writings.

3

Colonialism dehumanizes the colonized, demanding its reversal. Parallels in their description of colonial domination appear in their accounts of the subjective experience of colonialism. Fanon writes,

> [Colonialism] dehumanizes the native, or to speak plainly turns him into an animal. . . . [The native] knows that he is not an animal, and it is precisely at the moment he realizes his humanity, that he begins to sharpen the weapons with which he will secure its victory. ([1961] 1963, 42–43)

Similarly, Bourdieu ([1961] 1962, 151) writes that "respect and dignity" are the first demand of the dominated, because they have experienced colonialism as "humiliation or alienation." Echoing Fanon, he writes,

> The colonial situation thus creates the "contemptible" person at the same time that it creates the contemptuous attitude; but it creates in turn a spirit of revolt against this contempt; and so the tension that is tearing the whole society to pieces keeps on increasing. (134)

4

Colonialism uses its domination to dispossess the peasantry of their land. Both Fanon and Bourdieu concentrate on the destruction of the peasantry through the expropriation of land, the very foundation of their existence. Fanon writes,

> For a colonized people the most essential value, because the most concrete, is first and foremost the land: the land which will bring them bread and, above all, dignity. ([1961] 1963, 44)

Here is Bourdieu's parallel assessment of the centrality of land:

> The peasant can exist only when rooted to the land, the land where he was born, which he received from his parents and to which he is attached by his habits and his memories. Once he has been uprooted there is a good chance that he will cease to exist as a peasant, that the instinctive and irrational passion which binds him to his peasant existence will die within him. ([1961] 1962, 172)

While land is key in both, Bourdieu and Sayad's (1964) analysis in *The Uprooting* is far richer. There they study the resettlement camps created during the Algerian war, the result of forced removals conducted in the name of protecting the colonized from the national liberation movement, though clearly aimed at flushing it out of the rural areas by denying it the support of the people.

5

Only through revolution can the colonial order be overthrown. Fanon here stresses the importance of absolute violence. The order is held together by violence and therefore has to be overthrown through violence. This is how he puts it:

> The native who decides to put the program into practice, and to become its moving force, is ready for violence at all times. From birth it is clear to him that this narrow world, strewn with prohibitions, can only be called into question by absolute violence. ([1961] 1963, 37)

Although Bourdieu's idea of a caste system perhaps implies a more harmonious order than Fanon's racial order, he also has no doubt that the colonial system sows the seeds of its own destruction—a "great upheaval," in which "the great mass of peasants . . . have been carried along in the whirlwind of violence which is sweeping away even the vestiges of the past" (Bourdieu [1961] 1962, 188). Only revolution can achieve the end of colonialism:

> That only a revolution can abolish the colonial system, that any changes to be made must be subject to the law of all or nothing, are facts now consciously realized, even if only confusedly, just as much by members of the dominant society as by the members of the dominated society. . . . Thus it must be granted that the primary and indeed the sole radical challenge to the system was the one that system itself engendered; the revolt against the principles on which it was founded. (146)

6

The anticolonial revolution transforms consciousness, liquidating all forms of localism to build national solidarity. For Fanon, violence has a cathartic and unifying effect:

> We have said that the native's violence unifies the people. . . . Violence is in action all-inclusive and national. It follows that it is closely involved in the liquidation of regionalism and of tribalism. . . . At

the level of individuals, violence is a cleansing force. It frees the native from his inferiority complex and from his despair and inaction; it makes him fearless and restores his self-respect. ([1961] 1963, 94)

In Bourdieu's language, the war dissolves "false solicitude." Attempts at conciliation and all forms of concessions are merely tactics of the dominant to hold on to their power: "Attempts at trickery or subterfuge are at once revealed in their true light. The war helped to bring about a heightened awareness" (Bourdieu [1961] 1962, 153). Repression and war led to the spiraling of hostilities and the deepening of the schism between the two sides. The war became a cultural agent, dissolving resignation. It replaced symbolic refusal of colonial domination, for example, in the insistent wearing of the veil—what Bourdieu calls traditional traditionalism—with aggressive demands for rights to welfare and education. Pride, he says, replaces shame:

The feeling of being engaged in a common adventure, of being subject to a common destiny, of confronting the same adversary, of sharing the same preoccupations, the same sufferings and the same aspirations, widened and deepened the sentiment of solidarity, a sentiment which was undergoing at the same time a veritable transformation as the idea of fraternity tended to lose any ethnical or religious coloration and became synonymous with national solidarity. (162)

This is the "revolution within the revolution," the revolutionary transformation of consciousness, the substitution of an assertive solidarity for a resentful deference. How different is this revolution within the revolution from Fanon's account of the national liberation struggle?[4]

7

The anticolonial revolution leads either to socialism or barbarism. Fanon recognizes two paths out of colonialism: either national liberation based on peasant revolution leading to a socialist participatory democracy, or the taking of a national bourgeois road that will bring progressive degradation of the political order, ending in dictatorship and repression:

The bourgeois leaders of underdeveloped countries imprison national consciousness in sterile formalism. It is only when men and women are included on a vast scale in enlightened and fruitful work that form and body are given to that consciousness. . . . Otherwise there is anarchy, repression, and the resurgence of tribal parties and federalism. ([1961] 1963, 204–5)

Bourdieu, too, discovers a fork in the postcolonial road: socialism or chaos, which is not that dissimilar to Fanon's socialism or dictatorship.

A society which has been so greatly revolutionized demands that revolutionary solutions be devised to meet its problems. It will insist that a way be found to mobilize these masses who have been freed from the traditional disciplines and thrown into a chaotic, disillusioned world, by holding up before them a collective ideal, the building of a harmonious social order and the development of a modern economy capable of assuring employment and a decent standard of living for all. Algeria contains such explosive forces that it could well be that there now remains only a choice between chaos and an original form of socialism that will have been carefully designed to meet the needs of the actual situation. (Bourdieu [1961] 1962, 192–93)[5]

Both allow for the possibility of socialism, but for Fanon it is a long historical project, whereas for Bourdieu it is a spontaneous occurrence.

The two critics of colonialism converge to a surprising degree in their assessment of colonialism and its denouement. If Fanon was "speculative," "dangerous," and "irresponsible," then surely Bourdieu was no less so. The main difference, one might surmise, is that Fanon did not live to change his mind. But if he would have changed his mind, it is unlikely he would have followed Bourdieu. For, investigating further, we can see that their common understandings are located within very different theoretical-political frameworks—the one is a dissident within modernization theory and the other a dissident within Marxism.

BOURDIEU: BETWEEN TRADITION AND MODERNITY

Perhaps it is surprising to associate Bourdieu with modernization theory, given his concern with colonial domination. Nonetheless, there are close parallels with Durkheim's ([1893] 1984) Manichean worlds of mechanical and organic solidarity. At one extreme, Bourdieu constructs a harmonious order of self-reproduction through rituals of gift exchange and life cycle, and the unconscious reproduction of masculine domination as expressed in the division of the Kabyle house. This order, unsullied by colonialism, is dominated by a strong collective consciousness. The romantic redemption of ethnic culture has been defended by Bourdieu and his followers as reversing the contempt of colonialism for the culture of its subjects. Paul Silverstein (2004) refers to this as a structural nostalgia that can be a weapon in an anticolonial struggle.[6] More curious, it is from this vision of "traditional" society that Bourdieu draws many of his concepts—habitus, symbolic violence, misrecognition—to analyze French society.

Very different from this harmonious order was modern Algeria, beset by colonialism that created a stable but potentially revolutionary working class, a disoriented subproletariat, and a dispossessed peasantry. Here we find Durkheim's ([1893] 1984, Book III, chapter 1) abnormal forms of the division of labor that generate disorganization and conflict. On the one hand, there is the forced division of labor and the imposition of unequal conditions on the colonized, depriving them of opportunities for advancement and, indeed, leading to the anticolonial struggle. On the other hand, there is the anomic division of labor expressed in "allodoxia," the confusion of those caught between two opposed worlds—resulting in what Bourdieu would later call the "split habitus"—generating outbursts of irrational, messianic behavior:

> All these contradictions affect the inner nature of "the man between two worlds"—the intellectual, the man who formerly worked in France, the city dweller—is exposed to the conflicts created by the weakening of the traditional systems of sanctions and by the development of a double set of moral standards. . . . This man, cast between two worlds and rejected by both, lives a sort of double inner life, is a prey to frustration and inner conflict, with the result that he is constantly being tempted to adopt either an attitude of uneasy overidentification or one of rebellious negativism. (Bourdieu [1961] 1962, 142–4)

These ideas of cultural lag—incomplete adaptation to modernity or being caught between the old and the new—lie at the core of the 1960s modernization theory of Clifford Geertz, Alex Inkeles, and Edward Shils, not to mention Talcott Parsons's pattern variables.[7] To explain the plight of the so-called new nations and the impediments to "modernity," these authors invoked the heavy weight of tradition and primordial attachments (kinship, tribe, religion) that were plunging countries into anomie. Bourdieu, no less than they, provides precious little evidence to back up his claims.[8]

More original is Bourdieu's adaptation of Weber's *The Protestant Ethic and the Spirit of Capitalism*. Drawing on Husserl's philosophy of time, Bourdieu ([1963] 1979) argues that modernity is an orientation to a rationally planned future, whereas tradition is encased by the repetition of the same patterns. He pins modernity onto the Algerian working class, which has the stability to think rationally and imaginatively about future alternatives, as opposed to the peasantry, which is stuck in an eternal present, what he calls a *traditional traditionalism*. The unstable, marginal, semi-employed or unemployed urban "subproletariat" and the rural proletariat displaced from their lands into resettlement camps live from hand to mouth. They exhibit a *traditionalism of despair*, oriented to the here and now but cognizant of alternative futures that they are denied.

Curiously, this leads Bourdieu, via Durkheimian notions of anomie, to the orthodox Marxist position that the Algerian working class, because it is rooted in stable employment, is revolutionary—in contrast to the uprooted peasantry or urban subproletariat who can only break out into spontaneous, senseless revolt:

On the one hand, there is the revolt of emotion, the uncertain and incoherent expression of a condition characterized by uncertainty and incoherence; on the other hand, there is revolutionary radicalism, springing from the systematic consideration of reality. These two attitudes correspond to two types of material conditions of existence: on the one hand the sub-proletarians of the towns and the uprooted peasants whose whole existence is constraint and arbitrariness; on the other hand the regular workers of the modern sector, provided with the minimum of security and guarantees which allow aspirations and opinions to be put into perspective. Disorganization of daily conduct prohibits the formation of the system of rational projects and forecasts of which the revolutionary consciousness is one aspect. (Bourdieu [1963] 1979, 62)

The uprooted may be a "force for revolution" but not a "revolutionary force" that self-consciously promotes and rationally organizes the transformation of society. The latter possibility is reserved for the working class:

To those who have the "privilege" of undergoing permanent and "rational" exploitation and of enjoying the corresponding advantages also belongs the privilege of a truly revolutionary consciousness. This realistic aiming at the future [*l'avenir*] is only accessible to those who have the means to confront the present and to look for ways of beginning to implement their hopes, instead of giving way to resigned surrender or to the magical impatience of those who are too crushed by the present to be able to look to anything other than a utopian future [*un futur*], an immediate, magical negation of the present. (63)

What a contrast to the French working class depicted in *Distinction* or *Pascalian Meditations*, whose members are driven by necessity, symbolically dominated and misrecognizing their conditions of existence. Bourdieu never explains this most obvious paradox. What is the source of the difference? Does it lie in the political structures of the two countries—the effects of symbolic as opposed to colonial violence—or does it lie in Bourdieu's positions in the political-intellectual fields of the two countries? A comparison with Fanon sheds light on both possibilities.

FANON: BETWEEN CAPITALISM AND SOCIALISM

If Bourdieu analyzes Algeria through the opposed lenses of modernity and tradition, Fanon sees Algeria through the prism of capitalism and socialism; if Bourdieu analyzes Algeria from the standpoint of a romantic past, Fanon sees Algeria from the vantage of a romantic future. They meet on the terrain of the present.

For Fanon, colonialism was a space of struggles. National independence is a struggle against the colonial power, Gramsci's *war of movement* conducted with violence, but it is also a struggle over the direction of postcoloniality, a *war of position* within the colonized. It is a struggle for hegemony between, on the one hand, the followers of the national bourgeoisie who want nothing more than to *replace* the colonizers and, on the other hand, the militants of the national liberation movement who want to *transform* the class structure.[9] The war of position for the future exists uneasily alongside the anticolonial war of movement, but if the latter pushes the former aside and the denouement of colonialism is left to look after itself, democratic socialism will never be victorious. So argues Fanon.

Bourdieu not only failed to separate the two moments of the anticolonial revolution, but he also did not pay sufficient attention to class as a potential political force. Fanon, again unknowingly following the footsteps of Gramsci, examined the balance of class forces behind the reformist national bourgeoisie and the revolutionary national liberation movement. At the heart of the national bourgeoisie lay traders, merchants, and small capitalists, together with their intellectuals recruited from teachers, civil servants, lawyers, nurses, and other professionals. The national bourgeoisie also had the support of the albeit-small colonial working class, which in Fanon's view was pampered and parasitic. It is here that Bourdieu and Fanon diverge dramatically: relative stability of the working class for Bourdieu meant revolutionary potential, while for Fanon it meant reformism.[10]

For Fanon, the revolutionary struggle depended on the dispossessed peasantry, because the latter had nothing to lose. Bourdieu considered this to be "pretentious foolishness" (cited in Le Sueur 2001, 284). The peasantry was "overwhelmed by the war, by the concentration camps, and by the mass deportations," and so to claim that it was revolutionary was "completely idiotic" (284). Bourdieu attempted to put the picture right with his book *The Uprooting*, written with Abdelmalek Sayad (1964), which dealt with the crisis of the displaced peasantry. Fanon was not as ignorant as Bourdieu made out, as he had done his own fieldwork among the Kabyle (Macey 2000, 234–36). He considered instinctive rebelliousness to come precisely from the expropriation of land, which Bourdieu had himself recognized as the source of "revolutionary chiliasm and magical utopias" ([1963] 1979, 70).

The more substantial difference between them comes with the next step in Fanon's argument. For the peasantry to be a revolutionary force, its volcanic energy had to be disciplined by intellectuals. They would be in plentiful supply—radicals expelled from the towns for exposing the venality of the native elites. Opposed to the bourgeois road, they would join the peasantry to forge a revolutionary movement. To Bourdieu, the idea of symbiosis between intellectuals and peasantry is a fantasy of the intellectual that not only cannot work but is also dangerous and irresponsible. One sees here the source of his animus against the myth of the "organic intellectual." It is very different from Bourdieu's own position as an engaged intellectual supporting the colonized from a healthy, objective distance.

Be that as it may, Fanon continues his analysis of the balance of class forces. There are two projects vying for the support of the colonized classes: the national bourgeois road centered on the native bourgeoisie and the working class, and the national liberation movement centered on the peasantry embracing and embraced by radical intellectuals. Fanon asks which of these two projects will succeed in winning the support of vacillating classes: on the one hand, traditional leaders in the countryside who are reformist by nature, a screen for the colonizers, but who are also accountable to their ever more militant followers, and on the other hand, the urban lumpenproletariat, recently uprooted from their villages, a volatile group easily manipulated by leaders with but the smallest concessions. The colonizers play their own role in shaping the balance between these two tendencies, and when they see the writing on the wall, they throw their weight behind the less threatening national bourgeoisie.

This analysis of the future, so alien to Bourdieu's backward-looking sociology, continues with Fanon's pessimistic but prophetic anticipations. Should the national bourgeoisie win the struggle for leadership of the anticolonial movement and come to power, they will not be able to build a true hegemony, which would require resources that they do not possess. They will become a dominated bourgeoisie—dominated by the metropolitan bourgeoisie—only capable of becoming an imitative and parasitical class, compensating for its backwardness with conspicuous consumption and the reversion to tribalism and racism:

> Because it is bereft of ideas, because it lives to itself and cuts itself off from the people, undermined by its hereditary incapacity to think in terms of all the problems of the nation as seen from the point of view of the whole of that nation, the national middle class will have nothing better to do than to take on the role of the manager for Western enterprise, and it will in practice set up its country as the brothel of Europe. (Fanon [1961] 1963, 154)

The national bourgeoisie starts out by copying Western institutions—political constitutions and outward manifestations of its economy—but degenerates from a multiparty democracy to a one-party state and then to a one-man dictatorship. Fanon expressed vividly what would indeed come to pass in postcolonial Africa. This was no empty speculation; it was how things turned out.

By painting the national bourgeois road in such dire colors, Fanon hopes to convince us that the only progressive road is that of national liberation—the revolutionary transformation of the class structure and the realization of a participatory socialism. But how feasible was this? Even if the revolutionary forces won hegemony, could they bring about Fanon's participatory socialism? Leaving aside colonial legacies that cannot be simply swept aside—the argument of Bourdieu and others—what about international forces? Fanon rather optimistically argued that postcolonial Africa can insist on and enforce reparations from Western capitalism, because the latter needs what Africa has to offer—not just its natural resources but also its consumer markets. Fanon was naive about the possibilities of participatory socialism, but the naïveté sprang from a desperation that saw the pitfalls of the national bourgeoisie.

Both Bourdieu and Fanon have a fascination with the peasantry and deploy that fascination for a critical analysis of contemporary societies. Bourdieu creates a romantic anthropology of the Algerian peasantry that becomes the basis for his functionalist analysis of symbolic violence in French society. Fanon has his own romance, projecting the peasantry as a revolutionary class that will usher in participatory socialism. It is a romance inspired by what he sees as the degeneration of postcolonial Africa if it follows the national bourgeois road.

BETWEEN REVOLUTIONARY OPTIMISM AND CRITICAL PESSIMISM

The conversation between Fanon and Bourdieu shows how theoretical influences circulate between colony and metropolis, but especially the influence of the colony on the metropolis. Nor are these isolated examples. Some of the great French intellectuals were shaped by experiences in colonial Africa—Foucault spent two formative years in Tunisia; Derrida and Camus grew up in Algeria—and the Algerian question continues to exert a powerful influence on French intellectual life, even now, more than fifty years after independence.

Thus, the conversation between Fanon and Bourdieu becomes more interesting if we extend it backward and forward in time beyond the Algerian experience to examine the theoretical effects of their personal trajectories between colony and metropolis. Here, we see a striking and unexpected convergence in their understandings of French society, especially if placed in the frame of colonialism. The very notion of symbolic violence, at the center of Bourdieu's sociology of France, implies a contrast with the material violence of colonialism, especially Algerian settler colonialism. Symbolic violence works through the habitus—the cumulative introjection of social structure into the human psyche and the inscription of social structure onto the body.

The parallels with Fanon are uncanny. *Black Skin, White Masks*, based on Fanon's experience of metropolitan racism, is a psychoanalytical understanding of the social-psychological dynamics of racial domination in which the colonized internalize the social structure and wrestle to find their place in that structure. It is a futile and rebuffed aspiration for interracial sexual liaisons and exaggerated efforts to be the perfect French citizen that make them targets of mockery, deepening their sense of inferiority. This is not the material violence of colonialism but the deeper symbolic violence of metropolitan racial domination. For Fanon, as indeed for Bourdieu, there is simply no effective response to symbolic violence, and so both end up with a critical pessimism with respect to France, which contrasts so vividly with the revolutionary optimism they both exhibit in Algeria.

The parallels become more even intriguing if one probes Bourdieu's great book of symbolic violence—*Distinction*. Here, the dominant classes are blessed with cultural capital, some more than others, and the dominated classes are bereft of such capital, but the middle classes—the petite bourgeoisie—are the great pretenders, aspiring to legitimate culture, over-conforming in their attempt to emulate the class to which they don't belong. The petit bourgeois is indeed the bourgeois "writ small":

> Even his bodily hexis, which expresses his whole objective relation to the social world, is that of a man who had to make himself small to pass through the strait gate which leads to the bourgeoisie: strict and sober, discreet and severe, in his dress, his speech, his gestures and his whole bearing, he always lacks something in stature, breadth, substance, largesse. (Bourdieu [1979] 1984, 338)

Bourdieu's contempt for the petite bourgeoisie who seek admission to an inaccessible world is strikingly parallel to Fanon's contempt for blacks who try to "whiten" themselves in order to assimilate into white society. Fanon is writing not about the working class but about members of the black middle classes, like himself, who emigrated to France as professionals of one sort or another. It is as if their own histories of exclusion, seared into their psyches, led the one (Bourdieu) to be a self-hating petit bourgeois and the other (Fanon) a self-hating black. This might also explain the venom behind Fanon's denunciation of the colonial national bourgeoisie as an imitative bourgeoisie, just as it might also explain Bourdieu's hostility to Fanon, whose revolutionary ardor is the intellectual's attempt to escape his habitus, to jump out of his skin.

There is, however, a profound asymmetry in the trajectories of these two intellectuals. Whereas Fanon starts out in France as a critical pessimist to become a revolutionary optimist in Algeria based on a romantic radical vision of the peasantry, Bourdieu starts out in Algeria as a revolutionary optimist to become a critical pessimist in France, deploying features of a romantic conservative vision of the peasantry. Each reacts against his previous experience. Fanon leaves behind the symbolic violence of racism in France primed to participate in revolutionary catharsis against colonial violence. Equally, Bourdieu is all too ready to abandon his equivocal revolutionary optimism, so that when he enters France he rejects Third World Marxism and adopts a critical pessimism based on another form of violence—symbolic violence. Toward the end of his life he breaks out of his critical pessimism by joining the calumniated working class, attacking the symbolic order associated with neoliberalism and forging new bonds with African intellectuals—a return of the repressed but without theoretical warrant.

5

PEDAGOGY OF THE OPPRESSED
Freire Meets Bourdieu

> Thus, in a society in which the obtaining of social privi-
> leges depends more and more closely on possession of
> academic credentials, the School does not only have the
> function of ensuring discreet succession to a bourgeois
> estate which can no longer be transmitted directly and
> openly. This privileged instrument of the bourgeois sociodicy
> which confers on the privileged the supreme privilege of
> not seeing themselves as privileged manages the more
> easily to convince the disinherited that they owe their
> scholastic and social destiny to their lack of gifts or merits,
> because in matters of culture absolute dispossession
> excludes awareness of being dispossessed.
>
> — BOURDIEU AND PASSERON, *REPRODUCTION IN EDUCATION,*
> *SOCIETY AND CULTURE*

For Bourdieu, education is symbolic violence par excellence. In a society where the dominant class can no longer invoke rights of blood to pass on their inheritance nor appeal to ascetic virtue as a justification of success, academic certification becomes the vehicle to justify and transmit its domination. Education attests and consecrates the merits and gifts of the bourgeoisie, while concealing their distinction as an outgrowth of their privilege—concealing it, that is, not only from themselves but also from the dominated, who see themselves as undeserving because unmeritorious. *Reproduction in Edu-*

cation, Society, and Culture, which brought Bourdieu and Passeron into the public eye both in France and abroad, offers a deeply pessimistic account of the role of education in upholding domination through simultaneously privileging and hiding the cultural capital inherited by children of the dominant class. It is designed to dispel illusions that schooling can ever be a vehicle of social transformation, although that didn't stop Bourdieu using his own place in the education field to advocate change.

Paulo Freire's *Pedagogy of the Oppressed*—the originating, most popular text of critical pedagogy—appeared in 1970, the same year that *Reproduction* was published in France. Neither makes any reference to the other, yet they both embark from a similar criticism of conventional pedagogy and its optimism about formal education's progressive contribution to social change. Freire sets out from the assumption that the dominated have internalized their oppression and that this domination is reinforced through a "banking" system of education in which teachers pour knowledge into the supposedly thirsty minds of their students. There is, however, an alternative pedagogy, Freire argues, based on dialogue between teacher and student around problems originating with the latter. This requires working with students outside of formal education (i.e., bringing education to their communities, neighborhoods, and villages).

Bourdieu and Passeron may not refer to Freire by name, but they condemn all such "populist pedagogies" as misguided. Rather than challenging domination, these pedagogies effectively consolidate symbolic violence. In their earlier book *The Inheritors* ([1964] 1979), they had advocated "rational pedagogy"—the attempt to counteract inequalities in the cultural preparation of different classes, not by making concessions to subjugated cultures but by inculcating dominant culture into disadvantaged groups. In *Reproduction* they now abandon this solution, freely admitting this to be a utopian project in the face of class domination, although even the attempt to realize it would have the benefit of unmasking the inequity of cultural preconditioning.

Here, then, are two antithetical approaches to the same problem, namely the reproduction of class domination via education. Where Bourdieu can only conceive of countering domination by creating universal access to the cultural achievements of bourgeois society (i.e., by extending bourgeois civilization to all), Freire sees in this the perfection of domination. He seeks an alternative pedagogy that extricates and cultivates the residue of good sense that remains within the oppressed despite internalized oppression—a pedagogy that starts out from their lived experience.

In the conversation that follows, I first examine the argument of Bourdieu and Passeron and then construct Freire's antithesis, before seeking a synthesis in Gramsci's writings on education and politics. Gramsci, after all, believed in the "common school" that would induct everyone into the dominant culture, thereby arming potential organic intellectuals with the wherewithal to identify, elaborate, and protect the good sense of the working class. In this view, Freire's separatist solution underestimates the broad power of ideological hegemony—a power that calls for contestation on its own terrain as well as the development of an alternative culture.

SCHOOLING AS SYMBOLIC VIOLENCE

Bourdieu had an interest in education throughout his life, which is perhaps fitting for a reflexive sociologist whose career was made by excelling in the academic world. This abiding fascination with education was surely stimulated by his own life of upward mobility—an anomaly his theory could not explain. His self-portrait—a son of a rural postal worker who made good through education—subscribes to the ideology of "merit" and "gift" that his sociological writings systematically discredit. Not surprisingly, he returns again and again to the question of education, which was central to his own life and also to French society in general.

In 1964, only four years after he had returned from Algeria, Bourdieu joined Jean-Claude Passeron to publish *The Inheritors*, which examined the critical but hidden role of cultural capital not only in selecting students for university but also in subjecting them to a pedagogy that privileged the culturally advantaged. They made the argument—provocative at the time—that even if there were equality of opportunity, even if the children of the wage laborer had the same chance of entering university as the children of the senior executive, still the university would reproduce the domination of the latter over the former. Teaching in the university presupposes and reinforces the privileged upbringing of the middle and upper classes. *The Inheritors* prefigures so much in Bourdieu's corpus—the relationship of different classes to culture as laid out in *Distinction* (Bourdieu [1979] 1984), the self-delusions of the academic world elaborated as scholastic fallacies and the idea of social structure as a game presented in *The Logic of Practice* ([1980] 1990) and *Pascalian Meditations* ([1997] 2000), the battle of the disciplines worked out in *Homo Academicus* ([1984] 1988), and the strategies through which the dominant class reproduces itself via the Grandes Écoles presented in *State Nobility* ([1989] 1996). But most significantly, *The Inheritors* is a prolegomenon to its theoretical deepening and detailed elaboration in *Reproduction in Education, Society and Culture*. Written with Jean-Claude Passeron, *Reproduction* is an uncompromising critique of education that brought both fame and infamy to its authors.

Education exemplifies symbolic violence. Schooling *secures* the active participation of students and teachers in the pursuit of credentials, which entails the learning of legitimate culture, while *obscuring* the reproduction of class domination that is the effect of such participation. Securing participation is education's technical function (learning), while obscuring class domination is its social function (class selection) (Bourdieu and Passeron [1970] 1977, 164–67). Thus, Bourdieu and Passeron criticize economists for emphasizing the technical functions of education at the expense of its social functions and critical theorists for focusing on the social at the cost of the technical functions of education. At the heart of symbolic violence is the *combination* of enthusiastic participation and systematic misrecognition. To examine one without the other is to misunderstand the symbolic power of education.

Central to their model of reproduction is the way the relative autonomy of the educational system has the effect of naturalizing its twofold arbitrariness: the imposition of a cultural arbitrary (legitimate culture) through an arbitrary power (class domination). The source of relative autonomy lies with the cadres of teachers, specially trained and recruited as professionals and thus vehement defenders of the autonomy of their practice, but it also lies in the standardization and routinization of education, in other words, subjection to its own principles of regulation. Relative autonomy gives the (false) impression of neutrality with respect to class, by rendering class selection invisible and thereby making it all the more profound.

The argument rests on the assumption that primary pedagogic work (pw) in the family produces an enduring and irreversible primary habitus that sets the opportunities for subsequent schooling:

> Insofar as *pw* is an irreversible process producing, in the time required for inculcation, an irreversible disposition, i.e. a disposition which cannot itself be repressed or transformed except by an irreversible process producing in turn a new irreversible disposition, primary *pa* [pedagogic action] (the earliest phase of upbringing), which is carried out by *pw* without any antecedent (primary *pw*), produces a primary habitus, characteristic of a group or class, which is the basis for the subsequent formation of any other habitus. (Bourdieu and Passeron [1970] 1977, 42)

The primary habitus, inculcated by the dominant classes, bestows cultural advantages on their children. The primary pedagogic work in the family transmits linguistic and cultural dispositions that take advantage of the symbolic mastery—abstract bookish learning—taught at school. The children of the dominated classes, on the other hand, having received a more functional, utilitarian upbringing, face an alien school environment and pedagogy. Although it appears neutral and universal, school learning presupposes the cultural capital of the dominant class and disparages the culture of the dominated. The power of the school system is redoubled by the labor market, which rewards academic success and in turn further consecrates the legitimate capital of the already privileged and denigrates the dominated culture:

> The more unified the market on which the value of the products of the different *pa*s [pedagogic actions] is determined, the more the groups and classes, which have undergone a *pa* inculcating a dominated cultural arbitrary, are likely to have the valuelessness of their cultural attainment brought home to them both by the anonymous sanctions of the labour market and by the symbolic sanctions of the cultural market (e.g. the matrimonial market), not to mention the academic verdicts, which are always charged with economic and symbolic implications. These calls to order tend to produce in them, if not explicit recognition of the dominant culture as the legitimate culture, then at least an insidious awareness of the cultural unworthiness of their own acquirements. (28)

To be sure, there are those, like Bourdieu, who manage to overcome their class background, but their accomplishments are only realized through an obsession with achievement, which further mystifies the relation between education and class. Such upward mobility also turns attention away from the more pervasive phenomenon characterizing education, namely the exclusion of so many from education at different levels, many of whom quietly eliminate themselves rather than go through the humiliation of being eliminated.

ALTERNATIVE PEDAGOGIES

The picture painted here is very different from that of Paul Willis (1977), for example, who writes of working-class children *rebelling* against the middle-class culture thrust upon them in school and *embracing* their own down-to-earth, manual, practical culture (with all its problematic sexism and racism); furthermore, it is this hostility to middle-class school culture that makes them enthusiastic to reenter the working class. This rebellion exhibits what Willis calls a "partial penetration"—the lads are not deceived by the bias of the school but nevertheless still end up reproducing their own subordination. Willis proposes the creation of schools where teachers would validate working-class culture, elaborating it into a full-blown critique of capitalism. Bourdieu and Passeron dismiss any such sociological relativism as a populist illusion:

> This could lead students to demand that the parallel cultures of the disadvantaged classes should be given the status of the culture taught by the school system. But it is not sufficient to observe that school culture is a class culture; to proceed as if it were only that, is to help it remain so. (Bourdieu and Passeron [1964] 1979, 72)

The populist illusion recognizes the social function of education but misses the technical function, namely the inescapable importance of acquiring credentials for survival. Increasingly, working-class jobs will not be available to working classes who do not have basic schooling. Thinking perhaps of himself, Bourdieu mocks the very idea of endorsing working-class culture as paternalistic and insulting to the ambitions and capacities of the dominated.

If *popular* pedagogies that celebrate class cultures of the dominated end up channeling the disadvantaged back to the bottom of society, *soft* pedagogies that focus on alternative ways of teaching ignore and further mystify the importance of class:

> The ideologies of *pa* [pedagogic action] as non-violent action— whether in Socratic and neo-Socratic myths of non-directive teaching, Rousseauistic myths of natural education, or pseudo-Freudian myths of non-repressive education—reveal in its clearest form the generic function of educational ideologies, in evading, by the gratuitous negation of one of its terms, the contradiction between the objective truth of *pa* and the necessary (inevitable) representation of this arbitrary action as necessary ("natural"). (Bourdieu and Passeron [1970] 1977, 13)

The soft pedagogies become ideologies that do not recognize the role they play in the reproduction of class domination. As we shall see, Freire's problem-based dialogic pedagogy, although not mentioned explicitly, is clearly one of those ideologies that supposedly hides from itself its own implication in class domination.

So what then is the solution? In *The Inheritors*, Bourdieu and Passeron ([1964] 1979) draw the logical conclusion and prescribe a "rational pedagogy," which not only cancels out the inequality of access to education but also counteracts the advantages of the dominant-class habitus by inculcating the relevant aspects of that habitus in all classes. But by the time they write *Reproduction*, they have changed their minds:

> It may be wondered whether a type of secondary *pw* [pedagogic work] which, conversely, took into account the distance between the preexistent habitus and the habitus inculcated, and was systematically organized in accordance with the principles of an explicit pedagogy, would not have the effect of erasing the boundary which traditional *pw* recognizes and confirms between the legitimate addressees and the rest. Or, to put it another way, whether perfectly rational *pw*—i.e. *pw* exerted ab novo in all domains on all the educable, taking nothing for granted at the outset, with the explicit goal of explicitly inculcating in all its pupils the practical principles of the symbolic mastery of practices which are inculcated by primary *pa* only within certain groups or classes, in short a type of *pw* everywhere substituting for the traditional mode of inculcation the programmed transmission of the legitimate culture—would not correspond to the pedagogic interest of the dominated classes (the hypothesis of the democratization of education through the rationalization of pedagogy). But the Utopian character of an education policy based on this hypothesis becomes apparent as soon as one observes that, quite apart from the built-in inertia of every educational institution, the structure of power relations prohibits a dominant *pa* from resorting to a type of *pw* contrary to the interests of the dominant classes who delegate its PAu [pedagogic authority] to it. ([1970] 1977, 53–54)

What Bourdieu and Passeron present as the only solution in *The Inheritors*—true democratization of education—they now dismiss as utopian. Even utopias have their function in alerting us to the true nature of reality, but in *Reproduction*, Bourdieu and Passeron bend the stick in the opposite direction to demonstrate that there cannot be any alternative education so long as the class structure is what it is. This sounds like a call for revolution, but of course there is never a hint of that in their writing—so different from Paulo Freire, for whom education and revolution are intimately connected.

PEDAGOGY OF THE OPPRESSED

Paulo Freire began his interest in education through the development of literacy campaigns so that peasants could participate in Brazilian education. *The Pedagogy of the Oppressed*, which first appeared in 1970, is a manifesto for Third World revolution that parallels Fanon's *The Wretched of the Earth*. You might say that it is an elaboration of the relation between radical intellectuals and peasantry that we found so unelaborated in Fanon. Like Fanon, Freire had far more faith in the revolutionary potential of the peasantry than of the working class, which "lack revolutionary consciousness and consider themselves privileged" (Freire 1970, 148). For Freire, critical pedagogy is a necessary part of revolution.

Freire and Bourdieu start out from similar places—domination—although Freire uses a word with a more revolutionary connotation—oppression. Where Bourdieu thematizes symbolic violence in France, as opposed to material violence in the colonies, Freire thematizes internal, as opposed to external, oppression. The counterpart to symbolic violence is *internal oppression*—the introjection of the oppressor into the psyche:

> The very structure of their thought has been conditioned by the contradictions of the concrete, existential situation by which they were shaped. Their idea is to be men; but for them, to be men is to be oppressors. This is their model of humanity. This phenomenon derives from the fact that the oppressed, at a certain moment of their existential experience, adopt an attitude of "adhesion" to the oppressor. Under these circumstances they cannot "consider" him sufficiently clearly to objectivize him—to discover him "outside" themselves. This does not necessarily mean that the oppressed are unaware that they are downtrodden. But their perception of themselves as oppressed is impaired by their submersion in the reality of oppression. (Freire 1970, 45)

Leaving aside the question of masculinizing the oppressor and oppressed, at first glance this is no different from Bourdieu's notion of social structure being inscribed on the body or internalized in the habitus. Yet, of course, whereas Bourdieu does not see how education could ever liberate the dominated, for Freire this is exactly the purpose of critical pedagogy.

Still, they agree that formal education only reproduces domination/oppression. But here they begin to diverge, since for Bourdieu, class domination is socially invisible, being the product of formally neutral education, whereas for Freire it lies in the pedagogy itself—the so-called banking model, in which knowledge is deposited in the student as object and in which teacher is teacher and student is student, and what unites them is a relation of unidirectional authority that inhibits creativity, promotes adaptation, isolates consciousness, suppresses context, nurtures fatalism, and mythologizes and naturalizes domination. Students are subject to a cultural invasion by professionals so that "the invaded come to see their reality with the outlook of the invaders" (Freire 1970, 153). For Bourdieu's socio-analysis, Freire substitutes a heavy dose of psychoanalysis.

But Freire is more optimistic than Bourdieu, for he sees within the psyche two selves, the humanistic individual and the oppressor, the true self and the false self:

> The oppressed suffer from the duality which has established itself in their innermost being. . . . They are at one and the same time themselves and the oppressor whose consciousness they have internalized. The conflict lies in the choice between being wholly themselves and being divided; between ejecting the oppressor within and not ejecting them; between human solidarity or alienation; between following prescriptions or having choices; between being spectators or actors; between acting or having the illusion of acting through the action of the oppressors. . . . This is the tragic dilemma of the oppressed which their education must take into account. (1970, 48)

For Freire, then, critical pedagogy must eject the oppressor within, which can only be accomplished through a problem-centered dialogue between teacher and student, in which each learns from the other—for the educator too must be educated. When placed in their own context, tackling their own problems, the oppressed can develop critical faculties through collaboration with others. The interrogation of the folk theory (or thematic universe) of the oppressed leads from problems (or generative themes) to a decoding that focuses on context and thus the historical totality. At the heart of such a pedagogy is the dialogue not only between intellectual and oppressed but between action and reflection as well. To veer in one direction or another—activism or verbalism—is to threaten the critical process. Liberation comes through acts of solidarity and collective attempts at social transformation guided by an emergent understanding of historical constraints and possibilities. As in Marx and Fanon, ultimately it is struggle that dissolves inner oppression.

All too little is said about the teacher, who must forge a pedagogy *with* and not *for* the oppressed. Freire does acknowledge the danger that, coming from the oppressor class, teachers bring with them prejudices about the oppressed:

> Certain members of the oppressor class join the oppressed in their struggle for liberation, thus moving from one pole of the contradiction to the other. Theirs is a fundamental role, and has been so throughout the history of this struggle. It happens, however, that as they cease to be exploiters or indifferent spectators or simply the heirs of exploitation and move to the side of the exploited, they must always bring with them the marks of their origin: their prejudices and their deformations, which include a lack of confidence in the people's ability to think, to want, and to know. Accordingly these adherents to the people's cause constantly run the risk of falling into a type of generosity as malefic as that of the oppressors. . . . [They] truly desire to transform the unjust order; but because of their background they believe that they must be the executors of the transformation. They talk about the people but they do not trust them; and trusting the people is the indispensable precondition for revolutionary change. (1970, 60)

Through Bourdieu's eyes, "the pedagogy of the oppressed" is a dangerous fantasy of intellectuals who think they can, first, overcome their own habitus as intellectuals (a dominated fraction of the dominant class) and, second, and even more difficult, foster the transformation of the habitus of the dominated. Critical pedagogy is an intellectualist illusion that privileges "conscientization" (consciousness raising). It misunderstands the depth of oppression, for it conspires to do what educational ideologies generally do, that is, focus on the pedagogic relation and thereby obscure its class underpinnings. Freire might retort that Bourdieu is focused on the transmission of the dominant culture and cannot see beyond a banking model of education. When education is taken to the dominated, conducted on their terrain, and grounded in their problems and issues—rather than enrolling the dominated into the alien schools of the oppressor class—then emancipatory action is possible. Is there a resolution between these mutually opposed positions? I am going to seek one in an unlikely place—the writings of Antonio Gramsci.

GRAMSCI'S COMMON SCHOOL AND
THE WAR OF POSITION

If one were to place Gramsci within this conversation between Freire and Bourdieu, it would most likely be on Freire's side. Like Freire, Gramsci's optimism lies in the postulated good sense of the dominated qua working class that springs from its place in production. Cultural invasion there is, but never to the extent of blotting out that good sense at the core of common sense—a good sense that needs elaboration by organic intellectuals engaged in dialogue with the working class (i.e., dialogue not in formal schooling but in the workplace, in the community). Despite manifest differences in their views about the revolutionary potential of peasantry and proletariat, the centrality of the political party, civil society, and much more—largely due to Gramsci's far richer contextualization of struggle—nonetheless, Gramsci and Freire do share a faith in the capacity of the dominated to see through and then struggle against their domination. This shared revolutionary optimism contrasts with Bourdieu's critical pessimism, especially in *Reproduction*.

Therefore, one may be surprised to discover that Bourdieu's rather than Freire's ideas are anticipated in Gramsci's notes on education. The latter were written in the context of the fascist regime's call, on the one hand, for vocational education and, on the other, for an active pedagogy that downplays conventional instruction. Gramsci not only reasserts the importance of traditional pedagogy, but he insists on extending it to all classes. He calls for the introduction of the "common school," which would bestow classical education (Bourdieu's legitimate culture) on all to close the cultural gap between classes. Prefiguring Bourdieu and Passeron, Gramsci writes,

> In a whole series of families, especially in the intellectual strata, the children find in their family life a preparation, a prolongation and a completion of school life; they "breathe in," as the expression goes, a whole quantity of notions and attitudes which facilitate the educational process properly speaking. They already know and develop their knowledge of the literary language, i.e. the means of expression and of knowledge, which is technically superior to the means possessed by the average member of the school population between the ages of six and twelve. Thus, city children by the very

fact of living in a city, have already absorbed by the age of six a quantity of notions and attitudes which make their school careers easier, more profitable, and more rapid. (1971, 31)

Gramsci goes even further down Bourdieu and Passeron's road in calling attention to the bodily hexis that gives the intellectual classes advantage in the school:

Undoubtedly the child of a traditionally intellectual family acquires this psycho-physical adaptation more easily. Before he[1] ever enters the class-room he has numerous advantages over his comrades, and is already in possession of attitudes learnt from his family environment; he concentrates more easily, since he is used to "sitting still," etc. (42)

Being a hunchback from a poor rural family, Gramsci is perhaps even more aware than Bourdieu of the inherited disadvantages of class—not just the economic but the cultural disadvantages that he emphasizes here. Perhaps Gramsci was thinking of himself and the enormous discipline it took to write the *Prison Notebooks*—so meticulously presented and worked out—when he wrote about the importance of bodily training early on in life:

In education one is dealing with children in whom one has to inculcate certain habits of diligence, precision, poise (even physical poise), ability to concentrate on specific subjects, which cannot be acquired without mechanical repetition of disciplined and methodical acts. Would the scholar at the age of forty be able to sit for sixteen hours on end at his work-table if he had not, as a child, compulsorily, through mechanical coercion, acquired the appropriate psycho-physical habits? (37)

Gramsci may have prefigured the argument of *Reproduction*, but his response was very different. Where Bourdieu and Passeron pose the idea of a "rational pedagogy," only to dismiss it as utopian, Gramsci builds the idea into a concrete conception of the "common school," whose raison d'être is to equalize cultural capital across classes:

In the basic organization of the common school, at least the essentials of these conditions [of the families of intellectuals] must be created—not to speak of the fact, which goes without saying, that parallel to the common school a network of kindergartens and other institutions would develop, in which even before the school age, children would be habituated to a certain collective discipline and acquire pre-scholastic notions and attitudes. In fact, the common school should be organized like a college, with a collective life by day and by night, freed from the present forms of hypocritical and mechanical discipline; studies should be carried on collectively, with the assistance of teachers and the best pupils, even during periods of so-called individual study, etc. (31)

We note here a Freirean flavor with the emphasis on collective discipline and collaborative studies, which is not without significance for the future society Gramsci is imagining. Not surprisingly, and again anticipating the arguments of Bourdieu and Passeron, Gramsci points to the centrality of the teacher—the pivotal conveyor of the dominant culture to the children of the dominated classes:

In the school, the nexus between instruction and education can only be realised by the living work of the teacher. For he must be aware of the contrast between the type of culture and society which he represents and the type of culture and society represented by his pupils, and conscious of his obligation to accelerate and regulate the child's formation in conformity with the former and in conflict with the latter. (35–36)

We see that the idea of the common school is not as far-fetched as Bourdieu and Passeron claim. Indeed, examples of such schooling could begin with the notorious boarding school, normally the privilege of the dominant classes. Interestingly, Bourdieu himself attended one. He may have hated it but it seems to have worked, bringing him from the culturally deprived Béarn to the pinnacle of French higher education. Why does he not reflect sociologically on his own schooling as a flawed expression but an expression nonetheless of rational pedagogy, instead of bemoaning the humiliations he suffered? After all, Bourdieu himself writes that changing habitus requires a comprehensive process of countertraining, involving repeated exercises (Bourdieu [1997] 2000, 172). This can't be much fun.

Moving farther afield, one might recall the not unsuccessful attempts to reverse class differences in the Soviet Union, or the more thoroughgoing kibbutzim. The passage above, with its reference to a network of "kindergartens and other institutions" and the collective life of learning, anticipates such modern-day experiments as the Harlem Children's Zone, which cordons off an urban area and provides children and their families with extensive social services to counteract cultural disadvantage. Better to examine the attempts to realize a rational pedagogy and the obstacles it confronts as demonstration of the limits of possibility—and the truth of one's theory—than to dismiss it as a worthless utopia!

Their insights into education are very similar, but the projects of Gramsci and Bourdieu are very different. Bourdieu and Passeron are contemptuous of those who harbor the illusion that schooling can be a "mechanism of change" capable of "creating discontinuities" and "building a new world" ([1970] 1977, 65). Yet this is precisely what Gramsci has in mind, which is why he wants to subject everyone—not just the children of intellectuals and the dominant classes—to classical education. He wants everyone to learn Latin as a way of developing objectivity and disinterestedness, as an appreciation of logic but also of a sense of history, so we can recognize who we are. Schools can play a progressive role in countering folk beliefs and "localistic" ties, inherited from a feudal world, that refuse to disappear, thus preparing citizens for their role in politics and civil society:

> Scientific ideas were intended to insert the child into the *societas rerum*, the world of things, while lessons in rights and duties were intended to insert him into the State and into civil society. The scientific ideas the children learnt conflicted with the magical conception of the world and nature which they absorbed from an environment steeped in folklore; while the idea of civic rights and duties conflicted with tendencies towards individualistic and localistic barbarism—another dimension of folklore. (Gramsci 1971, 33–34)

Gramsci envisions the common school as a school for democracy, "forming [the child] during this time as a person capable of thinking, studying, and ruling—or controlling those who rule" (40).

Gramsci was concerned not only to bring children into the modern world but also to advance the project of social transformation, which brings him into direct engagement with Freire. In the field of education, we might say that Freire represents a war of movement that seeks revolutionary opposition to oppression, which is appropriate where civil society is less developed. The advance of a war of position in worlds with a strong civil society requires an extended battle on the terrain of bourgeois hegemony, and for that one needs the weapons of a classical education. The struggle for the common school, therefore, is part of such a war of position. It would be the crucible of the organic intellectuals of the future—intellectuals who would elaborate the good sense of the working class *and* contest the bourgeois ideologies that they had mastered.

CONCLUSION

Bourdieu and Passeron make every effort to debunk any notion that the school can be a vehicle of social transformation. Their critique of Freire would focus on his failure to see the broader importance of class domination within which schooling takes place and how the pedagogy of the oppressed leaves that domination unchanged. Moreover, Bourdieu and Passeron would be very skeptical that members of the dominant class could ever leave their habitus behind when they engage the peasantry or that the habitus of the peasantry could be transformed.

Recognizing Bourdieu and Passeron's critique of the "pedagogy of the oppressed," namely the penetration of capitalist culture, Gramsci would call for the common school as part of a war of position in civil society, forging intellectuals who are equally at home with legitimate culture as they are with the culture of the dominated class. Gramsci himself, even when in prison, never lost touch with his rural family and his working-class associates. But that did not prevent him from being steeped in the dominant Italian culture, so that much of the *Prison Notebooks* can be seen as a dialogue with Benedetto Croce, Giovanni Gentile, Luigi Pirandello, Machiavelli, and others. South Africa provides an interesting example of schools imparting a dominant culture that is then deployed *against* the dominant classes. Nationalist leaders such as Mandela and Tambo were in no way deceived by their missionary education, but it became a sort of "common school" that armed them for the struggle against apartheid. Interestingly, Robben Island was known as a "university of struggle," a school for so many of the leaders of the anti-apartheid movement.

Gramsci understood that you cannot extricate schooling from broader historical processes. The fight for the common school was part of a fight for the broader transformation of society. Again, this is not a strange idea in South Africa, where schools and universities have been at the forefront of the transformation of society. The Soweto rebellion was organized against the dominant culture and became a catalyst in the struggles to overthrow apartheid. Even if Bourdieu and Passeron would make colonial societies an exception, we only have to turn to May 1968 to see the ways in which French students could be a force for social change and challenge the existing order. The same can be said of the US student movements of that era.

It is worth noting that neither *Reproduction*, which appeared in 1970, nor the epilogue to the English translation of *The Inheritors*, written in 1979, refers to the French student uprising. For all the talk of the devaluation of credentials and the bamboozling of a generation in the original text of 1964, this epilogue seeks to show how student frustration was accommodated and class reproduction secured. Only in *Homo Academicus*, written in 1984, does Bourdieu address the student revolt, relying on the same framework of the devaluation of credentials and the mismatch of objective chances and subjective expectations, opportunities, and aspirations, while downplaying the self-understanding of the participants and the ideologies that galvanized the rebellion. Still, finally, there is an attempt at studying the place of education in what was the unfolding crisis of French society.

Once we adopt a broader theoretical canvas and forsake dry statistics for historical process, we quickly grasp the ways in which education becomes a terrain of struggle that fosters both social change and social reproduction. Despite himself, Bourdieu must have believed this, as he was so deeply committed to the advance and teaching of sociology as a progressive form of education, whether in school, university, or the pages of *Le Monde* or of his own widely read books. Once again, Bourdieu's practice was at odds with his theory.

THE ANTINOMIES OF FEMINISM
Beauvoir Meets Bourdieu

If the scholarly principle of her literary "vocation," of her emotional "choices" and even of her relation to her own status as a woman offered to us by Toril Moi have but little chance of appearing as Simone de Beauvoir, this is because she is separated from this by the philosophy of Jean-Paul Sartre to whom she delegated, in a way, her capacity to do philosophy. . . . There is not a better example of the symbolic violence that constitutes the traditional (patriarchal) relationship between the sexes than the fact that she will fail to apply her own analysis on relations between the sexes to her relationship with Jean-Paul Sartre.

She loves this destiny [*aggrégation* in philosophy] like she loves he who embodies the realisation of what she would long to be: Normalien, instituted by the rite of the concours in a superman socially authorised to despise the inferior castes . . . a philosopher who is sure of being one—sure to the point of destroying, for the sole pleasure of shining or of seducing, which are the same thing, this is the project of Simone de Beauvoir.

— BOURDIEU, "APOLOGIE POUR UNE FEMME RANGÉE"

Bourdieu very rarely refers to Simone de Beauvoir (1908–86), but when he does it is with undisguised contempt, reminding us of his treatment of Fanon. Of course, both had a close relation to Jean-Paul Sartre, Bourdieu's imagined combatant and intellectual archrival. The passages above are drawn from Bourdieu's preface to the translation of Toril Moi's biography of Beauvoir. In this preface, written under the mocking title, "Apology for a dutiful woman,"[1] Bourdieu claims that Beauvoir had no significant ideas of her own independent of Sartre and then reduces her to a project of his own (Bourdieu's) projection—to be a philosopher dismissive of those beneath her.

This strategy of *reductionism* justifies the silencing of Beauvoir. If her ideas are an emanation of Sartre's, then there's no need to take them seriously. Bourdieu thereby exercises the very symbolic violence he condemns, namely the masculinist practice of *silencing* women. The final move in this denigration is to *appropriate* as his own Beauvoir's ideas from *The Second Sex* ([1949] 1989)—a foundational classic in the analysis of masculine domination as an expression of symbolic violence. Bourdieu's *Masculine Domination* ([1998] 2001) is but a superficial and diminutive gloss on *The Second Sex*. Reductionism, silencing, and appropriation are three stages in the labor of producing one's own distinction through the conquest and erasure of others. In this conversation, I attempt to recover Beauvoir's voice so that she can enter into a conversation with Bourdieu.

ON SILENCING BEAUVOIR

These strategies of combat, doubtless not fully conscious but deeply embedded in Bourdieu's academic habitus, come into full view in *Masculine Domination*—a book that is full of references to a diverse array of second-wave feminists. Beauvoir, however, receives a single dismissive footnote:

> For a specific illustration of what is implied by this perhaps somewhat abstract evocation of the specific forms that masculine domination takes within the educational institution, see Toril Moi's analysis of the representations and academic classifications through which Sartre's hold imposed itself on Simone Beauvoir. (Bourdieu [1998] 2001, 86)

Once again he opportunistically exploits Toril Moi's (1994) biography of Beauvoir. He focuses on Moi's first two chapters, which do indeed place Beauvoir in her relation to Sartre and then in relation to the French intellectual field, but he ignores Moi's subsequent chapters devoted to the interpretation and original contributions of *The Second Sex*.

Moreover, Bourdieu claims that Beauvoir does not analyze her relation to Sartre, yet *The Second Sex* contains precisely that. Whether one looks at the chapter on love or on the independent woman, she is examining her own relation to Sartre, or her imagined relation to Sartre. Her prize-winning novel, *The Mandarins* (1956), is a thinly veiled dissection of her two major relations, one with Sartre and the other with the American poet Nelson Algren. And then there are the four volumes of memoirs. Moreover, even as she undertakes such a self-analysis, she does not make the mistake of universalizing her own situation as an intellectual woman; she recognizes how different she is from others, who are trapped in domesticity. If there is one thing one cannot accuse Beauvoir of, it is a failure of reflexivity. Paradoxically, it is Bourdieu, the great exponent of reflexivity, who systematically fails the test of reflexivity. We never discover any reference to, let alone analysis of, his relations with women (or men), even in his own *Sketch for a Self-Analysis*. Total silence.

Of course, Bourdieu is not alone in this silencing of Beauvoir, as Moi (1994, chap. 7) has herself shown. When *The Second Sex* first appeared in 1949 it became an instant national scandal. There was public outrage at the bluntness with which Beauvoir—one of France's leading intellectuals—dealt with male domination and female complicity. Everyone seemed incriminated in her uncompromising indictment of the oppression of women. Subsequently, feminists have been loath to refer to her work, no matter how much they have borrowed from her. It became a sacrilegious text of unpleasant revelations, whose reading would often take place in secret. Plagiarize from it, yes, but to take it seriously is to taint one's intellectual and/or feminist reputation. Influential though it was for second-wave feminism, homage to Beauvoir was all too often paid in silence.

Why then is Bourdieu, the advocate of reflexive sociology, complicit in this collective amnesia? It is especially surprising given that the silencing of women is precisely a strategy of domination that he explicates, and seemingly condemns, in *Masculine Domination*. In a section fittingly entitled, "Masculinity as Nobility," Bourdieu ([1998] 2001, 59) writes of "the virtual denial of their [women's] existence" in which "the best intentioned of men (for symbolic violence does not operate at the level of conscious intentions) perform discriminatory acts, excluding women, without even thinking about it, from positions of authority." He denounces the silencing of women, but that does not give him pause when invoking Beauvoir's supposed "dutiful" relation to Sartre to justify his own suppression of her understanding of masculine domination.

That would be bad enough, but he would at least be following the crowd in expunging her work from the recognized intellectual field. Bourdieu, however, is doubly guilty in that Beauvoir prefigured not only so much of second-wave feminism but also so much of what Bourdieu himself had to say about masculine domination fifty years later. Moreover, she does so in far richer, more complex, subtle detail and, as we shall see, always seeking paths beyond masculine domination. Yet not a single acknowledgment of *The Second Sex* finds its way into Bourdieu's *Masculine Domination*, although there are ample references to second-wave feminism, particularly the Anglo-Saxon feminists who took so much from Beauvoir.

The argument of this conversation, therefore, is that *Masculine Domination* is a pale imitation of the ideas of *The Second Sex*.[2] Nor should such a convergence be surprising. After all, both Bourdieu and Beauvoir were implacable enemies of domination, always seeking to reveal its hidden and manifest contours. Both were uncompromising in their denunciation of the mythologies of the naturalization and eternalization of domination. Both were vocal enemies of identity politics, of all forms of essentialism, and, thus, of difference feminism. Both denounced any attempt to romanticize the resistance or culture of the dominated. To recover and then celebrate the particularity of women, or any other oppressed group, from within the field of its domination is to affirm that domination. Rather, they both insisted that domination is overcome by giving the dominated equal access to the universal.

Here, therefore, I wish to restore Beauvoir's originality, showing how Bourdieu's categories and arguments not only already existed but were far better elaborated in *The Second Sex* and, moreover, how Beauvoir goes beyond him by always gesturing to freedoms beyond domination—and all this despite her book predating his by half a century.[3]

SYMBOLIC VIOLENCE

Apart from the strategic importance for any theorist of "distinction" to pronounce on such a central trope of modern social thought, why is Bourdieu interested in masculine domination? For him, it is

> the prime example of this paradoxical submission, an effect of what I call symbolic violence, a gentle violence, imperceptible and invisible even to its victims, exerted for the most part through the

purely symbolic channels of communication and cognition (more precisely misrecognition), recognition, or even feeling. (Bourdieu [1998] 2001, 1–2)

For Beauvoir, masculine domination is the supreme form of othering, of which race and class are also examples:

> [Woman] is simply what man decrees. Thus she is called "sex," by which is meant that she appears essentially to the male as a sexual being. For him she is sex—absolute sex, no less. She is defined and differentiated with reference to man and not he with reference to her; she is the incidental, the inessential as opposed to the essential. He is the subject, he is the Absolute—she is the Other. (Beauvoir [1949] 1989, xxii)

Already here we see that Beauvoir gives more agency to men in the constitution of women, although she will show how men are also dominated by their domination. Still, the effect is the same: "She [woman] has no grasp even in thought, on the reality around her. It is opaque to her eyes" ([1949] 1989, 598).

Symbolic violence is not a matter of combining force and consent; it operates far more deeply through the internalization of social structure via those "schemes of perception and appreciation" that are constitutive of habitus:

> So the only way to understand this particular form of domination is to move beyond the forced choice between constraint (by forces) and consent (to reasons), between mechanical coercion and voluntary, free, deliberate, even calculated submission. The effect of symbolic domination (whether ethnic, gender, cultural or linguistic, etc.) is exerted not in the pure logic of knowing consciousness but through the schemes of perception, appreciation and action that are constitutive of habitus and which, below the levels of the decisions of the consciousness and the controls of the will, set up a cognitive relationship that is profoundly obscure to itself. Thus, the paradoxical logic of masculine domination and female submissiveness, which can, without contradiction, be described as both *spontaneous and extorted*, cannot be understood until one takes account of the *durable effects* that the social order exerts on women (and men), that is to say, the dispositions spontaneously attuned to that order which it imposes on them. (Bourdieu [1998] 2001, 37–38)

A fish is so attuned to the water in which it swims and without which it could not exist that it does not recognize the water for what it is and takes it for granted as natural and eternal. So it is with masculine domination. It is interesting, therefore, to read how Beauvoir explains her own discovery of masculine domination. Writing her memoirs in 1963, she reflects back on the moment of epiphany. It was 1946 and she was having a conversation with Sartre about writing her memoirs:

> I realized that the first question to come up was: What has it meant to me to be a woman? At first I thought I could dispose of that pretty quickly. I had never had any feeling of inferiority, no one had ever said to me: "You think that way because you're a woman"; my femininity had never been irksome to me in any way. "For me," I said to Sartre, "you might almost say it just hasn't counted." "All the same, you weren't brought up in the same way as a boy would have been; you should look into it further." I looked, and it was a revelation: this world was a masculine world, my childhood had been nourished by myths forged by men, and I hadn't reacted to them in at all the same way I should have done if I were a boy. I was so interested in this discovery that I abandoned my project for a personal confession in order to give all my attention to finding out about the condition of women in the broadest terms. I went to the Bibliothèque Nationale to do some reading, and what I studied were the myths of femininity. (Beauvoir [1963] 1964, 94–95)

In this rendition, Beauvoir, by an act of self-conscious willpower, pursues the origins and reproduction, the architecture and archaeology of masculine domination, all laid out in *The Second Sex*. This discovery of what had been unrecognized or misrecognized appears here as a quite conscious process—as indeed it was for Bourdieu, who claims to have discovered the structures of masculine domination through scientific observation of its elementary forms among the Kabyle. On the other hand, one might argue that Beauvoir's consciousness did not transform her practice of femininity. She does not escape the dilemma of being complicit in masculine domination, as *The Mandarins*—the novel of her two lives, the one among Parisian intellectuals and the other with her American lover, Nelson Algren—makes clear. She is far more honest about her own complicity than Bourdieu, who retreats to Virginia Woolf (1927) when he wants to talk about the concrete practices of male domination.

Like Bourdieu, Beauvoir is under no illusion about the depth of female subjugation: "The bond that unites her [woman] to her oppressors is not comparable to any other. The division of the sexes is a biological fact, not an event of history" (Beauvoir [1949] 1989, xxv). So it is easily presented as natural, inevitable, and eternal. "They have no past, no history, no religion of their own; and they have no such solidarity of work and interest as that of the proletariat" (xxv). They have no awareness of themselves as an oppressed collective. "When man makes of woman the *Other*, he may, then, expect her to manifest deep-seated tendencies toward complicity" (xxvii). Thus, Beauvoir sees masculine domination as a *special type* of domination that is stronger and deeper than class or racial domination, for the latter occupy spaces from which oppositional identities can be formed. "Having no independent domain, she cannot oppose positive truths and values of her own to those asserted and upheld by males: she can only deny them" (611). In one of his rare comparative moments, Bourdieu seems to think the opposite, namely that masculine domination is the *prototype* of symbolic violence but that class domination is its deepest expression (Bourdieu [1979] 1984, 384). Yet for both—and this is the important point here—masculine domination is the purest form of symbolic violence, that is, domination not recognized as such, or when it is recognized, that does not affect the unconscious practical sense.

Finally, one might surmise that the revulsion that greeted *The Second Sex*, as well as its subsequent silencing, speaks to the unconscious levels it excavates and the resistance, whether among the dominators or the dominated, to recognizing deeply internalized hierarchies. Thus, as we shall see in detail, Beauvoir's treatment of masculine domination embraces the notion of symbolic violence, but it also seeks to transcend it. In demonstrating my claim that there is nothing in *Masculine Domination* that does not already exist in a more elaborated form in *The Second Sex*, I have organized the following sections along the thematic lines of *Masculine Domination*.

NATURALIZATION, OR REVERSING CAUSE AND EFFECT

At the heart of masculine domination is its naturalization, which gives rise to the reversal of cause and effect. If it were the case that the differences between men and women are inherent, as though these two beings were different human species, then we could indeed say that the gender division of labor merely reflects differences in natural abilities and talents. We could say, for example, that women are by their nature emotional and men by their nature rational. In reality, what is presumed to be cause—the natural differences between men and women—is actually the effect of historical forces and socialization. Thus, Bourdieu writes,

> The biological appearances and the very real effects that have been produced in bodies and minds by a long collective labour of social-ization of the biological and biologicization of the social combine to reverse the relationship between causes and effects and to make a naturalized social construction ("genders" as sexually character-ized habitus) appear as the grounding in nature of the arbitrary divi-sion which underlies both reality and the representation of reality and which sometimes imposes itself even on scientific research. ([1998] 2001, 3; see also 22–23)

Beauvoir goes into far more detail. Indeed, part 1 of *The Second Sex*, entitled "Destiny," devotes successive chapters to the biological, psycho-analytical, and historical materialist foundations of masculine domination. While there are those who ground masculine domination in the biological differences between men and women, after examining biological evidence in excruciating detail, Beauvoir finds this view wanting. Biological differ-ences there are, and women experience their bodies very differently than men—for women the body is an alien force outside their control, whereas men are at home with their body—yet these experiences are not given ana-tomically but are shaped by society and upbringing. In the final analysis, biological differences cannot explain the subjugation of women, which is the cumulative product of social and economic forces, most importantly the relation of production to reproduction. Biology is not destiny.

Psychoanalysis represents a major advance in that the body exists no longer in and of itself but as lived by the subject. In a subjectivist flourish, Beauvoir writes, "It is not nature that defines woman; it is she who defines herself by dealing with nature on her own account in her emotional life" ([1949] 1989, 38). While psychoanalysis gives the framework within which to study the dynamics of gender, it does not explain the origins of masculine domination nor its persistence, resting as it does on the assumption of the patriarchal father. Beauvoir's next chapter, therefore, turns to historical ma-terialism and, in particular, Engels's claim that private property is at the root of masculine domination. While acknowledging the influence of economic forces, she rejects Engels's argument on the grounds that it never explains the very constitution of male and female subjects. Rejecting, therefore, both the "sexual determinism" of Freud and the "economic determinism" of Engels, she presents a history of male domination by integrating the biological and psychoanalytic into a materialist analysis of history:

> In our attempt to discover woman we shall not reject certain contributions of biology, of psychoanalysis, and of historical materialism; but we shall hold that the body, the sexual life, and the resources of technology exist concretely for man only in so far as he grasps them in the total perspective of his existence. (60)

In this way, Beauvoir dispenses with the scientific foundations for views that regard woman as by nature destined to be man's *Other*, showing them all to be fallacious. Yet she will also draw on these very same theories to reverse causality, showing how history and biography shape the concrete hierarchical relations through which man and woman produce each other.

THE HISTORICAL LABOR OF DEHISTORICIZATION

For Bourdieu, the naturalization of masculine domination lies with the matching of subjective and objective structures, the inculcation of a habitus by social structures, and the resulting harmonization of the two so that domination cannot be recognized as such ([1998] 2001, 33). This matching of the subjective and the objective is not spontaneous but the result of a long historical labor that produces the effect of eternalization:

> It follows that, in order to escape completely from essentialism, one should not try to deny the permanences and the invariants, which are indisputably part of historical reality; but, rather, one *must reconstruct the history of the historical labour of dehistoricization*, or, to put it another way, the history of the continuous (re)creation of the objective and subjective structures of masculine domination, which has gone on permanently so long as there have been men and women, and through which the masculine order has been continually reproduced from age to age. In other words, a "history of women" which brings to light, albeit despite itself, a large degree of constancy, permanence, must, if it wants to be consistent with itself, give a place, and no doubt the central place, to the *history of the agents and institutions which permanently contribute to the maintenance of these permanences*, the church, the state, educational system, etc., and which may vary, at different times, in their relative weights and their functions. (82–83; emphasis original)

Such a history that Bourdieu calls for in programmatic terms, Beauvoir had already attempted in part 2 of *The Second Sex*, itself divided into five chapters. She knows that a history of the second sex must be a history of the social production of masculine domination and its "naturalization," "eternalization," or, as Bourdieu calls it, "dehistoricization." Bourdieu's chapter 3, "Permanence and Change," does not compare to Beauvoir's ambition, scope, and accomplishment—heavily influenced by Engels's flawed history, to be sure, but an enormous achievement nonetheless. Included here is an anticipation of feminist appropriation of Lévi-Strauss's idea of women as objects exchanged among men in the pursuit of masculine politics, as well as a sophisticated analysis of how the second shift will reproduce rather than undermine masculine domination. Beauvoir prefigured the work of Gayle Rubin (1975) and Arlie Hochschild (1983), whose ideas Bourdieu subsequently takes up as though they were original to them.

In justifying his own intervention into gender studies, Bourdieu claimed as his contribution the focus on the reproduction of the structure of masculine domination outside the domestic sphere in agencies such as the church, the educational system, and the state (and, he might have mentioned, the economy), as if feminists had not explored these areas already. But even more to the point, *The Second Sex* itself recognized the importance of these arenas, both in the chapter "Since the French Revolution: The Job and the Vote" and in part 5, where Beauvoir describes "woman's situation."

Having drawn up a history of masculine domination, a history in which man defines woman as other, so Beauvoir asks how men have imagined women in their dreams, "for what-in-men's-eyes-she-seems-to-be is one of the necessary factors in her real situation" ([1949] 1989, 138). Part 3 of *The Second Sex* is devoted to the exploration of the myths men create about women to justify their subordination. It describes the struggles of men to realize themselves with, through, and against women, as well as the fantasies they create about women as nature, as flesh, as poetry. Woman is constituted as other, as slave and companion to man's fanciful desires for his own self-realization, as an idol to worship, as a distraction or compensation for the anxieties of his own entrapment in the cruel or noble competition with other men. Woman serves so many functions as other to man's projection of himself, both his limitations and his potentialities. Man cannot live without the mythology and reality of woman. Beauvoir discovers the most vivid expression of these imaginations in literature. There she also detects the possibility that man, seeing woman as necessary to his existence, defining himself in her mirror, also catches sight of a human being with her own needs with whom he might share a life of transcendence.

Even in his treatment of the Kabyle, there is no ethnographic counterpart in Bourdieu to Beauvoir's dissection of the creative literary outpourings of men. Although Bourdieu's conception of symbolic violence is one in which the dominated apply the dominant point of view to themselves, he never explores that dominant point of view in any detail. But it is here that Beauvoir not only discovers myths that ratify and eternalize domination but also catches glimpses of transcendence when men, caught in the grip of their dependence on women, recognize that their freedom can only be won with and through the freedom of women. The relentless pursuit of the sources of domination never blinds Beauvoir to the possibilities of liberation, so different from Bourdieu's notion of habitus as internalized social structure that preempts the possibility of any such vision. Important as they are in prefiguring alternatives, Beauvoir is under no illusion that such imaginations can be easily sustained against woman's bondage to immanence.

PRODUCING THE GENDERED HABITUS

The history of the collective unconscious has to be supplemented, says Bourdieu, by an understanding of the personal unconscious; we need both an ontogeny and a phylogeny. Here too Bourdieu offers general formulations:

> The work of transformation of bodies which is both sexually differentiated and sexually differentiating and which is performed partly through the effects of mimetic suggestion, partly through explicit injunctions and partly through the whole symbolic construction of the view of the biological body (and in particular the sexual act, conceived as an act of domination, possession), produces systematically differentiated and differentiating habitus. The masculinization of the male body and the feminization of the female body, immense and in a sense interminable tasks which, perhaps now more than ever, always demand a considerable expenditure of time and effort, induce a somatization of the relation of domination, which is thus naturalized. ([1998] 2001, 55–56)

Beauvoir devotes part 4 of *The Second Sex* to the formative years of the woman: childhood, the young girl, and sexual initiation. It opens with the sentence for which she has become famous (and famously misunderstood): "One is not born, but rather becomes, a woman."

No biological, psychological, or economic fate determines the figure that the human female presents in society; it is civilization as
a whole that produces this creature, intermediate between male
and eunuch, which is described as feminine. Only the intervention
of someone else can establish an individual as an *Other*. ([1949]
1989, 267)

It is painful even to read the way she describes what must, after all, have been
close to her own upbringing. She draws on an array of literatures to develop
a psychodynamic view of the way femininity is forced upon girls, the fantasies and anxieties of compulsory segregation in adolescence, and, finally, the
traumas of sexual initiation. From then on she has been made, she has been
painfully disciplined, to be woman.

Well, not always. Beauvoir insists that socialization can go awry.
She points out, anticipating the work of Nancy Chodorow (1978) twenty-
nine years later, that as a result of their upbringing, specifically being moth-
ered by women—but also in revulsion against aggressive masculinity—
from early on, alongside heterosexual dispositions, women develop strong
bonds with other women. This can lead to lesbian relations. She devotes
an entire chapter to "The Lesbian"—an enigmatic chapter, perhaps reflecting her own ambivalence—in which she wavers between, on the one
hand, lesbian sexuality as second best to heterosexuality (i.e., a casualty
of masculine domination) and, on the other hand, lesbian sexuality as a
liberated sexuality of mutual recognition. Of course, we must not forget
that in the France of 1949, lesbianism was a "forbidden" sexuality. It was
an extraordinary act of courage to even broach the subject, let alone affirm
its propriety.

Times have changed, so that today Bourdieu feels compelled to add
what seems to be an obligatory appendix—"Some Questions on the Gay
and Lesbian Movement"—in which he too wavers between seeing the gay-
lesbian movement as subversive of masculine domination and seeing it as
upholding dominant classifications. But Bourdieu simply takes lesbian and
gay sexuality as a given, whereas Beauvoir offers a rudimentary theory of
its emergence. Bourdieu's notion of socialization, of habitus—the bodily
inscription of social structure—misses all the ambiguities, resistances, and
contradictions so central to Beauvoir's more open and indeterminate analysis. In *Masculine Domination*, the limitations of the notion of habitus become particularly clear.

DOMINATION AND ITS ADAPTATIONS

Once the girl becomes a woman and enters as an adult into society, she faces the strictures of marriage and motherhood, and then the transition from maturity to old age. The story is always a bleak one, a story of domestic drudgery, boredom, and confinement. Isolated in a "living tomb," woman serves only to "assure the monotonous repetition of life in all its mindless factuality" (Beauvoir [1949] 1989, 604). The child becomes an obsessive focus of attention, both in resentment of and as compensation for woman's chains.[4] Working with a definite vision of the nuclear family and the male breadwinner, Beauvoir describes the woman's escape via adultery, friendship, or community as unsound evasions, each road paved with falsehood. This is the picture of the American woman in the 1950s that Betty Friedan would later paint in *The Feminine Mystique* (1963), a destiny against which the feminist movement would rebel.

Beauvoir is aware that domesticity is not necessarily woman's destiny. Escape from confinement and entry into the labor force is a necessary but not sufficient condition for liberation, since oppression easily follows her into the workplace. She is now bound in servitude to employer *and* patriarch. Nor does she think all is paradise for men. Indeed, just as Bourdieu insists that the dominators are dominated by their domination, so Beauvoir describes how men are also oppressed by their oppression, chained by their sovereignty.

Reflecting the shift that occurred over the subsequent fifty years in which women have become more mobile and less prisoners of domesticity, Bourdieu focuses more on the body in motion, the way the woman's body is a body for others, the way it is surveilled and self-surveilled, generating insecurity and anxiety. Women become objects in a market of symbolic goods. Not for nothing does he insist that masculine domination has no center but is diffused throughout society. Still, woman is not only object but, even in Bourdieu's rendition, has a subjectivity and a vision of men. Here he draws on Virginia Woolf's *To the Lighthouse* to capture the many ways in which women's dependency on men leads them into a supporting role, participating vicariously in men's games, a cheerleader of their men. The wife pacifies and protects the man against other men, trying to alleviate his anxieties and to comprehend the harshness of his domestic rule as a measure of his paternal love or as a response to the insecurities he faces.

Above all, women love men for the power they wield, the power denied to women:

Because differential socialization disposes men to love the games of power and women to love the men who play them, masculine charisma is partly the charm of power, the seduction that the possession of power exerts, as such, on bodies whose drives and desires are themselves politically socialized. Masculine domination finds one of its strongest supports in the misrecognition which results from the application to the dominant of categories engendered in the very relationship of domination and which can lead to that extreme form of *amor fati*, love of the dominant and of his domination, a *libido dominantis* (desire for the dominant) which implies renunciation of personal exercise of *libido dominandi* (the desire to dominate). (Bourdieu [1998] 2001, 79–80)

Here, too, Beauvoir had said it before in her extraordinary second chapter of Part VI of *The Second Sex*, "Women in Love," where she describes how women deify men, putting them on a pedestal in order to worship them. He is her representative in the outside world, his victories are her victories, his defeats her defeats. She idolizes him only to drag him down into her lair, demanding his everlasting attention. She realizes herself through him, but this love of the powerful man is doomed to disaster, either because man cannot sustain her expectations or because his desire is capricious and ephemeral:

Shut up in the sphere of the relative, destined to the male from childhood, habituated to seeing in him a superb being whom she cannot possibly equal, the woman who has not repressed her claim to humanity will dream of transcending her being towards one of these superior beings, of amalgamating herself with the sovereign subject. There is no other way out for her than to lose herself, body and soul, in him who is represented to her as the absolute, as the essential. Since she is anyway doomed to dependence, she will prefer to serve a god rather than obey tyrants—parents, husband or protector. She chooses to desire her enslavement so ardently that it will seem to her the expression of her liberty; she will try to rise above her situation as inessential object by fully accepting it; through her flesh, her feelings, her behaviour, she will enthrone him as supreme value and reality; she will humble herself to nothingness before him. Love becomes for her a religion. (Beauvoir [1949] 1989, 643)

Such are woman's attempts at salvation—idolatrous love, along with narcissism or mysticism—attempts to "transform her prison into a heaven of glory, her servitude into sovereign liberty" (628).

These notions of woman enclosed in domesticity sound rather antiquated, and Beauvoir herself recognizes that "today the combat takes a different shape; instead of wishing to put man in a prison, woman endeavors to escape from one; she no longer seeks to drag him into the realms of immanence but to emerge, herself, into the light of transcendence" (717). She thinks it will be transcendence, but it turns out to only intensify her subjugation, the one at home intensified by the one at work (680–81). Indeed, all these stratagems to realize herself, to become a subject, are illusory and self-defeating. They are what Beauvoir calls "justifications" and what Bourdieu calls "making virtue of necessity," adaptations of the dominated to their domination. Both paint a bleak picture in which women understand such adaptations as paths of freedom, whereas in fact they intensify subjugation.

But neither Bourdieu nor Beauvoir, but particularly Beauvoir, can leave women doubly imprisoned, objectively and subjectively. Both search for a possible escape from immanence, entrapment, and symbolic violence.

LIBERATION

Once again, Bourdieu adopts a notion of liberation surprisingly close to Beauvoir's. This is all the more astonishing as Bourdieu has generally scoffed at the attempt to formulate utopias. Yet in his postscript to *Masculine Domination*, he does just that, serving up a weak replica of Beauvoir's last chapter. The postscript begins by reasserting that "love is domination accepted, unrecognized as such and practically recognized, in happy or unhappy passions" (Bourdieu [1998] 2001, 109). Yet he then goes on to imagine the possibility of the suspension of domination in favor of mutual recognition:

> This is a world of non-violence, made possible by the establishment of relations based on full *reciprocity* and authorizing the abandonment and entrusting of self; a world of mutual recognition, which makes it possible, as Sartre says, to feel "justified in existing" . . . the world of the *disinterestedness* which makes possible deinstrumentalized relations, based on the happiness of giving happiness, of finding in the wonderment of the other, especially at the wonder he or she arouses, inexhaustible reasons for wonder. (110)

This is exactly what Beauvoir had elaborated in the last chapter of *The Second Sex*:

> To emancipate woman is to refuse to confine her to the relations she bears to man, not to deny them to her; let her have her independent existence and she will continue none the less to exist for him *also*: mutually recognizing each other as subject, each will yet remain for the other an *other*. (Beauvoir [1949] 1989, 731; emphasis original)

Even the expressions they use are the same, not only "mutual recognition" but the idea of the "gift of self." Beauvoir writes of genuine love through mutual recognition as "revelation of self by the *gift of self* and the enrichment of the world" (667; emphasis added), and Bourdieu follows with the true love of mutual recognition that can be found in "the economy of symbolic exchanges of which the supreme form is the *gift of self*, and of one's body a sacred body, excluded from commercial circulation" ([1998] 2001, 110–11; emphasis added).

Still, the difference is clear. For Bourdieu, liberation is thrown in as an obligatory and ill-fitting afterthought, perhaps a concession to the feminists he is trying to win over, perhaps a reflection of one of his own ongoing affairs, whereas it is Beauvoir's central concern, a subterranean stream running through the entire book that springs up in a final resplendent fountain of hope—there can be no domination without the possibility of liberation. She does not imagine a dissolution of the differences between men and women but instead imagines a plurality of such relations, "differences in equality": "New relations of flesh and sentiment of which we have no conception will arise between the sexes" (Beauvoir [1949] 1989, 730).

Whereas Bourdieu tells us nothing of the conditions for his "pure love," "art for art's sake of love" ([1998] 2001, 111), Beauvoir insists that authentic love requires structural equality that would, in turn, require access to abortion, contraception, and voting rights (remember this is France 1949), but also more radical ideas such as co-parenting ([1949] 1989, 726). Beauvoir is dismissive of that spurious "equality in inequality"—an equality of opportunity that becomes meaningless under unequal conditions. Instead, she affirms a socialist equality that does not yet exist (680)—a necessary (but not sufficient) condition of liberation. While she is only too mindful of the shortcomings of the Soviet Union with regard to the question of female emancipation, nevertheless she applauds its promise of equality, its imagination of equality (724). For Beauvoir, women's emancipation is not just an abstract utopia; it is a real utopia based on what she sees around her, what could be.

Beauvoir is clear that solitary individuals cannot successfully strive for transcendence in a capitalist society. The economically independent woman is a necessary, but certainly not sufficient, condition, as she makes amply clear in her penultimate chapter on the dilemmas of professionalism—contradictory pressures and double standards—that holds up well in the light of present-day research. For Beauvoir, liberation can only be a collective project and under economic conditions that provide for its possibility. And yet she does not see how women can strive together, collectively, for the transformation of the conditions of their existence. Indeed, the argument of *The Second Sex* rests on distinguishing masculine domination from race and class dominations. Whereas workers or blacks can forge an organic unity among themselves in opposition to a dominant group, not so with women, who orbit as individuals around individual men, complicit in their own subjugation, seeking the best possible partnership on the matrimonial market, subjugated in body and soul to masculine domination. The only hope for women, it would seem, is for the working class to first make its revolution and then—and only then—create the conditions for women to seek emancipation. It would be hard, therefore, for Beauvoir to comprehend the feminist movement to which her own book contributed so much. Feminist movements that express the genuine interests of women have never existed:

> The proletarians have accomplished the revolution in Russia, the Negroes in Haiti, the Indo-Chinese are battling for it in Indo-China; but the women's effort has never been anything more than a symbolic agitation. They have gained only what men have been willing to grant; they have taken nothing, they have only received. (Beauvoir [1949] 1989, xxv, but also 129)

So was the feminist movement she witnessed toward the end of her life another movement that was confined to the interests of men? Was this a movement conducted on the terrain of masculine domination, or did it challenge that domination?

Like Beauvoir, Bourdieu is also sensitive to the dilemmas of challenging domination from below. In writing about the gay-lesbian movement, Bourdieu analyzes the possibilities, but also the dangers, of struggles that successfully articulate the interests of an alternative sexuality. Once recognized, however, gay sexuality becomes invisible again and subject to many of the same oppressions as women. Querying the extent to which the feminist movement has eroded masculine domination, he enters a polemic against consciousness raising, which cannot be what it claims to be. The very language of consciousness is inappropriate for comprehending masculine domination that is inscribed deeply in an enduring habitus. "If it is quite illusory to believe that symbolic violence can be overcome with the weapons of consciousness and will alone, this is because the effect and conditions of its efficacy are durably and deeply embedded in the body in the form of dispositions" (Bourdieu [1998] 2001, 39). He continues:

> Although it is true that, even when it seems to be based on the brute force of weapons or money, recognition of domination always presupposes an act of knowledge, this does not imply that one is entitled to describe it in the language of consciousness, in an intellectualist and scholastic fallacy which, as in Marx (and above all, those who, from Lukács onwards, have spoken of "false consciousness"), leads one to expect the liberation of women to come through the immediate effect of the "raising of consciousness," forgetting—for lack of a dispositional theory of practices—the opacity and inertia that stem from embedding of social structures in bodies. (40)

The foundations of symbolic violence, therefore, lie not in a "mystified consciousness" but in "dispositions attuned to the structure of domination," so that the "relation of complicity" that the dominated "grant" to the dominant can only be broken through a "radical transformation of the social conditions of production of the dispositions that lead the dominated to take the point of view of the dominant on the dominant and on themselves" (42–43). But we have no idea what such a transformation entails or how it might occur.

Is Bourdieu's symbolic violence different from Beauvoir, who also sees women thinking in terms given to them by masculine domination? Woman's critical faculties are critically limited: "Having no independent domain, she cannot oppose positive truths and values of her own to those asserted and upheld by males; she can only deny them" (Beauvoir [1949] 1989, 611). You might call this absence of a "counter-universe" (617) "false consciousness" to be sure, but it is also deeply embedded, nurtured over a lifetime. Indeed, every page of *The Second Sex* is testimony to just how deep it is and the elaborate ways it is inculcated and reproduced. Moreover, let it be said that Beauvoir is no devotee of consciousness raising and is skeptical of programs for oppressed women to assert their own standpoint. She is deeply pessimistic about any good sense emerging within common sense. Like Bourdieu, she sees an ocean of bad sense, dotted with islands of momentary liberation.

FROM FEMINIST CRITIQUE TO FEMINIST MOVEMENT

We see now just how different both Beauvoir and Bourdieu are from Frantz Fanon's writings on Algeria that promote intellectuals' engagement in revolutionary activity. That was the theme of *The Wretched of the Earth*. Fanon's earlier book, *Black Skins, White Masks* ([1952] 1967), however, is the counterpart to *The Second Sex*. There, Fanon dissects the psychic consequences of racial domination, discovered when he came to France with a view of himself as a Frenchman and not a black Martiniquan. The shock of racism, just like the shock of sexism for Beauvoir, led Fanon to a devastating account of the situation of the racially oppressed, the mythologies that support racial domination, and the inauthentic responses to that domination, namely attempts to assimilate to whiteness that were doomed to failure. The analysis closely parallels the situation, myths, and justification linked to masculine domination found in *The Second Sex*.[5] More than Beauvoir does for women, Fanon emphasizes the virtues of the dominated culture, specifically the Negritude movement, as necessary to give dignity to blacks, but always his goal, like Beauvoir, is to transcend racism toward a universalism where race exists but not as an instrument of domination.

Black Skins, White Masks ends in despair, with no clear road to the universalism Fanon seeks, just as Beauvoir ends *The Second Sex* with a similar vain hope of liberation. Whereas Fanon would soon travel to Algeria, where the liberation movement becomes his key to universalism, Beauvoir would have to wait many years for the feminist movement, and even then she had to overcome her skepticism before declaring her support in 1972. She had always kept her distance from feminism, thinking that the woman question was subordinate to the socialist project, but when she realized that the Left had little interest in the emancipation of women; when she saw the continuing oppression of women in France, especially around rights of abortion; and when she became more familiar with the realities of women's position in the Soviet Union, she threw her intellectual and political weight behind an autonomous and radical feminism (Schwarzer 1984).

For Fanon, theory and practice come together in a revolutionary catharsis, whereas for Beauvoir they always remain in tension. Hers is a more contradictory position in which she dissects masculine domination yet in her own life finds herself falling into the same traps that she denounces as inauthentic. While she is writing *The Second Sex* she is having a passionate affair with Nelson Algren that bears all the marks of her analysis of "women in love"—knowing it to be an inauthentic and ultimately futile response to masculine domination. More successful, though never without its tensions, is the "brotherhood" of Sartre! Throughout her life, Beauvoir lives out, reflects on, and struggles with the contradictions between her theory and her practice.

Bourdieu, on the other hand, seems far less self-conscious about the contradictions between the moral implications of his theory of masculine domination and his practice, between the logic of theory and the logic of his own practice. He acknowledges that well-intentioned men can fall victim to deeply ingrained cognitive structures and unwittingly reproduce these, even when they think they are challenging them. He suggests this is true of Kant, Sartre, Freud, and Lacan, but he doesn't examine his own complicity in masculine domination. We have already noted how he dismisses Beauvoir, on the grounds that she is simply an appendage of Sartre. Yet, as I have shown, Bourdieu's work is but a pale imitation of Beauvoir's. He practices sexism in the very act of denouncing it.

Masculine domination runs deep in the unconscious of both men and women. But perhaps women, as the victims of domination, are in a better position to bring it to the surface. Even Bourdieu recognizes that women's insights into the life of men are often inaccessible to men themselves. Women see the games of men for what they are (Bourdieu [1998] 2001, 31, 75). They are more aware of the pitfalls of domination and how it leads to contradictory and inauthentic behavior. Notwithstanding their common concern to elucidate the structures of domination, Beauvoir's analysis is incomparably more profound than Bourdieu's, addressing rather than repressing the ambiguities and contradictions of approaching freedom from within the cage of domination.

THE INSIGHT OF THE OUTSIDER

If the habitus of masculine domination runs so deep, how is it than anyone, not least Beauvoir and Bourdieu, can even recognize it for what it is? If masculine domination is opaque and beyond the grasp of men and women, how have Bourdieu and Beauvoir managed to develop their insights (and, indeed, how have we managed to recognize them as insights)? Here, too, there is some convergence, and both rely on their position as outsider.

Bourdieu argues that masculine domination is most "magnified" in traditional societies like the Kabyle, and, while it is not recognized as such by the participants themselves, an outside ethnographer (like himself) can undertake "a socioanalysis of the androcentric unconscious that is capable of objectifying the categories of that unconscious" ([1998] 2001, 5). He then transplants his appreciation of the Kabyle androcentric unconscious to the more complex and differentiated unconscious structures of masculine domination found in advanced societies.

Just as Bourdieu's distance from, but connection to, Kabyle society gave him insight into its androcentric unconscious, so Beauvoir argues that it is her composite position as independent-woman-intellectual that gives her both distance from and insight into the subjugation of women—an insight denied to both intellectual men and dependent women.

> Very well, but just how shall we pose the question? And to begin with, who are we to propound it at all? Man is at once judge and party to the case; but so is woman. What we need is an angel— neither man nor woman—but where shall we find one? Still, the angel would be poorly qualified to speak, for an angel is ignorant of all the basic facts involved in the problem. . . . It looks to me as if there are, after all, certain women who are best qualified to eluci- date the situation of woman. . . . Many of today's women, fortunate in the restoration of all the privileges pertaining to the estate of the human being, can afford the luxury of impartiality—we even recognize its necessity. . . . Many problems appear to us to be more pressing than those which concern us in particular, and this detach- ment even allows us to hope that our attitude will be objective. Still, we know the feminine world more intimately than do the men because we have our roots in it, we grasp more immediately than do men what it means to a human being to be feminine; and we are more concerned with such knowledge. (Beauvoir [1949] 1989, xxxiii–iv)

Objectivity for Beauvoir, like Bourdieu, comes from being an outsider, located in a relatively autonomous space, but, crucially, she is also an insider connected to the subjects under interrogation.[6]

While Bourdieu's "outsider from without" connection to the Kabyle is different from Beauvoir's "outsider from within" connection to the experience of women, nonetheless they both have a notion of objectivity that is grounded in some segregated intellectual arena. For Bourdieu, it is the academy, defined by *skholè* and the competitive struggle for truth; for Beauvoir, it is the public sphere, epitomized by intellectual debate in the Parisian café or in journals like *Les Temps Modernes*. Such distance is necessary to avoid being mired in the misrecognition that accompanies symbolic violence—women seeing themselves through the eyes and with the categories of men. Thus, both are suspicious of movements based on the romanticization of resistance, for that would be the triumph of misrecognition or bad faith. Most fundamentally, they both agree that with some exceptions (like themselves), when it comes to appreciating the foundations of masculine domination, men and women are dominated by their "bad sense" and, specifically, women are complicit in their own subjugation.

They are, therefore, both traditional intellectuals demystifying masculine domination from on high. They are different not only from Fanon in Algeria, who is deeply engaged with revolutionary struggle, but also from Gramsci, who, like Bourdieu and Beauvoir, finds himself in what in the end proves to be a non-revolutionary context, but unlike them believes in the good sense of the oppressed, or at least the working class. Given the presumption of good sense, there is therefore a place for organic intellectuals who can elaborate that good sense (while also attacking bad sense), developing a war of position. We find analogous feminist intellectuals who see insight and good sense arising from the dominated. Patricia Hill Collins (1990), for example, argues that the most oppressed have the clearest view of the social structure and of their own position within domination and that they spontaneously generate cultures of resistance. She is specifically talking about poor black women in the United States. White women and black men, being in contradictory positions no less than white men, cannot see through the mists of domination. Collins, therefore, endorses the standpoint of an organic intellectual closely tied to communities of poor black women, elaborating their standpoints and their culture, transmitting these to wider publics. Consistent with this perspective, Collins (2005) is critical of contemporary, mainly male, black intellectuals such as Henry Louis Gates and Cornel West for being cut off from the communities they supposedly represent.

Indeed, there are strong traditions of feminism, very different from Beauvoir's, that have deep roots in women's communities. Beauvoir was the traditional intellectual who gave language and vision to the movement and thereby established the very possibility of organic intellectuals. It remains to be seen whether Bourdieu's critical role as a traditional intellectual will also contribute to a movement that forges a reciprocal connection between sociology and its publics—a position he himself adopted in later life, despite his oft-stated contempt for organic intellectuals.

7

THE SOCIOLOGICAL IMAGINATION
Mills Meets Bourdieu

It is the political task of the social scientist—as of any liberal educator—continually to translate personal troubles into public issues, and public issues into the terms of their human meaning for a variety of individuals. It is his task to display in his work—and, as an educator, in his life as well—this kind of sociological imagination.

— MILLS, *THE SOCIOLOGICAL IMAGINATION*

Political competence, inasmuch as there can be a universal definition of it, undoubtedly consists in the ability to speak in universal terms about particular problems—how to survive dismissal or redundancy, an injustice or an accident at work, not as individual accident, a personal mishap, but as something collective, common to a class. This universalization is possible only by way of language, by access to a general discourse on the social world. This is why politics is in part bound up with language. And here again, if you like, we can introduce a bit of utopia to attenuate the sadness of sociological discourse, and convince ourselves that it is not too naive to believe that it can be useful to fight over words, over their honesty and proper sense, to be outspoken and to speak out.

— BOURDIEU, "GIVING VOICE TO THE VOICELESS"

All this means that the ethno-sociologist is a kind of organic intellectual of humanity, and as a collective agent, can contribute to de-naturalizing and de-fatalizing human existence by placing his skill at the service of a universalism rooted in the comprehension of different particularisms.

— BOURDIEU, "A RETROSPECTIVE ON THE ALGERIAN EXPERIENCE"

So far, I have created imaginary conversations between Bourdieu and Marxism: how Bourdieu appropriated so much of Marx but took it in a direction unimagined by Marx, namely the political economy of symbolic goods; how in many ways Gramsci and Bourdieu are at loggerheads over the durability and depth of domination; how, despite their common views of colonialism, Bourdieu and Fanon clash over the means of its transcendence; how Freire and Bourdieu responded to the domination perpetuated by formal education in diametrically opposed ways; and, finally, how Bourdieu's understanding of masculine domination as symbolic power was a pale replica of Beauvoir's feminism. We turn now to another conversation, between Bourdieu and Mills. Both deeply ambivalent about Marxism, they shared similar sociological and political projects, despite living half a century apart and on different continents.

The quotes from Bourdieu and Mills above are chosen to underscore their convergent views on the relations between sociologists and their publics, a notion of the traditional intellectual who can potentially challenge domination by denaturalizing and de-fatalizing what exists, demonstrating the links between the taken-for-granted lived experience (the particular) and the social forces that constitute it (the universal). They differ, however, in that Bourdieu recognizes and lives out the contradictions between "science as a vocation" and "politics as a vocation," to use Max Weber's terms, since science rests on a *break* with common sense while politics rests on an *engagement* with common sense. Mills, on the other hand, would probably have as little tolerance for Bourdieu's scientific "jargon" as he did for Parsons's, since he doesn't see a fundamental break between science and common sense, seeing an easy passage from the sociological imagination (linking micro and macro) to the political imagination (turning personal troubles into public issues). We will return to this question in the conclusion to this conversation, but first we must build up the case that, despite their obvious differences, Mills is Bourdieu in the 1950s, decked out in American colors.

STRIKING CONVERGENCES

Bourdieu's major methodological text, *The Craft of Sociology* (written with Jean-Claude Chamboredon and Jean-Claude Passeron in 1968), in many respects converges with C. Wright Mills's famous elaboration of the sociological imagination in 1959. Indeed, one cannot but notice that the title of Bourdieu's book is borrowed from Mills's appendix, "On Intellectual Craftsmanship." Both books are critical of the divorce of theory from empirical research; both emphasize social science research as process—a modus operandi rather than an opus operatum, as Bourdieu would say. Bourdieu follows Mills in attacking US sociology for its professionalism, its formalism, its empiricism, and its provincialism. Yet I cannot find any references to Mills in Bourdieu's writings, except the inclusion of a short extract—one of forty-four "illustrative texts"—from *The Sociological Imagination* (1959), in which Mills criticizes public opinion research for creating its own spurious object, an argument also found in *The Craft of Sociology* and one that Bourdieu will elaborate later in his career.

Given their similar methodological outlooks and empirical foci, the comparison of Bourdieu and Mills underlines how the world has changed since the 1950s (while in some ways reverting back to that era), as well as the abiding differences between the United States and France. Still, there are parallels in the political context that shaped their writing. In the United States, the years immediately after the Second World War witnessed the continuity of the radicalism that had begun in the 1930s, but it wasn't long before reaction asserted itself in the form of McCarthyite witch hunts, a broad anticommunism, American triumphalism, and the "end of ideology." Just as Mills confronted the swing away from the political configuration of the New Deal, much of Bourdieu's writings can be seen as coming to terms with the denouement of the 1960s and the rightward turn in the 1980s and 1990s. Both sustained a critique of the present at a time when progressive alternatives were in retreat, though more so in the US of the 1950s than in France of the 1980s.

Biographically, Bourdieu and Mills came from very different backgrounds—the one grew up the son of a postal employee in a village in the French Pyrenees, the other from middle-class stock in Texas. More interesting, however, they both began as philosophy students but quickly turned from abstract and abstruse intellectual preoccupations to a more direct engagement with the world. For Mills, his interest in pragmatism gave him a particular stance on sociology that was opposed to structural functionalism and survey research, just as Bourdieu reacted against the pretensions of Sartre and his circle, as well as against social reform sociology.

Like Bourdieu, who developed a knee-jerk reaction against the Marxism of the communist intellectuals who surrounded him at the École Normale Supérieure, Mills had his Marxism refracted through the milieu of New York leftism. Only late in his short life would Mills take up a serious engagement with the history of Marxism. Like Bourdieu, he borrowed many ideas from Marxism, but, also like Bourdieu, he never quite identified with its political project as he saw it. Thus, both were hostile to the Communist Party and were never members, although—again—both exhibited sometimes overt and sometimes covert sympathies for democratic variants of socialism.

Both openly recognized the influence of Weber, with whom they shared a preeminent concern with domination, its reproduction and its repercussions. Like Weber, they never spelled out any future utopia. Both had only a weakly developed theory of history: Mills focused on the shift from a nineteenth-century aristocratic order (alongside putative democratic publics) to the new regime of power elite and mass society, while Bourdieu subscribed to modernization theory based on the differentiation of relatively autonomous fields, analogous to what Weber called value spheres.

Mills and Bourdieu were reflexive sociologists inasmuch as they dissected the academic and political fields in which they operated—although they were more adept at applying that reflexivity to others than to themselves. Both were invested in the sociology of knowledge, both a sociology of sociology and a sociology of the academy. Mills's dissertation was a study of the history of pragmatism—the secularization and professionalization of philosophy. Following in the footsteps of Veblen, Mills was always critical of the American system of higher education but, again like Bourdieu, took advantage of its elitist aspects that gave him the space and autonomy to develop his distinctive sociology. Still, both felt themselves to be outsiders in the academy and from this vantage point wrote their savage criticisms, lambasting the establishment and generating the hostility of their colleagues and a following among new generations of students.

Both were public sociologists and also major public intellectuals, not just in their own countries but across the world. Both served their scholarly apprenticeships as professionals but soon sought out wider audiences. Neither hesitated to enter the political arena as an intellectual, and their careers displayed a steady movement from the academy into the public sphere. Mills was writing in an era of relative political passivity, and his notions of mass society reflect this. Like Beauvoir, he inspired a movement he never anticipated—in his case the New Left of the 1960s. It remains to be seen whether Bourdieu will inspire such a movement—certainly his political writings and addresses have played an important role in public debate in France. Both held out hope for intellectuals as an independent force that would pioneer progressive politics in the name of reason and freedom.

CLASSES AND DOMINATION

Bourdieu has come to be known for his metatheoretical framework—centering on fields, habitus, and capital as well as the master idea of symbolic violence—that transcended his own empirical projects, a theoretical framework that has been taken up by others. Mills's only venture into broader theoretical issues was *Character and Social Structure*, written with Hans Gerth (Gerth and Mills 1954). It advanced a social psychology with a notion of "character," parallel to but far richer than Bourdieu's "habitus," that was tied to a concept of "institutional order" corresponding to Bourdieu's notion of field. Covering a similar terrain to but more critical and far more accessible than Parsons's *The Social System* (1951), *Character and Social Structure* never captured the same audience—perhaps because the authors were two outlaws with limited influence and following at the time. It is now a largely forgotten text, unlike Mills's empirical critiques of US society and his invitation to the sociological imagination, which have inspired successive generations of students. These assaults on the class structure of the US have definite parallels in Bourdieu's corpus, although Bourdieu's work is more theoretically self-conscious than that of Mills. In both cases their impact transcended sociology, not just in reaching the public realm but in spreading to other disciplines beyond sociology.

The three major works of Mills to address US society in the 1950s dealt sequentially with labor and its leaders (*New Men of Power*, 1948), the new middle classes (*White Collar*, 1951), and the dominant class (*The Power Elite*, 1956). Mills's framework for studying US society does develop over the decade of his writing, but his portrait shows a clear continuity: ever-greater concentration of power in a cohesive economic-political-military elite; a burgeoning new middle class of professionals, managers, sales workers, and bureaucrats; and, finally, a pacified working class betrayed by its leaders. These are also the three classes treated in Bourdieu's monumental *Distinction*. Whereas Mills works his way up the social hierarchy, Bourdieu works his way down, from the dominant classes to the petty bourgeoisie and finally to the working class. Both study the way the dominant classes impose their will on society, but where Mills focuses on the concentration of resources and decision-making in the power elite, Bourdieu takes this concentration of power and wealth for granted, instead focusing on how domination is hidden or legitimated by the classifications the dominant class uses to establish its distinction.

Bourdieu, therefore, focuses on symbolic violence—the exercise of domination through its misrecognition. Simply put, the dominant class distinguishes itself by its cultural taste. Whether this be in art, architecture, music, or literature, the dominant class presents itself as more refined and more at ease with its cultural consumption than the petite bourgeoisie, whose taste is driven by emulation, and the working class, whose lifestyle is driven by economic necessity. The distinction of the dominant class actually derives from its privileged access to wealth and education, but it is presented as innate, thereby justifying its domination in all spheres of life. According to Bourdieu, the popular aesthetic of the working class—its concern with function rather than form, with the represented rather than the representation—is a dominated aesthetic, bereft of genuine critical impulse. Bourdieu's innovation, therefore, turns on viewing class not just as an economic-political-social formation but also as a cultural formation. Class members possess cultural capital as well as economic capital, so that a class structure is a two-dimensional space defined hierarchically by the total volume of capital, but also horizontally (within class) by the composition of capital (i.e., the specific combination of economic and cultural capital). He shows how this class structure is mirrored in the distribution of cultural practices and patterns of consumption.

It is interesting to compare this vision of class structure with Mills's *Power Elite*, where he describes the dominant class as three interlocking sets of institutions—economic, political, and military. He calls them "domains," but he might as well have called them fields. He also writes about their distinction and their ruling-class lifestyle, inherited through families, acquired in elite schools and colleges, and developed through networks of self-assurance. Mills even devotes a chapter to "celebrities" who distract attention from the concentration of power. Symbols of prestige hide the power elite from public view. This is all quite parallel to Bourdieu, but ultimately the emphasis is very different. Mills is less interested in the relation between cultural and economic-political elites—between the dominant and dominated fractions of the dominant class, as Bourdieu puts it—and more interested in the changing relations among the three pillars of the power elite, in particular the ascendancy of the military (the warlords) over the economic and political elites. This different emphasis reflects the very different place of the United States and France within the world order—the one a dominant military power, the other a cultural nobility.

If there is divergence in their conceptualizations of the dominant class, there is more convergence in their respective discussions of the middle classes. A theme that threads through both discussions is the insecurity of the middle class, trying to maintain its position within the stratification system. As the gap between the middle classes—especially the old middle classes subject to deskilling but also the new middle classes subject to bureaucratization—and the working class closes, so the status panic of the former intensifies. As a form of capital, education becomes more important than property in asserting middle-class distinction. Thus, *White Collar* makes much of the rising importance of education, in addition to the role of the mass media and the illusory world it creates. Mills devotes considerable space to the fate of the intellectuals and their loss of independence through bureaucratization, becoming a technocracy, serving power and unresponsive to publics. Mills describes, in terms directly analogous to those of Bourdieu, how the academic field is looking more and more like an economic market, invaded by the logic of corporate capital.

On the subject of the working class, both Bourdieu and Mills have much less to say. Bourdieu's more ethnographic *The Weight of the World* (Bourdieu et al. [1993] 1999) has a richer, if untheorized, exploration of working-class life than does *Distinction*, which is reliant on survey research. The culture of the working class is a dominated culture, responsive to the pressing needs of economic necessity and the prestige of the dominant culture. Mills's analysis of the working class is thinner, since *The New Men of Power* is devoted more to labor leaders than to the led, utilizing survey research. The argument is very similar to the one Bourdieu makes in *Language and Symbolic Power* (1991)—the representatives of subordinate classes enter the field of power, where they engage in a competitive game among themselves, and the logic of the field of power trumps their accountability to the dominated. Mills describes how labor leaders, through their negotiations, are co-opted onto the terrain of the business class. They seek to attach themselves to the lower levels of the power elite. Both Mills and Bourdieu, therefore, see leaders manipulating the led—representation becomes rhetoric used to simultaneously pursue and hide games within the higher reaches of society. Bourdieu's essays ([1982] 1990, [1984] 1993) on public opinion follow Mills's critique of mass society.

Yet alongside Mills's critique is always an alternative political vision, albeit a political vision that becomes more utopian over time. *The New Men of Power* describes the absorption of labor leaders into the power elite, accomplices of the "main drift," but it also maps out the political field of the immediate postwar period as an array of publics that includes the Far Left (Leninist Left), the Independent Left (more critical than interventionist), the Liberal Centre (which might include support for trade unions), the Communists (which he sees as antidemocratic fifth columnists), the Practical Right (which supports class war against unions and leftists), and Sophisticated Conservatives (corporate liberals tied to the military-industrial complex who see unions as a stabilizing force that manages discontent). Like so many commentators of his time, Mills expected capitalism to undergo another "slump" that would force the hand of the Sophisticated Conservatives but also attract popular support to a true Labor Party that would organize worker control and democratic planning.[1] Socialism, he asserted, had been derailed by social democracy, petty trade unionism, and communism. In line with this program, Mills hoped for a new type of intellectual, a "labor intellectual," independent of but committed to the working class, capable of forging a new vision and a new collective will.

Mills's political optimism did not last long. Reaction swept across the country, so that when he turned to *White Collar* (1951) he came up with a much bleaker scenario. There he refers to the middle classes as a rearguard, without a will of their own, siding with the prevailing forces in society, and, pending a slump, those prevailing forces lay with the power elite. When it comes to *The Power Elite* (1956), Mills is consumed by despair. Denouncing the "higher immorality" and "organized irresponsibility" of the dominant classes, his political imagination turns from the bleak future to the radiant past. He contrasts the mass society he sees around him with a democracy of publics—the founding dream and early practice of American society. Mills never reconciles himself to the present, never withdraws from the intellectual battle for another world.

If there was always a strong utopian element in Mills's writings—at first projected onto leftist political forces and then as emancipatory projects buried in history—one is hard-pressed to find any equivalent in the writings of Bourdieu, who saw his public jeremiads as being adequately political in their own right. They would be less effective if connected to utopian thinking. In part, this was because of the historic role of French intellectuals, starting with Zola, and the openness of the public sphere to such intellectuals—so different from their more marginal place in US politics. No less important, Bourdieu was always opposed to conjuring up false hopes in the transformative potential of the dominated classes. His political engagement around issues of human rights, labor rights, education, and so forth was firmly rooted in the concrete present. Bourdieu mobilized his analysis of the subjective experience of domination, largely absent in Mills's writings, against what he regarded as the misguided illusions of leftist intellectuals. Bourdieu refused speculative connections across the yawning gap between hope and reality, the yawning gap that separated Mills's utopian disposition and his sociological analysis, the unrecognized distinction between Mills's political imagination and sociological imagination.

THE SOCIOLOGICAL IMAGINATION

The refusal to confront the gap between sociological imagination and political imagination—indeed, the confusion of the two—can be found in *The Sociological Imagination*, one of the most widely read and inspiring introductions to sociology. *The Sociological Imagination*, published in 1959, just three years before Mills died, looks two ways—back to sociology and forward to politics. When looking back to sociology, it is a devastating and memorable indictment of professional sociology for the sins of abstracted empiricism and grand theorizing. Abstracted empiricism refers to survey research divorced from any historical or theoretical context, typified in Mills's mind by the work of his titular boss, Paul Lazarsfeld, with whom he had a most rocky relationship. Abstracted empiricism approximates to market research and exemplifies the bureaucratization of sociology, and more generally how intellectuals were increasingly serving the corporate world as consultants and experts and as orchestrators of public opinion. Grand theory, on the other hand, refers to the hegemony of structural functionalism within the world of theory—formal theory, arcane and inaccessible to the uninitiated. According to Mills, grand theory is an elaborate but empty architecture of mundane yet unsubstantiated claims.

Against abstracted empiricism and grand theory, Mills celebrated the sociologist as craft worker, uniting in one person the development of sociological theory through engagement with empirical data. He paints a romantic image of the lone sociologist uncorrupted by the academic environment—a self-portrait of his isolation in and alienation from the academic world. This image is an absurdly unsociological critique of professional sociology—a Manichean struggle between God and the Devil—but one that justified his own abandonment of that world.

If the first romance in *The Sociological Imagination* is with the sociologist as craft worker, the second is with the sociologist as "independent intellectual," looking outward to politics rather than inward to academia. Here too are two positions to avoid: on the one hand, the sociologist as adviser to the prince—the technician, the consultant—and, on the other hand, the philosopher-king who aspires to rule the world. In the political realm, the adviser to the prince and the philosopher-king are the counterparts to the abstracted empiricist and the grand theorist in the academic realm, while the independent intellectual is the counterpart of the craft worker. The independent intellectual speaks *to* publics and *at* rulers, maintaining a distance from both. Here indeed is Mills's notion of the public sociologist—a concept he describes but does not name—for him a traditional rather than an organic intellectual.

The connection between the craft worker and the independent intellectual is made through the idea of the sociological imagination that famously turns private problems into public issues. But here the slippage begins: between, on the one hand, the *sociological imagination*—i.e., the connection between social milieu and social structure, micro and macro—and, on the other hand, the never-specified *political imagination* that connects private troubles to public issues. It is one thing to demonstrate that unemployment is not a problem of individual indolence but one of the capitalist economy; it is another matter to turn that sociological understanding into a public demand or a social movement for security of employment. Indeed, appreciating the broad structural determinants of one's personal troubles is as likely to lead to apathy and withdrawal as to engagement. *The New Men of Power*, *White Collar*, and *The Power Elite* each attempts to bridge the divide between sociology and politics but in an abstract way, as though sociological imagination inevitably leads to political engagement. Political imagination cannot be reduced to sociological imagination, as Bourdieu knows only too well.

The first problem concerns the very existence of publics for Mills's public sociologist to address. His writings all point to the disappearance of publics and the rise of mass society, so with whom, then, will the public sociologist converse? Bourdieu recognizes the dilemma quite explicitly, albeit in a specific way. The argument is laid out in *The Craft of Sociology*, which speaks directly to Mills's sociologist as craft worker. It criticizes both existentialism (the counterpart to Parsons's structural functionalism) and the reaction to it in the form of imported American empiricism. Like Mills, Bourdieu engages in is a continual dialogue of theory and empirical research: the one cannot exist without the other. Bourdieu rarely indulges in flights of political fancy;[2] his claims are always empirically grounded. Yet, he closely follows Gaston Bachelard, the French philosopher of science, by insisting on the break between science and common sense, or what Bourdieu calls *spontaneous sociology*. For sociology, such a break with common sense is especially important, because its subject matter deals with familiar problems about which everyone has an opinion. Throughout his academic life, Bourdieu will be fighting against what he regards as amateurish commentators—"doxosophers"—who claim to know better than professional sociologists.

Although the home of sociology, France has always had difficulty developing an autonomous professional sociology and separating itself from social reform and public discourse. In this sense, the academic context of Bourdieu is very different from that of Mills. The former faces the struggle to create a science against common sense, while the latter is suffocated by professionalism and struggles to reconnect his science to common sense. This accounts, at least in part, for their opposed genres of writing, the latter always straightforward and accessible, the former dominated by complex linguistic constructions and the coining of esoteric concepts.[3] For a renewal of sociology to be accepted by the French academic pantheon, it was necessary to adopt the style of writing of the discipline with the highest distinction, namely philosophy. While denouncing the detachment of philosophy from everyday reality, Bourdieu nevertheless replicates a philosophical rhetorical style to claim sociology's legitimacy within the academic world, but the result can be separation from the wider publics he seeks to reach. He is only too aware of the gap between sociology and politics, even as he tries to overcome that gap in his later years. Mills suffers from the opposite problem—by making his books accessible and by resisting the idiom of science and high theory, he loses credibility within the world of sociology and mistakes his sociological imagination for political imagination.

Still, reacting to opposite challenges—Bourdieu embracing science against common sense, Mills embracing common sense against formalistic science—they converge on a common understanding of methodology, represented in the idea of craftwork as the interactive unity of theory and research. Likewise, Bourdieu, no less than Mills, is committed to the idea of the independent intellectual. Moreover, his targets are the same as Mills's. On the one hand, he denounces the philosopher-king, or what he calls the "total intellectual," epitomized by Jean-Paul Sartre, and, on the other hand, he denounces the advisers to the king—the technocrats, experts, consultants to the state, and servants of power. The philosopher-king—the public intellectual as total intellectual—has a certain reality in France that it does not have in the United States. Notwithstanding the higher appreciation of the intellectual in France, Bourdieu nonetheless faces the same dilemma as Mills. Neither sees a public out there that he can address. Mills talks of a mass society, atomized, withdrawn, and alienated from politics and public discussion, whereas for Bourdieu the problem is, if anything, even more serious. The habitus is so deeply inculcated that the dominated are unreceptive to criticism of domination. Furthermore, the independent intellectual faces the power of the media and its own mediators. Bourdieu lost no opportunity to attack the media's power to determine the message, to even shape the research that becomes the message. Although Mills was also aware of the power of the media, he never wrote such a broad assault on the media as Bourdieu carries out in *On Television* ([1996] 1999).

Whether they sought it or not, both—but Bourdieu more than Mills—became celebrities in their own time for their angry oppositional views. They became media events in their own right, and the more they railed against the establishment, the more celebrated they became! Yet both were opposed to the idea of the organic intellectual who would circumvent the media and engage directly with publics. In theory, both opposed the organic intellectual on the grounds that it compromised their independence, yet their actual practices were quite different.

Mills rarely participated in any collective demonstration or protest, refused to sign petitions, and generally avoided the people he somewhat contemptuously dismissed as the masses. He was a pure intellectual, speaking out to the people from his pulpit. Bourdieu, however, was very different. He was always ready to initiate or sign a petition, he would talk to all sorts of publics, and he could be found addressing workers on picket lines. He had no allergy to the people in whose name he spoke. Quite the contrary, he had enormous sympathy for those at the bottom of social hierarchies, vividly expressed in *The Weight of the World*, which describes the plight of the lower classes and immigrants under modern capitalism. Here lies the paradox— according to his theory, such unmediated engagement is not only a futile but a dangerous activity. Yet he also saw this practice of public sociology as developing a political imagination out of his sociological imagination. Mills was always truer to the idea of the traditional intellectual, standing aloof from the individual and collective struggles below, but even he, in the last three years of his life, compromised his independence in a desperate political partisanship.

FROM SOCIOLOGY TO POLITICS

The Sociological Imagination (1959) was Mills's farewell to sociology. In the remaining three years of his life he became a public intellectual, writing two short polemical books intended to capture the public imagination. The first was *The Causes of World War Three* (1958), a continuation of the arguments of *The Power Elite* but written for an even broader public. It condemned "crackpot realism" and "organized irresponsibility" not just in the United States but in the Soviet Union too. Together, these power elites were ushering in World War III. He ends the book with an appeal to intellectuals to fight against the insanity of "rationality without reason," calling instead, you might say, for Bourdieu's "realpolitik of reason."

The second book was of a very different character. If *The Causes of World War Three* diagnosed the way the power elites of the two superpowers were heading toward the annihilation of the human race, *Listen, Yankee*, written in 1960, pointed to an alternative scenario—a socialism that was neither capitalist nor communist. The Cuban Revolution served to make the alternative real—a "concrete fantasy" intended to galvanize a collective political imagination. *Listen, Yankee* is based on Mills's short, intense visit to Cuba in 1960. He spent three-and-a-half long days with Fidel Castro and nearly a week with the head of the Institute for Agrarian Reform. In his account of the Cuban Revolution through the eyes of its leaders, Mills points to the already ongoing and remarkable experiments in economic planning, education expansion, welfare provision, and land reforms—experiments that would be institutionalized as the mark of Cuban socialism. He undertakes a class analysis of the social forces that are driving the social transformations and the counter-revolutionary forces opposing it, not least the support being given to the counter-revolution by the United States. He describes the challenges Cuba faced both domestically and internationally. The open hostility of the United States, Mills says, was driving Cuba into the arms of the Soviet Union, which led to intensified US military threats. *Listen, Yankee* addresses the US public, befuddled by the jingoist media and ignorant of the destructive path of US imperialism throughout Latin America, but particularly in Cuba—imperialism justified under the Monroe Doctrine. The Cuban Revolution should be seen, he argued, as a reaction to Yankee supremacy, an experiment in true democracy, an experiment that all people of conscience can learn from, an experiment they must defend.

It was only two years before the end of his forty-six-year life that Mills discovered the potential of Third World revolutions. He was ahead of his time. In its class analysis, in its understanding of colonialism and imperialism, in its vision of socialism, *Listen, Yankee* is a precursor to Fanon's *The Wretched of the Earth*, which appeared the following year—the same year that its author died at the age of thirty-five. These two sadly curtailed lives—Mills's and Fanon's— ended within three months of each other, inspiring in their different ways social movements across the world. Both saw the key role of intellectuals in forging revolution, but Mills came to this idea late in life, only when he began traveling abroad, especially to Latin America, where he discovered, firsthand, the significance of revolutionary theory, which he had previously dismissed as a Marxist ruse.

Just as Mills became ever more outspoken and radical during the last three years of his life, so in the last decade of his life Bourdieu also became more angry, more public, more accusatory. He had always seen sociology— or, at least, his sociology—as having political consequences in the sense that it revealed the hidden bases of domination; nonetheless, his denunciations took on polemical force when faced with the conservative turn of politics in France and elsewhere. His book *On Television* ([1996] 1999) and then the two short collections of essays *Acts of Resistance* (1998) and *Firing Back* ([2001] 2003) spoke out against neoliberalism and the tyranny of the market. He established his own press, Liber-Raisons d'Agir, to publish such politically motivated and publicly accessible books. His magazine, *Actes de la recherche en science sociales*, had always had a broad intellectual audience. He became a major intellectual spokesman of a broad left front in France but also worked to develop what he called an Internationale of intellectuals. He could be found on picket lines with workers, as well as writing open letters to prominent leaders protesting against violations of human rights. He was committed to intellectuals as an independent collective force, to the intellectual as an "organic intellectual of humanity," as he once called it. Mills had a similar vision of intellectuals as a "third force," an idea he had formulated as early as the Second World War when he taught at the University of Maryland, a view that stuck with him until his dying days. In *Listen, Yankee* he wrote of Cuba as a cultural center of the world, proposing to establish a "world university" and with it create an international community of progressive intellectuals. The parallels between Mills and Bourdieu are perhaps astonishing, but then they are also expressing the unconscious desires of intellectuals on the road to class power.

Yet here is the paradox: Bourdieu recognizes that ideas can have only limited effect on social change. The dominated, who have an interest in a critical sociology, cannot grasp its meaning, because their submissive habitus is so deeply inscribed, whereas those who can grasp its meaning have no interest in the message. There is a contradiction, as I have said before, between Bourdieu's logic of theory and his logic of practice. His theory says such interventions are futile, yet his actions imply that such interventions might dislodge public discourse and thus disrupt symbolic violence. In the final analysis, his own political engagement contradicts his attacks on such notions as ideology and consciousness as too thin to grasp the depth of domination. Thus, despite his theory, Bourdieu subscribes to the idea of the organic intellectual engaged directly with publics, as well as the traditional intellectual speaking from the tribune, addressing humanity. He feels compelled to supplement his sociological analysis with political engagement. We need to make sense of this by unleashing Bourdieu on Bourdieu, but first we must ask how irreversible and how universal is symbolic violence.

THE TWOFOLD
TRUTH OF LABOR
Burawoy Meets Bourdieu

Like the gift, labour can be understood in its *objectively* twofold truth only if one performs the *second reversal* needed in order to break with the scholastic error of failing to include in the theory the "subjective" truth with which it was necessary to break, in a first para-doxal reversal, in order to construct the object of analysis. The objectification that was necessary to constitute wage labour in its objective truth has masked the fact which, as Marx himself indicates, only becomes the objective truth in certain exceptional labour situations: the investment in labour, and therefore miscognition of the objective truth of labour as exploitation, which leads people to find an extrinsic profit in labour, irreducible to simple monetary income, is part of the real conditions of the performance of labour, and of exploitation.

— BOURDIEU, *PASCALIAN MEDITATIONS*

The defining essence of the capitalist labor process is the simultaneous obscuring and securing of surplus value. How does the capitalist assure himself of surplus value when its production is invisible?

— BURAWOY, *MANUFACTURING CONSENT*

Tucked away toward the end of Bourdieu's masterpiece, *Pascalian Meditations*, are four startling pages under the heading "The Twofold Truth of Labour" (Bourdieu [1997] 2000, 202–5). They are startling, first, because they deal with the labor process, a topic Bourdieu rarely broached, and, second, because his interpretive framework follows Marxist orthodoxy, a framework he generally dismissed as anachronistic and misguided.

His argument is presented in typically intricate form in the quotation above. Let me translate. In constituting the object of knowledge—i.e., the notion of wage labor—Marx breaks with the subjective (lived) experience of workers that they are paid for a full day's work, for eight hours in an eight-hour day. In reality workers are exploited and only receive wages that are equivalent to a portion of the working day, say five hours, leaving three hours as surplus labor, which is the basis of profit. So far, this is straightforward Marx. But, says Bourdieu, it is not enough to make this first break— first reversal—with lived experience to produce the objective truth of exploitation; it is further necessary to make a second break, a second reversal, this time *against* the "objective truth" in order to reincorporate the "subjective truth"—the lived experience of workers. It is one thing to discover the objective truth of labor (i.e., exploitation); it is another to show how exploitation is sustained by workers themselves.

More concretely, how is it that workers work sufficiently hard so as to produce surplus value and thus make exploitation possible, even while it is invisible? The answer, Bourdieu claims, lies in the workers' "investment in labour," through which they find an "extrinsic profit in labour, irreducible to simple monetary income," with the result that exploitation is ensured even as it is not experienced as such. In other words, in the organization of work there is "a miscognition of the objective truth of labour as exploitation," which induces the hard work that is the foundation of exploitation. Further—and here too Bourdieu follows Marxist orthodoxy—the less autonomy a worker has, the less room for meaningful investment in labor and the more likely workers will see themselves as exploited, that is, the more likely there is a convergence of objective and subjective truths.

I find these pages startling not only for their focus on labor and their unqualified embrace of the Marxist theory of exploitation, but also for their convergence with the argument I made in *Manufacturing Consent* (1979)—an ethnography of an industrial plant in south Chicago where I worked as a machine operator for ten months in 1974 and 1975. In *Manufacturing Consent* I formulated the twofold truth of labor as follows: if surplus labor is *obscured* (the objective truth of capitalist work, first break), then the question becomes how it is *secured* (the subjective truth of capitalist work, second break). Marx assumed it was secured through coercion, the fear of loss of the job, but under advanced capitalism, I argued, there were employment guarantees and legal constraints on managerial despotism that made the arbitrary application of coercion impossible. So management now had to persuade their employees to work hard—it had to manufacture consent. But how? The answer, I argued, was that the protection of workers not only posed a new challenge to the generation of surplus value, it also contained the solution to that challenge: the protection gave workers a certain autonomy on the shop floor that allowed them to "invest in labour" through constituting work as a "game." In my case it was a piece-rate game that we called "making out." The game compensates workers for their intrinsically boring work by giving them "extrinsic profits"—emotional satisfaction and symbolic rewards. I had taken Gramsci's ideas to the workplace to argue that consent rather than fear ruled the shop floor. Under advanced capitalism, workers are subject to what I called a hegemonic rather than a despotic regime of production.

I used the game metaphor as Bourdieu sometimes used it—as a way of understanding the reproduction of social structure and its underlying patterns of domination. Games obscure the conditions of their own playing through the very process of securing participation. Just as one cannot play chess and at the same time question its rules, so one cannot play the game of "making out" on the shop floor and at the same time question its rules—rules that are socially sanctioned by workers and shop floor management alike. This is the twofold truth of the game—the truth of the outsider studying the game and the truth of the insider playing the game. To the outsider the obsessive pursuit of the game appears ridiculous, but the sociologist as outsider can see its meaning in the way it "secures" the effort to makes capitalism possible, a truth that is "obscure" to the worker. As I worked on the shop floor I operated with the truth of the machine operator; as a sociologist I interrogated those experiences for the objective truth underlying the game of making out. My sociology, however, did not affect the way I worked on the shop floor.

How had Bourdieu arrived at a seemingly identical formulation to my own? How could I be using the language of hegemony and consent, which implies a conscious recognition of domination, to describe what, indeed, looked more like symbolic violence and misrecognition? Thus began years of fieldwork into the complex and fascinating texts of Bourdieu, leading to the conversations of this book in addition to a reassessment of my understanding of the nature of advanced capitalism and its durability as well as the nature of state socialism and its fragility. On the one hand, it compelled a critique of Gramsci for overlooking the *mystification* that characterizes advanced capitalism. On the other hand, it led to a critique of Bourdieu for projecting *misrecognition* as universal—the result of the incorporated and embodied habitus—rather than seeing it as mystification (i.e., something socially produced and historically contingent).

The question I bring to Bourdieu is deceptively simple: How durable is domination?—which divides into three related questions. If the habitus of subjugation is universal and deep (i.e., there is misrecognition), how can domination be challenged? If, on the other hand, subjugation is historical and contingent (i.e., there is mystification), when does domination become transparent? And under what conditions, if any, does the objective truth of the sociologist converge with the subjective truth of the worker? Here I address these questions through an examination of the stability of workplace regimes in advanced capitalism and state socialism.

HOMO HABITUS VS. HOMO LUDENS

Bourdieu is always seeking to transcend antinomies: subject and object, micro and macro, voluntarism and determinism. All too often, however, he does not so much transcend the antinomy as combine the two opposed perspectives. Such is the case, I believe, for his conception of structure and agency, where he combines *Homo habitus* and *Homo ludens*.

Sometimes, Bourdieu starts with *Homo habitus*—with habitus, as we have seen, being the notion that the human psyche is composed of "the durably installed generative principle of regulated improvisations," producing "practices which tend to reproduce the regularities immanent in the objective conditions of the production of their generative principle" (Bourdieu [1972] 1977, 78). Here the emphasis is on doxic submission, but one that allows for improvisation within limits. We might call this a deep notion of social reproduction.

On other occasions, Bourdieu starts with *Homo ludens*—individuals whose character is given by the games they play, giving rise to a notion of social structure as rules that guide individual strategies. Human beings are players motivated by the stakes and constrained by the rules that define the game. This is a contingent notion of social reproduction that depends on the continuity of a particular game embedded in a particular institution. The only assumption it makes about human beings is that they are game players seeking control of their environment.

Bourdieu has both a contingent notion and a deep notion of social action, alternating between the two and often fusing them—*Homo ludens* and *Homo habitus*. For Bourdieu, game playing accompanies deeply inculcated, almost irremovable dispositions, which vary from individual to individual, depending on their biographies. Here, however, I want to oppose rather than merge these two notions of human action: on the one hand, *Homo habitus*, for whom social structure is internalized, and on the other hand, *Homo ludens*, for whom social structure is a set of external constraints to be negotiated. Is submission deeply engraved in the psyche or the product of institutionally ordered practices? Bourdieu wants it both ways, but the result is a notion of social structure that can never change and a pseudoscience that is unfalsifiable.

In adopting *Homo ludens* and the idea of mystification rather than *Homo habitus* and the idea of misrecognition, I show how social structures are more malleable and unstable than Bourdieu admits, although some more so than others. Thus, I argue that capitalist hegemony requires and obtains mystification as its precondition, which makes it relatively stable, whereas state socialism, unable to produce such a mystification, could not sustain hegemony and instead alternated historically between coercion and legitimation—an unstable arrangement that, in the final analysis, proved to be its undoing. The comparative analysis of advanced capitalism and state socialism shows the limits of both Bourdieu and Gramsci—the first too pessimistic about the possibilities of social change, the second too optimistic about such change.

MYSTIFICATION VS. MISRECOGNITION

My disagreement with Bourdieu turns on the crucial distinction between *mystification* and *misrecognition*. When Karl Marx writes about the mechanism through which exploitation is hidden in the form of wage labor or about commodity fetishism and the way the market obscures the human labor that goes into the commodity, he insists that this happens automatically and independently of the particular characteristics of any individual who experiences it—male or female, black or white. Thus, Marx and Engels famously write in *The German Ideology* ([1845–46] 1978, 154), "If in all ideology men and their circumstances appear upside-down as in a *camera obscura*, this phenomenon arises just as much from their historical life-process as the inversion of objects on the retina does from their physical life-process." There is no psychology here—there is only the "historical life-process." Individuals are both the carriers and the effects of social relations, so if they experience things upside down, then this is the consequence of the social relations into which they enter. *Mystification* is the term we use to describe the social process that produces the gap between experience and reality *for all who enter a specific set of social relations.*

We can find examples of mystification in Bourdieu, most notably his repeated analysis of the gift economy in which the gift is experienced by givers and receivers as an act of generosity, while to the outside "scientist" it may be viewed as an act of self-interested economic behavior—an act that will reap its rewards—or as the collective creation of social bonds of interdependence. Bourdieu says that the scientists who impose their views on the agents misunderstand the nature of the gift exchange, which depends on the coexistence and separation of the subjective truth (an act of generosity) and the objective truth (building symbolic domination or social solidarity). But how are the two truths sustained? In *Outline of a Theory of Practice*, Bourdieu ([1972] 1977, 1–9) focuses on the separation in time of successive gift giving, so that the gift appears to be an isolated act of generosity. Thus, any attempt at immediate reciprocity is regarded as a crude violation of the basic norms. Here the structuring of exchange as a process evolving over time explains the misrecognition or, more precisely, the mystification.

When he turns to the gift exchange in *Pascalian Meditations*, however, the emphasis is more on the inculcation of perceptions and appreciations (habitus) that are shared by gift giver and receiver. This habitus of generosity is at the foundation of the gift economy, a habitus that is being replaced by the calculative disposition, making gift exchange rarer and more difficult to sustain. Insofar as the gift economy depends on the prior inculcation of a certain habitus, so we are shifting from mystification that is the product of social processes to misrecognition that is the result of an individual's internalized habitus (which in turn mediates and reflects social processes).

Reading *Pascalian Meditations*, Bourdieu's climactic theoretical work, I was struck by how much it sounded like Talcott Parsons's sealing of the social order. Individuals internalize the norms of the social order: "Incorporated cognitive structures attuned to the objective structures" secure "doxic submission to the established order" (Bourdieu [1997] 2000, 178); or, in other words, there is a mutual adjustment of position and disposition, of resources and expectations, of habitat and habitus. "The schemes applied to the world are the product of the world to which they are applied" (147), which guarantees the unknowing, unconscious adaptation to the world:

The agent engaged in practice knows the world but with a knowledge which, as Merleau-Ponty showed, is not set up in the relation of externality of a knowing consciousness. He knows it, in a sense, too well, without objectifying distance, takes it for granted, precisely because he is caught up with it; he inhabits it like a garment [*un habit*] or a familiar habitat. He feels at home in the world because the world is also in him, in the form of habitus, a virtue made of necessity which implies a form of love of necessity, *amor fati*. (141–42)

Just as Parsons (1951) acknowledges the existence of "deviance" when role expectations are not complementary, so Bourdieu acknowledges that there can be mismatches between habitus and field—misfirings—that may or may not lead to new adaptations. But just as deviance is a residual category for Parsons, mismatches and misfirings are residual categories for Bourdieu. In both cases, the weight of the argument is to show the impossibility of contesting a social order, which means in Bourdieu's case bending the stick against Marxism, feminism, populism, and any other "ism" that celebrates transformation from below. It is not that some social orders lead to mystification and others to transparency, but that all social orders reproduce themselves through the inculcation of habitus and necessary misrecognition. We are all fish in water, unable to comprehend the environment in which we swim—except, of course, Bourdieu and his fellow sociologists.

The question we have to ask is whether social orders are held together by mystification, with the emphasis on *social relations independent of the particular individual,* or by misrecognition, constituted through a *deeply implanted habitus at least partially independent of the particular social relations into which an individual is inserted.* How can one discriminate between these alternative explanations for social order: a contingent domination dependent on social relations producing an *ideology as mystification* versus an internalized deep *symbolic violence that works through misrecognition*? Bourdieu clings to both notions, whereas I want to adjudicate between them. That requires a study that compares submission in different societies. In what follows, I undertake such a comparative analysis by reconstructing my studies of the subjectivities that arise from work organization and its regulation in advanced capitalist and state socialist workplaces. I show that mystification of domination is present in advanced capitalism but not in state socialism, explaining the durability of the one and the instability of the other. Symbolic violence based on misrecognition, however, being universal, cannot discriminate between societies. Bourdieu falsely generalizes from his conception of contemporary France and pre-capitalist Kabyle society to all social orders. He cannot—and, indeed, makes no attempt to—explain how it is that state socialism collapses while advanced capitalism endures. That is what I attempt to do in the following pages.

THE GRAMSCIAN MOMENT: MANUFACTURING CONSENT

I begin again with Antonio Gramsci, whose originality lay in a periodization of capitalism not on the basis of the economy but on the basis of its superstructures, and in particular on the rise of the state–civil society nexus that organized consent and absorbed challenges to capitalism. This was the story of the rise of capitalist hegemony in Europe. In the United States, by contrast, without parasitic feudal residues, Gramsci writes that "hegemony was born in the factory" and not in civil society—a streamlining of domination that allows the forces of production to expand more rapidly than elsewhere, what he calls Fordism.

Manufacturing Consent (Burawoy 1979) endeavored to elaborate on what Gramsci might have meant when he spoke of hegemony being born in the factory. The study was based on participant observation in a south Chicago factory where I was a machine operator for ten months, from July 1974 to May 1975. I was a wage laborer like everyone else, although it was apparent that I was from a different background, not least because of my limited skills and my strange English accent. I made no secret of my reason for being there: to gather material for my dissertation.

Influenced by the French structuralist Marxism of the 1970s and its appropriations of Gramsci, I argued that the theories of the state developed by Althusser, Poulantzas, and Gramsci could be applied to the internal workings of the factory. In my Chicago plant, an *internal state*[1] constituted workers as industrial citizens, individuals with rights and obligations, recognized in grievance machinery and in the details of the labor contract. Here I could see in miniature Poulantzas's "national popular state." At the same time, the internal state orchestrated what Gramsci called the concrete coordination of the interests of capital and labor through collective bargaining, which provided the material basis of hegemony. Capital granted concessions that were necessary for labor's consent—concessions, as Gramsci would say, that do not touch the essential. Finally, following Gramsci, but also Poulantzas's analysis of the dominant classes and their relation to the state, I saw factory management as a power bloc, made up of different divisions (fractions) under the hegemony of its manufacturing division.

As well as an internal state, there was also an *internal labor market* that reinforced the individualizing effects of the internal state. It gave workers the opportunity to bid on other jobs within the factory, which were then allocated on the basis of seniority and experience. This internal labor market gave individual workers power and leverage against management. If workers did not like their job or their supervisor, they could bid on and then move to an alternative job. Workers who somehow made themselves indispensable to their foremen could wield considerable power. Like the internal state, the internal labor market constituted workers as individuals and, through rewards based on seniority, tied their interest to capital. If it gave workers some power on the shop floor, it also cultivated their loyalty, since moving to another firm would put them at the bottom of the seniority ladder. Workers had another interest, therefore, in the success— profitability—of their enterprise, even at their own expense, as happened in the 1980s, when many US workers had to enter into concession bargaining just to keep their jobs.

The internal state and internal labor market were the conditions for a third source of consent, the constitution of *work as a game*—in my case, the game of making out, whose rules were understood and accepted by operators, auxiliary workers, and shop floor supervisors alike. It was a piecework game and the goal was to "make out" (i.e., make an acceptable percentage output, one that was not higher than 140 percent and not lower than 125 percent). The details need not detain us here; suffice it to say that constituting work as a game is common in many workplaces because it counters ennui and arduousness, and it makes time pass quickly, enabling workers to endure otherwise meaningless work. There were good psychological reasons to participate in such a game, but, just as important, the social order pressured everyone into playing the same game with more or less the same rules. We continually evaluated each other as to how well we were playing the game. It was also difficult to opt out without being ostracized.

Playing the game had two important consequences. First, the game certainly limited output through goldbricking (going slow when piece rates were difficult or impossible to make in the hope that the rates would be loosened) and quota restriction (limiting output to 140 percent so as to avoid rate increases), but it also got operators to work much harder, and often with ingenious improvisation. It was a game that favored the application of effort and thus increased profits for management, and with only small monetary concessions. Second, it contributed not only to profit but also to hegemony. The very act of playing the game simultaneously produced consent to its rules. As we've seen, you can't be serious about playing a game—and this was a very serious game for those who played it—if at the same time you question its rules and goals.[2]

If the organization of work as a game was the third prong of hegemony, it was effective in generating consent only because it was protected from the *arbitrary* application of coercion (punitive sanctions that ranged from disciplinary procedures to firing)—a protection that was made possible by the constraints imposed on management by the internal labor market and internal state. This three-pronged hegemony was a distinctive feature of advanced capitalism in which management could simply no longer hire and fire at will. No longer able to rely on the arbitrary rule of the despotic regime of production of early capitalism, management had to *persuade* workers to deliver surplus; in other words, management had to manufacture consent. Thus, the internal state and the internal labor market were the apparatuses of hegemony, constituting workers as individuals and coordinating their interests with those of management, applying coercion only under well-defined and restricted conditions. Management could not arbitrarily close down the game or violate its rules—at least, not if it wanted to uphold its hegemony.

A game has to have sufficient uncertainty to draw in players, but it also has to provide players with sufficient control over outcomes. A despotic regime, in which management applies sanctions in an arbitrary fashion, creates too much uncertainty for a game to produce consent. In short, the hegemonic regime creates a relatively autonomous arena of work with an optimal balance of certainty and uncertainty, so that a game can be constituted and consent produced. In a hegemonic regime, the application of force (ultimately being fired), whether it occurs as a result of a worker's violation of the rules or as a result of the demise of the enterprise, must itself be the object of consent. Thus, we have Gramsci's "hegemony protected by the armour of coercion" (1971, 263).

In short, the *economic* process of producing things constituted as a game is simultaneously a *political* process of reproducing social relations and an *ideological* process of producing consent to these relations, made possible by the relatively autonomous internal state and internal labor market. I advanced Gramsci's analysis by taking his account of the state and civil society into the factory, applying it to the micro-physics of power, and, further, adding a new dimension to organizing consent—the idea of social structure as a game.[3]

THE BOURDIEUSIAN MOMENT:
THE TWOFOLD TRUTH OF LABOR

The preceding account of manufacturing consent derives from Gramsci's theory of hegemony, but it overlooks the fundamental dilemma capitalists face: to secure surplus (unpaid) labor at the same time as its existence is obscured. The organization of consent is concerned only with the securing of surplus, but it coexists with the mystification of exploitation. This is none other than Bourdieu's twofold truth of labor: (1) the objective existence of exploitation, and (2) the subjective conditions of its simultaneous concealment and realization. It took my engagement with Bourdieu to realize that mystification is simply not part of Gramsci's theoretical toolkit. His idea of hegemony is not about mystification or misrecognition but largely about the rational and conscious basis of consent. At most, it is an account of the naturalization of domination, not the concealment of exploitation.

A Bourdieusian moment, therefore, is powerfully at work in my analysis of games. The peculiarities of the game of making out—and, indeed, all workplace games—lie in the way playing the game enlists workers not only in legitimating its rules and thereby producing surplus but also in mystifying the conditions of its existence (i.e., the relations of production between capital and labor). This is how Bourdieu presents the same point:

> Social games are in any case very difficult to describe in their twofold truth. Those who are caught up in them have little interest in seeing the game objectified, and those who are not are often ill-placed to experience and feel everything that can only be learned and understood when one takes part in the game—so that their descriptions, which fail to evoke the enchanted experience of the believer, are likely to strike the participants as both trivial and sacrilegious. The "half-learned," eager to demystify and denounce, do not realize that those they seek to disabuse, or unmask, both know and resist the truth they claim to reveal. They cannot understand, or take into account, the games of self-deception which make it possible to perpetuate an illusion for oneself and to safeguard a bearable form of "subjective truth" in the face of calls to reality and to realism, and often with the complicity of the institution (the latter—the university, for example, for all its love of classifications and hierarchies—always offers compensatory satisfactions and consolation prizes that tend to blur the perception and evaluation of self and others). ([1997] 2000, 189–90)

In "making out," workers secure "compensatory satisfactions and consolation prizes," winning freedoms at the margin that become the center of their lives on the shop floor. To the outsider, "making out" appears absurd; to the insider, it is what gives meaning to life. Through their small gains and the relative satisfactions these gains bring—"I'm so excited; today I made 129 percent on that lousy drilling job"—not only does alienating work become enchanting, but workers think they are outwitting management even as they are unwittingly contributing to their own exploitation. Management succeeds in securing surplus labor through the rebellion of workers against management. Bourdieu follows suit: "Workers may contribute to their own exploitation through the very effort they make to appropriate their work, which binds them to it through the freedoms—often minute and almost always 'functional'—that are left to them" ([1997] 2000, 203).

If both Bourdieu and I emphasize the concealing of the underlying social relations—and here we are continuous with the Marxist tradition from Marx through Lukács and the Frankfurt School, although, unlike them, Bourdieu considers the mystification to involve an almost unassailable misrecognition—how is it that it plays virtually no role in Gramsci, who instead develops a theory of rational consent to domination? The most general answer must be that he participated in revolutionary struggles at a time when socialist transformation was on the political agenda, when capitalism did appear to be in some deep organic crisis—although, in the end, it gave rise to fascism rather than to socialism. Capitalism was thus not the stable and enduring order it appeared to Bourdieu. For Gramsci, we can say, capitalism was more durable than it appeared to classical Marxism, but it appeared less durable than it appears to us today in our post-socialist pathos.

A more specific answer has to do with Gramsci's participation in the factory council movement and the occupation of the factories in Turin in 1919–20. As skilled workers, many of them craft workers, those involved experienced deskilling and separation from the means of production much more directly than the unskilled workers of today, who take for granted wage labor and the private ownership of the means of production. Moreover, the occupation of their factories and the collective self-organization of production through their councils meant that they understood only too well the meaning of capitalist exploitation. For Gramsci, whose experience of the working class was through the factory council movement, exploitation was hardly hidden and, on this occasion, the working class really did exhibit a good sense within the common sense. In Gramsci's eyes, the factory occupations failed because working-class *organs*—trade unions and the Socialist Party—were wedded to capitalism, that is, their interests were ultimately coordinated with those of capital. For Gramsci, this "betrayal" would have to be rectified by the development of a "Modern Prince"—the Communist Party—that understood and challenged capitalist hegemony. There was nothing hidden or unconscious about the consent of parties and trade unions to capitalism.[4]

Bourdieu makes the opposite argument, namely that craft workers are not the most likely but instead the least likely to see through their subjective experience to the objective truth of exploitation: "It can be assumed that the subjective truth is that much further removed from the objective truth when the worker has greater control over his own labour" ([1997] 2000, 203). Curiously, Bourdieu is at his most Marxist here in arguing that subjective truth converges with objective truth and exploitation becomes transparent as labor is deskilled. As barriers to labor mobility are swept away, workers lose any attachment to their work and can no longer win for themselves the freedoms that bind them to work. Fearing such stripped and homogenized labor, modern management tries to re-create those freedoms through participatory management: "It is on this principle that modern management theory, while taking care to keep control of the instruments of profit, leaves workers the freedom to organize their own work, thus helping to increase their well-being but also to displace their interest from the external profit of labour (the wage) to the intrinsic profit" (204–5)—i.e., the profits from partial control over work.

While Bourdieu seems to be following my argument about the mystification of social relations through compensatory game playing, he is actually saying something quite different. For him, the power of misrecognition is linked to the level of skill, whereas I argue it has to do with the political and ideological apparatuses of production. Thus, in my case, the internal labor market and internal state create attachments to the employer and restrictions on employer interventions, so workers will be able to carve out those workplace games that give them their subjective sense of freedom. That is to say, hegemonic regimes are the necessary and sufficient condition for the mystification of exploitation, no matter how unskilled the work may be. Indeed, the more labor is unskilled, the more important become the games of work as compensation for arduousness and estrangement.

In short, for Bourdieu the convergence of the objective truth (exploitation) and the worker's subjective experience of work *increases* with the degradation of work, whereas I argue the opposite. The craft worker of the nineteenth century, as described by E. P. Thompson (1963), exhibits deeper class awareness of exploitation than the autoworker of the twentieth century. Behind our differences lies a very different analysis of the basis of domination and subjugation.

CONDITIONS OF DOMINATION: INSTITUTIONS OR DISPOSITIONS

Instead of exploring the *institutional conditions* of mystification—the political and ideological apparatuses of the enterprise—Bourdieu turns to the *dispositional conditions* of misrecognition—"the effect of these structural factors obviously depends on workers' dispositions" ([1997] 2000, 203). In an earlier piece, he is most explicit:

> Differences in dispositions, like differences in position (to which they are often linked), engender real differences in perception and appreciation. Thus the recent changes in factory work, toward the limit predicted by Marx, with the disappearance of "job satisfaction," "responsibility" and "skill" (and all the corresponding hierarchies), are appreciated and accepted very differently by different groups of workers. Those whose roots are in the industrial working class, who possess skills and relative "privileges," are inclined to defend past gains, i.e. job satisfaction, skills and hierarchies and therefore a form of established order; those who have nothing to lose because they have no skills, who are in a sense a working-class embodiment of the populist chimera, such as young people who have stayed at school longer than their elders, are more inclined to radicalize their struggles and challenge the whole system; other, equally disadvantaged workers, such as first-generation industrial workers, women, and especially immigrants, have a tolerance of exploitation which seems to belong to another age. (Bourdieu 1981, 315)

The propensity to submission is not invariant but depends on the inculcated habitus. Those who have been socialized to industrial work or who come from oppressed conditions accommodate to it; those young people who have few skills but extended education and nothing to lose are likely to "radicalize their struggles and challenge the whole system," while immigrants and women are supposedly submissive beyond the pale. What sort of folk sociology is this, dependent on conventional wisdom and belied by history? We know that immigrants and women are quite capable of being militant and of organizing themselves into strong trade unions, whether this be in South Africa, China, Brazil, or the United States. Since we have no way of measuring "disposition" or "habitus" independent of behavior, the argument is simply tautological—immigrants and women are submissive because of their submissive habitus as demonstrated by their submissiveness.

The argument of *Manufacturing Consent* was directly opposed to this commonsense or "spontaneous" sociology. I tried to bend the stick in the other direction, showing that externally derived dispositions made no difference to the way people responded to production or to the intensity with which they were drawn into the game of making out. Our experience on the shop floor was more or less the same, irrespective of our "habitus." Thus, I was struck by my own absorption into the game that I knew to be furthering my exploitation. I was not coerced into hard work. As my day man told me on my first shift, "no one pushes you around here," and he was right. Nor could the extra money explain my devotion to hard work. Rather, it was the symbolic rewards and emotional satisfaction of making out that drove the rhythm of work.

Using quantitative and qualitative data, I showed that race, age, marital status, and education had little to do with performance at work, whereas the workplace attributes of seniority and experience made a significant difference (Burawoy 1979, chap. 9). Observing interactions on the shop floor, I argued that joking relations established between races underscored that differences in background and racial prejudices were not relevant within the workplace, even as they were relevant with regard to the institutional racism beyond the workplace. I contrasted the situation in a Chicago factory with the mining industry in Zambia, where racism was, indeed, institutionalized *within* the workplace in the form of the color bar, differential pay scales, and differential legal codes. I described that system as one of colonial despotism, many of whose elements continued into the postcolonial era, despite the democratization of the political sphere. Here racism was no joking matter, so to speak. While there is no denying that racial mindsets continue to exist, their significance at the point of production depends on the racial form of the political regime of production.[5]

So we arrive at my crucial difference with Bourdieu. In contrast to Gramsci, both of us recognize a fundamental gap between the objective and subjective truth of labor, but for Bourdieu this is achieved through *misrecognition* rooted in the individual's habitus, whereas I claim it is achieved through *mystification* rooted in the social relations into which men and women enter—a mystification that operates on all individuals, independent of their inherited dispositions. Symbolic violence through misrecognition rests on the bodily inculcation of social structure and the formation of a deep, unconscious habitus. There is no need for any concept of hegemony, because we are programmed to act out the social structure. Mystification, on the other hand, rests on individuals being inserted into specific social relations. Mystification is the necessary condition for a stable hegemony (i.e., for the organization of consent to domination).

If this is the difference that separates us, then examining consent/submission under different institutional complexes could corroborate or disconfirm our different theories. Thus, state socialism becomes a laboratory for the adjudication of our two theories. I will try to show that intensive inculcation from the party state and its institutions does not produce misrecognition, because these self-same institutions generate a transparency in their functioning. Without mystification, hegemony is not sustainable. In other words, as I will now show, the contradictions sowed by its institutions prove stronger than the incorporation of habitus.

THE PRECARIOUS HEGEMONY OF STATE SOCIALISM

I went in search of factory work in Hungary for two reasons. The first is that I missed the boat with the Polish Solidarity movement, 1980–81, which had absorbed my attention as an extraordinary working-class movement. When General Wojciech Jaruzelski declared martial law before I had even packed my bags, I did the next best thing—took up jobs in Hungary and asked why the Solidarity movement took place in Poland rather than Hungary and, more broadly, why in state socialism rather than advanced capitalism. What were the possibilities for a democratic socialism to emerge from such struggles against state socialism? The second reason drawing me to the socialist world was the specificity of my Chicago experience—was it the product of capitalism or of industrialism? Would I find the same work organization, factory regime, and working-class consciousness in the industries of state socialism?

Between 1982 and 1989 I spent my summers and three sabbatical semesters studying and working in Hungarian factories (Burawoy and Lukács 1992). I began in a champagne factory on a collective farm and moved to a textile factory on an agricultural cooperative, before graduating to industrial work in a machine shop very similar to the Chicago plant. Finally, I spent about eleven months in three separate stints working as a furnace man in the Lenin Steel Works of Miskolc. Based on this research, I concluded that the workplace regimes of advanced capitalism and state socialism were indeed very different: if the former produced consent, the latter produced dissent, which was the disposition that fired the Polish Solidarity movement but also the collective mobilization in East Germany in 1953, in Poland and Hungary in 1956, and even in Czechoslovakia in 1968.

The argument was a simple one: unlike capitalism, the appropriation of surplus under state socialism is a transparent process, recognized as such by all. The party, the trade union, and management are all extensions of the state to the point of production—extensions designed to maximize the appropriation of surplus for the fulfillment of plans. Being transparent, exploitation is *justified* as being in the interests of all. Like any process of legitimation, it is susceptible to being challenged on its own terms—the party state is vulnerable to the accusation that it is not delivering on its promises to serve the general interest. Whereas under capitalism legitimation is secondary, because exploitation is hidden, under state socialism it is primary, necessary to justify the open exploitation of state socialism, but it also becomes the latter's undoing.

Thus, the party state organizes rituals on the shop floor (what I called painting socialism) that celebrate its virtues—efficiency, justice, equality—yet all around workers see inefficiency, injustice, and inequality. Workers turn the ruling ideology against the rulers, demanding that they realize the claims of their socialist propaganda. The state socialist bureaucratic regime of production sows the seeds of dissent rather than consent. As regards the organization of work itself, the key games that dominate work are those involving the negotiation with management over the fulfillment of plan targets, so that the relations of exploitation are not obscured but define the relations among the players. Furthermore, given the shortage economy—shortages of materials, their poor quality, the breakdown of machinery, and so forth, all of which stem from the central administration of the economy—the games at work aim to cope with those shortages, demonstrating the hollowness of official claims about the efficiency of state socialism. Moreover, this adaptation to shortages requires far more autonomy than the bureaucratic apparatus regulating production will allow. Work games are transposed into games directed at the system of planning, bringing the shop floor into opposition to the production regime and the party state.

Far from social structure indelibly imprinting itself on the habitus of the worker and thus inducing doxic submission, the state socialist regime systematically produces the opposite—dissent rather than consent, even alternative organization to despotic controls. Indeed, more broadly, state socialism generated its own counter-socialisms from below—the cooperative movement in Hungary, Solidarity in Poland, and the civics in *perestroika* Russia. From the beginning, state socialism was a far more unstable order, not because its socializing agencies were weaker—far from it—but because of the contradictions generated by the institutions themselves. State socialism was held together by a precarious hegemony that was always in danger of slipping back into a despotism that relied on secret police, tanks, prisons, and show trials. In other words, where advanced capitalism organized simultaneously the mystification of exploitation and the consent to domination, now we see how the hegemony of state socialism—the attempt to present the interests of the party state as the interests of all—is a fragile edifice that was always threatened by the transparency of exploitation.

Bourdieu's notion of symbolic violence ensured through a deeply inscribed misrecognition cannot explain the instability of state socialism. Within Bourdieu's framework of internalization, there is no reason to believe that symbolic violence through misrecognition is any shallower or weaker in state socialism than in advanced capitalism. Quite the contrary: the coordination among fields—economic, educational, political, and cultural—should have led to a far more coherent and submissive habitus than under capitalism, where such fields have far greater autonomy and are more contradictory in their effects. An analysis of the logic of institutions and their immediate effects on the individual and on collective experience goes much further in explaining the fragility of state socialism.

FOLLOWING BOURDIEU: THE POWER OF FIELDS

Bourdieu never paid much theoretical attention to one of the signal events of his time—the collapse of the Soviet Union. I have found only one sociological writing by Bourdieu on state socialism—the four-page text of an address he gave in East Berlin on October 25, 1989, just two weeks before the fall of the Berlin Wall, amid massive demonstrations. Curiously, according to the published article, Bourdieu invoked the concepts of political and cultural capital to describe the tensions among the communist elites (Bourdieu [1989] 1998). Still, his notion of field can help us explain the dramatic demise of communism, so long as we drop the notion of habitus.[6]

Recall that Bourdieu's theory of social change rests on the discrepancy between position and disposition, between opportunities and expectations within a given field.[7] This is precisely what I described above for Hungarian workers—they were led to expect the wonders of socialism, yet they found themselves in a world of its inversions. Neither they nor the dominant class, trying as it might with reform after reform, could bring reality into conformity with its ideology. The discrepancy was not due to some psychic lag between an inherited habitus and a rigid field ("hysteresis," as Bourdieu would call it) but was generated by the field itself. State socialism created expectations it could not fulfill. As the gap between official ideology and reality widened, and as attempts to reduce the gap violated that official ideology (as in market reforms), so the ruling class lost confidence in its capacity to rule and the enactment of socialist ideology became a meaningless ritual. Without capacity or belief, the dominant class's hegemony collapsed. Again, there is no need to resort to the existence of a deep-seated habitus that resists change.

This line of argument can also be used to shed light on the timing of the collapse. To understand the dynamics of 1989 we have to look at the Soviet bloc as a transnational political field dominated by the Soviet Union, which defined the terms of competition among the dependent states—much as the state defines the terms of competition among elites. This certainly captures the way in which state socialism dissolves. The Soviet Union changed the rules of the game and then the national governments (themselves divided) acted in anticipation of the reaction of the others. Thus, the Hungarian government of Németh, being the first to discover how the rules had changed, opened its border with Austria, allowing East German tourists to flood into the West. At this point Honecker's East German government miscalculated. Faced with throngs of East Germans who had arrived in Prague to claim refugee status, Honecker got the hard-line Czechoslovakian government to bottle up the East Germans in sealed trains that went across Germany to the West. Honecker sought to humiliate these "traitors" going to the West, but the strategy backfired; it only intensified the exodus. Influenced by the Solidarity sweep of the Polish elections and the movements in Hungary, as well as huge demonstrations against the party state, Egon Krenz realized that Honecker had to go, but in so doing he laid the basis of his own burial in the rubble of the Berlin Wall. All this inspired the Czechoslovakian people to assemble in Wenceslas Square in the hundreds of thousands to listen to Václav Havel and other dissidents. After the Czechoslovakian party wilted, only Romania's Ceaușescu remained obdurate, putting down protest with violence and ultimately succumbing to a palace coup that put an end to him and his dictatorship. This thumbnail sketch of the events of 1989 shows how national actors acted strategically in a common transnational field. Strategy, as Bourdieu insists, only becomes conscious in exceptional crisis times when rules are in flux.

This would require much further elaboration, but it indicates the importance of studying the *interaction* of fields—something Bourdieu never addresses systematically—in this case the field of transnational relations within the Soviet bloc (itself nested in a larger field of international relations) and the political field within each nation.[8] Underlying these interfield dynamics, however, is the underlying instability of the state socialist order, unable to create a stable hegemony due to the palpable transparency of exploitation and domination.

FOLLOWING GRAMSCI: THE GOOD SENSE OF SOCIALIST WORKERS

Just as Bourdieu's field analysis can be usefully reconstructed to shed light on the unfolding crisis of the Soviet order, so reconstructing Gramsci also illuminates what transpired in 1989. Let me return to the shop floor and to the methodological issues raised by Bourdieu in the epigraph that opened this conversation. There, Bourdieu writes of the double truth of labor and that it was not enough to construct the objective truth by breaking with common sense (first reversal); it was also necessary to break with this objective truth to understand how common sense both produced and concealed the objective truth (second reversal). That was how I approached the Chicago factory, first recognizing the underlying truth of surplus labor and then trying to understand how that surplus labor was experienced subjectively in a way that explained how it was produced. Unpaid labor was simultaneously obscured and secured through constituting work as a game, itself made possible by the internal labor market and internal state.

Like Bourdieu, I did not believe that my fellow workers grasped the conditions of their subordination in the way a sociologist might, but even if they did, it would have made little difference. In other words, I did not find any Gramscian good sense within the common sense of workers, so instead of trying to convince my fellow workers of my Marxist theory—a daunting project indeed—I sought to persuade my fellow academics of the superiority of my theory of the labor process and of manufacturing consent. This was so very different from my experience in Hungary, where my fellow workers—no less hostile to Marxism—nonetheless were possessed of "good sense," not because they were superior beings but because the institutions created the basis of good sense. Therefore, I did not have to make a *break* with common sense, but instead I *elaborated* its kernel of good sense, including the immanent critique of state socialism, through dialogue with my fellow operators, contextualizing it in terms of the political economy of state socialism.

Here in Hungary, Bourdieu's strict opposition of science and common sense was replaced by Gramsci's (1971, 333) account of dual consciousness— i.e., a practical consciousness stemming from production and an ideological consciousness superimposed by the party state or inherited from the past. I was riveted to the practical consciousness of my fellow workers "implicit" in their activity, which united them "in the practical transformation of the real world." I paid less attention to the ideologies, "superficially explicit or verbal . . . inherited from the past and uncritically absorbed," which included racist, sexist, religious, and local sentiments. Yet it is true that these latter sentiments formed powerful bonds among workers, often overwhelming their incipient class consciousness.

Together with my collaborator, János Lukács, we focused on the capacity and necessity of workers to autonomously and flexibly organize production in the face of shortages. We defended this practice against managers who strove to appropriate control from the direct producers through bureaucratic procedures. Incensed by our claims, these managers insisted that we redo our study. This was not a Gramscian tension within the consciousness of workers but a struggle between workers and management, and once again it would be the "explicit and verbal consciousness" perpetrated and perpetuated by management that ultimately prevailed. By the time Hungarian socialism entered its final years, bombarded by bureaucratic managers, workers had lost any confidence in the very idea of socialism and certainly had little imagination of an alternative democratic socialism, even though some such imagination had been implicit in the logic of their own practice. Inspired by the "good sense" of workers and what he saw as a great potential for some sort of worker-owned enterprises, in the immediate years after the collapse of state socialism, Lukács worked with labor collectives to create the foundations of an alternative to capitalism, but this withered on the vine as capitalist ideology gained the upper hand.

In short, the analysis of state socialism—how it generated dissent and ultimately collapsed—does not call for a theory of deep-seated habitus but can remain at the level of social relations of production. State socialism could not sustain its precarious hegemony, and the attempts to shore up such a hegemony only hastened its demise. Equally, as we saw earlier, the reproduction of durable domination under capitalism does not require the *inculcation* of social structure. Such submission that exists can be explained by the configuration of institutions that elicit consent to domination based on the mystification of exploitation. *Homo habitus* is not necessary to explain submission and resistance; *Homo ludens* is sufficient.

THE LOGIC OF PRACTICE:
BEYOND GRAMSCI AND BOURDIEU

My argument can be summarized by referring back to the notion of *false consciousness*. For Gramsci, the problem with false consciousness lies not with consciousness but with its falseness. That is to say, Gramsci believed that workers actively, deliberately, and consciously collaborate in the reproduction of capitalism and consent to domination. They understand what they are doing; they simply have difficulty appreciating that there could be anything beyond capitalism. Yet at the same time, by virtue of their position in production, workers also possessed a critical perspective on capitalism and an embryonic sense of an alternative—one that could be jointly elaborated in dialogue with intellectuals. They have a *dual* consciousness rather than a *false* consciousness.

If for Gramsci the questionable part of false consciousness was its "falseness," for Bourdieu the problem lies not with "falseness" but with "consciousness" that denies the depth of symbolic violence—a domination that settles within the unconscious through the accumulated sedimentations of social structure.

> In the notion of "false consciousness" which some Marxists invoke to explain the effect of symbolic domination, it is the word "consciousness" which is excessive; and to speak of "ideology" is to place in the order of *representations*, capable of being transformed by the intellectual conversion that is called the "awakening of consciousness," what belongs to the order of *beliefs*, that is, at the deepest level of bodily dispositions. (Bourdieu [1997] 2000, 177)

So, for Bourdieu, consent is far too thin a notion to express submission to domination and must be replaced by the idea of misrecognition, which is embedded within the habitus.[9] Because the dominated internalize the social structure in which they exist, they do not recognize it as such. They have, in Gramscian terms, only bad sense. Only the dominators—and then only privileged intellectuals—can distance themselves from, and thus objectivize, their relation to social structure. Only they can have access to its secrets. And not all intellectuals, to be sure—only those who are reflexive about their privileged place in the world and who use that reflexivity to examine the lives of others.

In adjudicating between these positions, I have argued that both are problematic. Gramsci does not recognize the mystification of exploitation upon which hegemony—i.e., consent to domination—rests. In other words, capitalist workers do suffer from "false consciousness," but this falseness emanates from the social structure itself, which is where I depart from Bourdieu. Insofar as we participate in capitalist relations of production, we all experience the obscuring of surplus labor, independent of our habitus. Mystification is a product of the social structure itself and is not so deeply implanted within the individual that it cannot be undone, whereas Bourdieu's misrecognition is lodged deep within the individual psyche, tending to harmonize habitus and field.

Accordingly, Bourdieu cannot explain why symbolic violence is effective in some societies but not in others. Thus, why did state socialism, where one would have expected submission to be most deeply embedded, systematically produce dissent? For Bourdieu, social change, if it occurs at all, springs from the mismatch of habitus and field, but there is no systematic account of how this mismatch is produced, whether it is produced *situationally* through a cultural lag (hysteresis)—i.e., through habitus cultivated in one field clashing with the logic of another field—or *processually* through the very dynamics of social structure. Nor is there an analysis of the consequences of that mismatch in terms of whether it produces accommodation or rebellion. In other words, Bourdieu points to the *possibility* of social change but has no *theory* of social change. We will examine this question in the next and final conversation of Bourdieu with Bourdieu.

In the end, habitus is an intuitively appealing concept that can explain any behavior, precisely because it is unknowable and unverifiable. Bourdieu never gives us the tools to examine what a given individual's habitus might be. It's a black box. We infer the habitus from behavior—a shoplifter is a shoplifter because he/she has the habitus of a shoplifter. We only know the habitus from its effects; there is no theory of its components or how they are formed as in psychoanalytical theory. In short, habitus is not a scientific concept but a folk concept with a fancy name—a concept without content that might equally well be translated as character or personality.

Far more than Bourdieu, Gramsci is concerned with social transformation. He sees this as taking place through the breakdown of hegemony and the creation of a new subaltern hegemony, whether this comes through organic crises (balance of class forces) or through the war of position mounted from below on the basis of the kernel of good sense, or, what is more likely, a combination of the two. What my research suggests is that there is more to hegemony than the concrete coordination of interests or the ties linking state and civil society—there is more to hegemony than consent. There are non-hegemonic foundations of hegemony, namely the mystification of exploitation, which is why hegemony is so effective in advanced capitalism and so precarious in state socialism.

Because exploitation was so transparent in state socialism, it gave more scope for intellectuals to engage with workers in the elaboration of alternative "hegemonies" from below—the Hungarian worker councils in 1956, the Prague Spring of 1968, the Polish Solidarity movement of 1980–81, the market socialism of Hungary's reform period of the 1980s, the effervescence of civil society under Soviet *perestroika*. These alternative hegemonies were formed by different configurations of the relations between intellectuals and workers. They were eventually swept away, but they did provide the embryos of alternative socialist social orders. Intellectuals had more scope to join with workers to be sure but, by the same token, they posed a bigger threat to the regime and thus became the target of repression.

We live in depressing times of capitalist entrenchment when the failure of actually existing socialism has buttressed dominant capitalist ideologies. We should not compound the forcefulness and eternalization of the present by subscribing to unsubstantiated claims about the deep internalization of social structure, reminiscent of the structural functionalism of the 1950s and its "oversocialized man." Remember, those theories were overthrown by a critical collective effervescence that structural functionalism did not, but also could not, anticipate.

THE WEIGHT
OF THE WORLD
Bourdieu Meets Bourdieu

It is quite illusory to think that symbolic violence can be
overcome solely with the weapons of consciousness and will.
— BOURDIEU, *PASCALIAN MEDITATIONS*

I would say that the interview can be considered a sort of
spiritual exercise that, through forgetfulness of self, aims
at true conversion of the way we look at other people in
the ordinary circumstances of life.
— BOURDIEU, *THE WEIGHT OF THE WORLD*

It is likely that those who are "in their right place" in the
social world can abandon or entrust themselves more,
and more completely to their dispositions . . . than those
who occupy awkward positions, such as the *parvenus* and
the *déclassés*; and the latter are more likely to bring to
consciousness that which, for others, is taken for granted,
because they are forced to keep watch on themselves and
consciously correct the "first movements" of a habitus that
generates inappropriate or misplaced behaviours.
— BOURDIEU, *PASCALIAN MEDITATIONS*

Bourdieu's most acclaimed and successful work of public sociology is *La
Misère du Monde* (1993), translated into English as *The Weight of the World*

(Bourdieu et al. [1993] 1999)—a best-selling, popular, and accessible vo-luminous book that was turned into a film.[1] It is a collection of sixty-nine in-depth interviews—fifty-four in the English edition—with people from many walks of life: farmers, blue-collar workers, service workers, lawyers, social workers, teachers, students, and immigrants. The interview-ers are sociologists—Bourdieu's colleagues as well as himself—who come from backgrounds similar to their respondents in order to facilitate mutual trust and understanding. The interviewers also write lengthy interpretative essays introducing each excerpted interview.

The interviews themselves offer a richly textured account of lives from the underbelly of French society, while the introductions summarize the content of the interview as well as giving context. The two perspectives neatly dovetail, so that there is no break between the interviewer's sociol-ogy and the interviewee's lived experience. The introductory essays don't refer to Bourdieu's conceptual triad (capital, habitus, and field). Except possibly in the case of the more right-wing respondents, there is no attempt to offer an interpretation of the world that is at odds with the participants' understanding. What has happened to symbolic violence—the necessary false visions that are at odds with those of the sociologist? What has hap-pened to the twofold truth—that of the sociologist and that of the partici-pant? What has happened to the great divide between the logic of theory and the logic of practice that can only be understood from the standpoint of theory? What has happened to Bourdieu's strong notion that the domi-nated cannot comprehend their subjugation? In short, what has happened to "misrecognition," so key to the reproduction of domination? *The Weight of the World* appears to be a direct challenge to Bourdieu's conception of sociology.

The Weight of the World suggests there are two Bourdieus[2]—one who puts the sociologist on a pedestal, making insight into the world the privilege and monopoly of the sociologist, as opposed to one who descends into the life of participants, crediting them with the capacity to see the world through the eyes of the sociologist. *The Weight of the World* makes the paradox acute: the sociologist-interviewer and the participant-interviewee present their understandings alongside each other, yet rarely do their sepa-rate interpretations conflict. The "twofold truth"—dividing the scientist from the participant—so emphasized in *Reproduction, Distinction, Outline of a Theory of Practice, The Logic of Practice,* and *Pascalian Meditations* simply evaporates. Instead of being mired in misrecognition, participants can, with a little help, become sociologists of their own lives.

The divide between works that give credence to the perspective of the participant and those that don't runs through Bourdieu's oeuvre. We have already studied his inconsistent approach to Algeria—the self-mystifying world of the Kabyle versus the transformative consciousness of the anticolonial movement. Turning to France, the serious engagement with workers' movements and more broadly social movements against neoliberalism as found in *Acts of Resistance* and *Firing Back* contrasts with the major treatises where subjects are depicted as misrecognizing their own subjugation.

Great theorists display great contradictions. Such contradictions can be used to dismiss a theory as confused. Bourdieu contradicts himself over the key concept of symbolic violence and, therefore, some will say, his theory cannot be taken seriously. That's the approach of the dismissive critic. On the other hand, contradictions can be repressed or denied so as to behold the theorist in pristine perfection. In this view Bourdieu's scholarship assumes a finished and flawless form, taking on biblical status. All one has to do is to put him to work, apply his ideas. That's the devotion of the acolyte or disciple. Alternatively, there is a third approach in which contradictions are investigated to initiate, deepen, and advance a theoretical tradition. Here Bourdieu is no transcendent God: he is a human situated in history and society; his works do not assume a seamless whole. They are inspirational because they are imperfect, providing challenges for his followers.

I take this last approach to *The Weight of the World*, exploring possible interpretations of the Bourdieusian paradox, interpretations consistent with an evolving research program. In this approach it is important to consider Bourdieu's scholarship as a whole and not piecemeal. The oeuvre is not a supermarket from which we pick out whatever items we please and as our taste dictates, but a jigsaw puzzle in which the meaning of each part rests on its contribution to the whole.

THE DISRUPTION OF SYMBOLIC VIOLENCE

The most obvious interpretation of *The Weight of the World* is that there is no paradox. It was never intended as a sociological analysis but simply as a representation of subjugated populations through their own telling of their own vivid experiences. As Bourdieu writes in *Firing Back* ([2001] 2003, 22), "*The Weight of the World* . . . brought to light new forms of social suffering caused by state retrenchment, with the purpose of compelling politicians to address them." In his postscript to *The Weight of the World* he also underlines how science can contribute to a political project. Rather than portray the subjugated as victims of their own habitus, Bourdieu and colleagues present them as wrestling with forces they don't control—the neoliberal policies of the socialist governments under Mitterrand.

Undoubtedly, this is a political project but what is the scientific project? One is looking for a sociological interpretation that goes beyond the self-understanding of the participants. There are forays in that direction, but they are not so much moving behind and beyond the lived experience as loose generalizations of that experience. So the book is divided into the following themes: "The Space of Points of View" (the world looks different from different places in the social structure); "Site Effects" (relation between physical space and social space); "The Abdication of the State" (the changing character of the state and its effects); "On the Way Down" (the consequences of downward mobility); "Outcasts on the Inside" (the result of democratizing access to schools); and "The Contradictions of Inheritance" (intergenerational relations). Again, there is a noticeable absence of references to habitus, capital, and field, and there's hardly a whiff of misrecognition and symbolic violence.

Perhaps, *The Weight of the World* is simply an expression of the logic of practice, making the logic of theory a separate endeavor. This seems to fit with Bourdieu's claims in *Pascalian Meditations*, his final theoretical treatise, in which *The Weight of the World* offers a methodological innovation—the extended interview as a device to induce a "quasi-theoretical" narrative by "assisting those respondents who were furthest from the scholastic condition in an effort of self-understanding and self-knowledge which . . . is ordinarily reserved for the world of *skholè*" ([1997] 2000, 60). This still leaves unexamined the relation between the logic of practice and the logic of theory.

I do not reject either of these interpretations—that *The Weight of the World* is a political tract or that it awaits sociological analysis—but both make the theory of symbolic violence irrelevant to the project of the book. An alternative approach is to run with the paradox, asking how it is that the respondents in *The Weight of the World* develop a sociological perspective. The task, then, is to explain how the world has become transparent to the participants themselves, how the understanding of the participant converges with the analysis of the sociologist. In this view, *The Weight of the World* is not sidestepping the question of symbolic violence but announcing its dissolution. There are two possible conditions for its dissolution.

We have already had a hint of the first. It focuses on the interviewer-as-sociologist who becomes the "midwife" of truth, as Bourdieu says in the methodological essay "Understanding," appended to *The Weight of the World*:

> Like a midwife, the sociologist can help them [respondents] in this
> work [bringing to light what is deeply buried] provided the sociolo-
> gist has a deeper understanding both of the conditions of existence
> of which they are the product and of the social effects that can be
> exercised by the research relationship (and through it by the posi-
> tion and primary dispositions of the researcher). . . . This craft is a
> real "disposition to pursue truth" . . . which disposes one to impro-
> vise on the spot, in the urgency of the interview, strategies of self-
> representation and adaptive responses, encouragement and op-
> portune questions, etc., so as to help respondents deliver up their
> truth or, rather, to be delivered of it. (*ww*, 621)

Using a "Socratic method" of interviewing, the sociologists draw their subjects toward a broader vision of their life, but only because the interviewers
are deliberately chosen for their "social proximity and familiarity" (610)
with the life experiences of the respondents. The interviewer has to be a sociologist somehow connected to the life of the respondent. In other words,
the interviewer is an "organic intellectual" but not the "organic intellectual"
Bourdieu disparages for foisting their views, reflecting a particular habitus,
onto the working class with a very different habitus (Bourdieu [1979] 1984,
372–74). This only leads to a downward spiral of mutual misunderstanding,
whereas Bourdieu's matching of the habitus of interviewer and interviewee
leads to an upward spiral of mutual enlightenment. Bestowing such power
on the interviewer-sociologist still flies in the face of Bourdieu's scorn for
consciousness raising. So what other conditions are necessary for the re-
shaping of habitus?

Under what circumstances might the sociologist-interviewer overcome resistance to disclosing "those aspects of the social determinants
of their [respondents'] opinions and their practices which they may find
it most difficult to openly declare and assume" (*ww*, 616)? Although *The
Weight of the World* is not explicit about this, examination of the interviews reveals a common thread, namely a tension between expectations
and opportunities, aspirations and resources, dispositions and positions, or
in Bourdieusian language, habitus and field. Elsewhere Bourdieu ([1997]
2000, 159–63; [1979] 1984, 142–68; [1984] 1988, chaps. 4 and 5) regards
this disjuncture as the source of *allodoxia*, a state of confusion that, under
the direction of the interviewer as socio-analyst, can lead subjects to become aware of the conditions of their existence, of the broader forces shaping their worlds. I have reorganized the interviews from *The Weight of the*

World to highlight different disjunctures that disrupt the smooth operation of symbolic violence: (1) declining opportunities facing farmers and factory workers; (2) rising aspirations induced by education and immigration; and (3) contradictory positions held by professionals disrupting the smooth operation of symbolic violence. If successful, the sociologist as socio-analyst brings clarity to confusion.

If symbolic violence dissipates in the face of *allodoxia*, how, then, is domination nonetheless sustained? Here I draw on Bourdieu's theory of politics based on symbolic dispossession. The dominated can only partake in politics, says Bourdieu (1991, chaps. 7–10; [1979] 1984, chap. 8), by delegating their power to others—leaders, organizations, parties—who claim to speak on behalf of the dominated but who also act on their own behalf within the elevated field of power, where the competition among representatives leads to *misrepresentation*. While misrecognition may give way to recognition, this does not imply a corresponding transition from misrepresentation to representation. Instead, as I will suggest, we get recognition without representation.

In short, this conversation of Bourdieu with himself brings to light different sources of *allodoxia*, which sets the conditions for respondents to recognize their subjection under the questioning of the sociologist-interviewer. At the same time, it is a recognition without representation, a dull subjugation to forces out of their control, in the absence of effective organs of representation. What emerges is a political sociology of suffering that increasingly defines an era of precarity.[3]

DECLINING OPPORTUNITIES: FARMERS AND FACTORY WORKERS

In *The Bachelors' Ball* Bourdieu ([2002] 2008a) returns three times to his homeland in the Béarn (1962, 1972, and 1989) to describe the plight of farmers who face the loss of their patrimony because of forces beyond their control—the land is poor, government subsidies are falling, and the European Union quotas intensify competition. Women do not see a future in rural existence that condemns them to arduous labor. They seek a new life in towns, replete with consumerist temptations and a chance to advance their opportunities through education. The bachelors left behind are discredited and humiliated, that is, if they too don't abandon the farm for the city.

In *The Weight of the World* Bourdieu interviews two aging farmers, also from the Béarn, struggling to make ends meet (381–91). Pierre's son has remained loyal to his inheritance and works the land with his father, but he is not married. Pierre realizes that no woman would marry his son, whose inheritance is now a losing proposition. Sizing up the situation, Henri's son adopts a different strategy. He decides to abandon his father and his inheritance to seek his fortune in the town with his new urban wife, living with his in-laws. He refuses his inheritance, effectively murdering his father and all he stood for. Both farmers face a reality which is at odds with their deepest dispositions—dispositions cultivated by a life dedicated to farming and the expectation that their patrimony will continue as it has for generations. They are forced to problematize a world they had taken for granted. They go into internal exile, reflecting on their disappearing inheritance.

In an interview with a different Pierre, this time a garrulous and despondent entrepreneur who inherited a wine dealership in rural eastern France, Patrick Champagne (*WW*, 392–407) describes another form of disinheritance. It seems Pierre let his dealership run down and now blames the French taxation structure, the European Union, and the strangulation by supermarket chains for his downfall. He denounces the Pieds-Noirs from North Africa, who together with Arabs, have brought ruin to the French people. He is jealous of his sister and brother, who are doing very well for themselves, having married into upper-class families. The interview turns into a tirade about the state of the world that melds both truth and paranoia. Champagne writes, "He doesn't need to understand what's going on since he knows it already. Except that everything pushes him to reject these transformations and carries him on to a failure that he knows is inevitable" (*WW*, 396). Pierre has no time for socialists like Mitterrand and is more inclined to support right-wing politicians, especially Jean-Marie Le Pen. There is no neat fit between habitus and field, between expectations and opportunities—they are deeply at odds with one another, driving Pierre into an escapist politics.

We find a similar account of disinherited factory workers. In several interviews (*WW*, 257–66, 267–81, 282–96, 321–37), Michel Pialoux and Stéphane Beaud describe the downward spiral of permanent workers at the Peugeot plant in Sochaux and the precarious "temporary" workers who replace them. The old working class, solidary and political, cannot adapt to the new conditions—new industrial relations, new pressures, new work organization, and the spreading distrust even among the unionists. The temp workers, who are recruited from all over France, are resentful of the old-timers they are slowly replacing—jealous of the better conditions the permanents still retain, disaffected by the uselessness of their trade certificates, saying that even immigrants get a better deal than they do. Gerard, an activist old-timer, worrying about his two sons, tries to encourage them to take the academic rather than the vocational track in school. If they take the vocational track, very easily his sons could end up as temps. Hamid, an immigrant and a devoted shop steward, expresses his anger with fellow workers for not standing up to the company, for allowing the company to erode working-class solidarity. The young workers turn on him as a wind-bag, always complaining about management, handing out leaflets. Even his own buddies have lost interest in the union.

If the farmers of the Béarn are losing their patrimony as the next generation leaves for the towns or stays behind but is unable to create heirs, the workers of Peugot are being disinherited by a successor generation that has lost touch with working-class culture in the face of despotic management policies. The habitus that used to be handed on from father to son cannot cope with declining agriculture or Japanese-style management. In both cases, there is a despondent recognition, expressed with a mixture of anger, nostalgia, humiliation, and cynicism. The scholar-interviewers may decorate the lived experience of their respondents with a coat of sociology, but they don't contradict it. There is no sign of misrecognition, naturalizing domination, or even making a virtue of necessity. Let us now turn from those who are downwardly mobile to those who aspire to upward mobility.

EXPANDING ASPIRATIONS: STUDENTS AND IMMIGRANTS

In *Reproduction in Education, Culture and Society*, children of the dominant classes, inculcated with symbolic mastery, adapt well to the school, whereas those coming from dominated classes with practical mastery are shunned and shamed. The "arbitrary culture" of the school emphasizes meritocracy and scholastic achievement, thereby privileging those with a privileged background. The relative autonomy of the school presents "the arbitrary culture" as universal, and the privileged students appear as simply gifted while the underprivileged are made to appear dumb. That is the basis of misrecognition. They are eliminated from the school or, more likely, eliminate themselves. Because the school does not overtly distinguish class, so qualifications become all the more important in channeling students into the labor market, thereby securing as well as obscuring class domination.

This original account of symbolic violence and misrecognition is quite different from the accounts in *The Weight of the World* (*ww*, 421–26, 427–40, 441–54), where democratization of access to the lycée led, on the one hand, to heightened student aspirations and, on the other hand, to devaluation of the credential and, thus, more limited opportunities. As children of the working class are subject to processes of internal tracking into less valued curricula, they begin to recognize the biases of the school and how the school is systematically thwarting their aspirations. Teachers are no longer awarded unimpeachable authority but bear the brunt of hostile and rebellious students who see the school as a swindle (463–83, 484–87). As Bourdieu writes, "This is the contradiction of a social order that has a growing tendency to give everything to everybody" but only in the form of simulacra, keeping the real goods for the few (*WW*, 426). He describes how schools perpetuate illusions, how students cling to hopes of success, leading to anxious submission or powerless revolt. Sylvain Broccolichi (*WW*, 441–54) interviews three girls going through the lycée—two from the working class and one from the middle class. They describe how the struggle to enter the prestigious streams—the competition, remote teachers, pressure from parents, endless homework—all leads to protest. The contrast between the comforting and supportive experience in their previous school and the anonymity of the lycée feeds their critique even if they do not see it in class terms.

Behind student aspirations are those of their parents. Bourdieu (*WW*, 6–22) interviews parents of two teenage girls whose future is uncertain. The father, LeBlond, is the latest of several generations of steel workers, now part of an aging labor force facing a new order of discipline, deskilling, and lower wages, but he still has employment security. Bourdieu interweaves the biography of the steelworker with an unemployed Algerian. Pushed into the subproletariat, he has no security and lives an impoverished existence from hand to mouth. He thinks of returning to Algeria but he knows that is unrealistic. His children are academic failures, objects of discrimination. LeBlond himself expresses a subdued racism in complaining about the cultural practices of his Algerian neighbors. In the next interview, Abdelmalek Sayad (*WW*, 23–36) describes the mutual hostility and incomprehension between an immigrant family and their white neighbors.

Yet there are also those who struggle against racism. In an interview conducted by Bourdieu himself (*WW*, 60–76), a French youth tries to protect his Algerian friend from the racism of the housing projects where they both live. In their representation, the youths are unable to project themselves beyond the immediacy of their relations, a representation fostered, perhaps, by the interviewer's remoteness.

Like those of students, immigrant stories are ones of aspirations dashed by the obduracy of social structures. As an Algerian, as well as Bourdieu's long-term research assistant and collaborator, Abdelmalek Sayad was able to get inside the skin of immigrants and render their accounts sociological. In one interview, entitled "The Curse" (*WW*, 561–79), Abbas—an old and lonely Algerian immigrant widowed by his wife and orphaned by his children, who are now absorbed into French society—recalls his father's dismay when he (Abbas) departed for France at an early age. At first, Abbas had considered it just a short-term move to obtain some badly needed income, but his father warned him of the curse of migration, the polluting power of money, and the liability of betraying the homeland. Abbas's father had been disinherited of his own patrimony, forced to become a seasonal laborer in Algeria. When his father was killed in the Algerian war, Abbas found himself in France cut off from his home. His wife joined him and a new struggle for survival began in an alien land. Ostensibly, his children did well, but the curse followed them—his son, an engineer, doesn't like to work, and his daughter, suffering a mental breakdown from being locked up in the home, has abandoned him. From Abbas's point of view his family is no family, just a collection of individuals going their separate ways. His original sin follows him and whomever he touches. France has devoured him and his family.

This is a perspective of an immigrant, but what about the perspective of his children? In a separate interview Sayad (*WW*, 580–89) presents the perspective of the succeeding generation in the heroic story of Farida. Her father, fearful of the corrupting influence of French society, followed her every day to school and, for the rest of the time, he imprisoned her in the home. Hostile to her father but also to his accomplice, her mother, Farida rebelled by retreating into her own space and devoting her life to reading. When her cousin invited her to stay, and with her father relenting, she seized on this opportunity as a route out of isolation. She then took a secretarial job and moved into her own apartment. When her mother was hospitalized with a liver disease, it was Farida who looked after her. She blazed a trail for her younger sisters and brothers—her sisters went to university, and her brothers gave their silent consent; she established a close and devoted relation to her mother; and even her father began to accept her independence. Sayad treats this as a case of socio-analysis in which a sociological examination of self becomes the road to emancipation.

> If encountering unequal situations often reinforces the dominator in his sociocentrism, it obliges the dominated person (colonized, black, Jew, woman, immigrant, etc.) to work at clarifying the relationship, which means working upon oneself. It is a necessary, one might even say vital, practice which imposes an inclination to socioanalysis, this predisposition ends up by becoming "second nature" and guides all the individual's acts and gestures. (*WW*, 581)

In this view the dominated are no longer mired in irreversible misrecognition. Quite the opposite: by virtue of their *subjugation*, the subaltern becomes the sociologist, gaining clarity into their circumstances. From being trapped by her environment, Farida wends her way toward emancipation, drawing others after her.

CONTRADICTORY LOCATIONS: PROFESSIONAL WORKERS AND ORGANIC INTELLECTUALS

So far we have seen how dispositions come up against structures when exogenous forces close down opportunities (farmers and autoworkers) or when inflated aspirations are blocked (students and immigrants). There is a third situation in which subjective disposition and objective circumstances clash—one that appears frequently in *The Weight of the World*—for individuals located at the intersection of competing fields. Bourdieu writes,

> This explains the way that narratives about the most "personal" difficulties, the apparently most strictly subjective tensions and contradictions, frequently articulate the deepest structures of the social world and their contradictions. This is never so obvious as it is for the occupants of precarious positions who turn out to be extraordinary "practical analysts": situated at points where social structures "work," and therefore worked over by the contradictions of these structures, these individuals are constrained, in order to live or to survive, to practice a kind of self-analysis, which often gives them access to the objective contradictions which have them in their grasp, and to the objective structures expressed in and by these contradictions. (*ww*, 511)

Once again misrecognition dissolves, giving way to the transparency of objective structures, when people are placed in contradictory positions. Bourdieu (*ww*, 189–202) offers the example of the social worker, who presents an astute account of her predicament. She was very effective in her previous job, allocating apartments to the needy, until her success threatened local politicians, whereupon she was transferred to another municipality. In her new job, bureaucratic infighting frustrated her organizational skills. She understood only too well how she was caught between needy clients and an unresponsive bureaucracy.

In an interview with a sentencing judge with social concerns, Bourdieu (*ww*, 203–5) describes the judge's battle with the prosecuting magistrate, public prosecutor, and director of the prison who have conflicting interests governed by the logic of their own office. The judge recognizes his place under cross-pressures of the left hand and right hand of the state. Remi Lenoir (*WW*, 239–54) offers an interview with another judge caught between his commitment to justice and conformity to the powers that be, appalled by the cover-ups and laziness he sees all around him. From their position judges have to wrestle with the contradictory logics of the legal field and the call for justice.

Of all the interviews with professionals, those with teachers are the most revealing. Overworked and underpaid, they are only too aware of the disaster that follows increasing student enrollments when resources and labor market opportunities remain unchanged (Sylvain Broccolichi and Françoise Œvrard, *WW*, 455–62). Rosine Christin's (*WW*, 484–87) interview with Collette, who is teaching in a collège (junior high), presents a graphic description of the anarchy in schools located in poorer neighborhoods—the graffiti, the disrepair of buildings, the challenge of getting students into the classroom and then getting them to sit down and focus on learning, their rudeness if not impertinence. This is a far cry from Bourdieu and Passeron's ([1970] 1977) elaboration of symbolic violence according to which teacher and curriculum are endowed with unquestioned legitimacy and the stamp of authority.

Sylvain Broccolichi's (*WW*, 488–91) interview with a teacher in a vocational high school paints a similar picture of degradation. Rejected by society, students see no value in their credentials, and teachers compete with gangs for the control of the school. The school responds with a bevy of psychologists, counselors, and social workers. In a moving interview, conducted by Gabrielle Balazs and Abdelmalek Sayad (*WW*, 492–506), a dedicated principal describes the "institutional violence" that has gripped his collège in one of Lyon's poorest neighborhoods. The principal recounts his efforts to patrol the premises, prevent the invasion of youth gangs, and keep the school clean of drugs. However, the last thing he wants is for his school to become a police station. He sees all too clearly how it has become the focus of despair for children of North African immigrants—with few job prospects and scavenging for existence. Far from suffering from misrecognition, the principal oversees what is effectively a sociological laboratory where exclusion and violence converge. The school and the neighborhood beyond are dominated by hard material violence, reminiscent of colonialism, not the soft symbolic violence described in *Reproduction in Education, Society and Culture*, *Distinction*, or even *Pascalian Meditations*.

The professional classes—social workers, teachers, lawyers—find themselves in a contradictory position as agents of the state, responsible for regulating insurgent populations. At the intersection of antagonistic fields they are forced to reflect on the wider social order. Similarly, there are those who emerge from below to represent the subaltern. Mme. Tellier (*WW*, 88–94) became a political actor after being involved in a factory takeover. She entered municipal politics, becoming responsible for sports activities. She then opened her own sports shop, which was vandalized in riots. She attributes the violence to social causes—the absence of jobs and meaningless schooling—not to the victims and still less to their "habitus." Tellier's political engagement led to militant sociology, similar to an upwardly mobile Tunisian blue-collar worker who partakes in a tenants' association. He also refuses to blame the riots on the rioters, pointing to the provocation of the National Front, which was trying to make political hay at the expense of the left-wing mayor. He is incensed by the picture of immigrants painted in the media.

Here then are two examples of organic intellectuals, spokespersons of the maligned, similar to the street educator interviewed by Bourdieu and Balazs (*WW*, 206–12). Working closely with drug addicts, he builds ties to the mayor, a judge, social workers, and pharmacists, trying to create job opportunities for these unemployed youth. But as soon as he steps out of line and engages in oppositional politics, the local power elites descend on him like a ton of bricks. He is embraced as long as he is attending to addicts, forging individual solutions, but as soon as he crosses from social control into political organization, he is stopped dead in his tracks. The astute critical sociology that springs from his daily practice on the streets makes him a frustrated spokesman of the subaltern.

Whether officially representing the state and "cooling out" the subaltern, or representing the subaltern and frustrated by local power structures, these actors are caught between contradictory forces. They contest the mythologies put about by the press and struggle on behalf of their co-residents, their neighbors, and their community, leading them to a festering critique of domination. At no point does the sociologist qua interviewer contest their understanding of the world. There is not a hint of misrecognition.

RECOGNITION WITHOUT REPRESENTATION

There is a sort of antinomy inherent in the political sphere which stems from the fact that individuals—and this is all the more true the more they are deprived—cannot constitute themselves (or be constituted) as a group, that is

as a force capable of making itself heard, of speaking and
being heard, unless they dispossess themselves in favour
of a spokesperson. . . . In fact, isolated, silent, voiceless
individuals, without either the capacity or the power of
making themselves heard and understood, are faced with
the alternative of keeping quiet or of being spoken for by
someone else.

—BOURDIEU, "DELEGATION AND POLITICAL FETISHISM"

In order to pursue their collective interests the subaltern must first dispossess
themselves of their own political voice, delegating representation to others
who actually speak for themselves as much as for those they represent. The
delegates, according to Bourdieu, operate in the field of politics, where they
compete with other elites to accumulate political capital. Inasmuch as the
subaltern don't possess material and cultural resources to directly defend
and expand their own interests, they are unable to impose their will on their
spokespeople. To advance their interests in the field of politics, "representative" organs such as parties, trade unions, and associations compete with
one another. In so doing they *may* bring benefits to those they supposedly
represent, not through direct representation but through a "homologous"
competition in the field of power.

When the subaltern recognize their subjugation, are they more
likely, more able to directly represent themselves outside the field of power?
For the most part, *The Weight of the World* confirms Bourdieu's bleak hy-
potheses that "recognition" of their own subjugation is no guarantee of
"representation." If there is one theme that threads through the suffering
expressed in the interviews it is political alienation. Here and there we catch
glimpses of independent political engagement as a reaction against an unresponsive state bureaucracy, against the decline of the industrial working
class, against violence in schools. Several interviewees speak of their impo-
tence before misrepresentation by the media—Patrick Champagne's (*WW*,
213–19) account of the way public opinion is forged against the experiences
of the subaltern, Abdelmalek Sayad's (*WW*, 219–21) analysis of the way the
state turns political issues into technical problems, through cost-benefit
analysis of immigration. The subaltern don't speak, they are spoken for.
When they do have access to the media, as in the case of the Tunisian worker
who, as head of a tenants' committee, participates in filming of the housing
projects, their views are distorted or ignored (*WW*, 95–105).

When representatives try to directly defend the interests of the subaltern, they seem to only experience frustration, whether it is Hamid, the committed shop steward (321–37), the social worker who distributes housing (189–202), the street educator who works with drug addicts (206–12), the judge who tries to be sensitive to social concerns (203–5), or the school principal who tries to bring order into the school (492–506). In each case attempts at fermenting change are stymied by the rigidity of state bureaucracy, which ensnares the reformer. Although political struggles in the community may give rise to recognition, it does not reverse political dispossession or undo misrepresentation. There is, in short, no civil society made up of institutions, organizations, and movements that can represent the interests of the subaltern. Indeed, Bourdieu studiously avoids the concept of civil society, with its optimistic politics, as ill-fitting the political alienation conjured up by the interviews.

What then is *The Weight of the World*—as a work of sociology that found resonance with French publics? As opposed to public opinion polls that are constructed to endorse the dominant view of society (Bourdieu [1984] 1993), *The Weight of the World* becomes a political intervention from below—a representation of political dispossession as experienced by the subaltern and as witnessed by an army of street-level workers whose labors are made all the more difficult as the center of gravity within the state shifts from the left hand to the right hand. It is, indeed, a case of intellectuals forging an uneasy alliance with the subaltern to challenge dominant cultural representations.

CONCLUSION: TWO BOURDIEUS OR THE END OF SYMBOLIC VIOLENCE?

In searching for antecedents to *The Weight of the World* I am led back to Bourdieu's early writing on Algeria, in particular *Algeria 1960*, where he describes the working classes of Algiers, and *Le déracinement* (*The Uprooting*), which describes the effects of resettlement camps. For Bourdieu the colonial situation is exceptional in that it represents an external imposition of "modern" norms and values, thereby disrupting "traditional" society. It is an anomalous situation that highlights all that is taken for granted in the social order of capitalism, all that has been repressed in the long historical processes of its formation and stabilization. Rather than the anomie that is the result of the "clash of civilizations" in urban Algeria, Bourdieu draws on his conception of the Kabyle as a self-reproducing society for concepts that illuminate the stability of French society. Habitus, capital, misrecognition, and symbolic violence all derive from his idealized portrait of the Kabyle. It is a strange and brilliant move to see in Kabylia the elementary forms of symbolic violence just as Durkheim saw in the Australian tribes the elementary forms of religion. And yet, *The Weight of the World* suggests that modern France may be closer to the colonial context of urban Algeria than to precolonial Kabylia.

Bourdieu develops his key concepts in his study of Kabylia, but one in particular is missing, namely the concept of "field"—a reflection of the undifferentiated character of a "traditional" society. At the end of *Outline of a Theory of Practice* Bourdieu argues that symbolic violence requires much hard work to uphold the notions of honor and status in order to obscure underlying traditional hierarchies, whereas in a modern society *institutional differentiation spontaneously leads to its own misrecognition*: participation in education, consumption, art, work, and politics involves absorption into a hierarchical ordering homologous to class domination but, at the same time, obscuring that domination. Differentiation generates symbolic violence independent of human will.

But only at a secondary level does Bourdieu see that differentiation involves people moving between different structures, institutions, and fields so that there is continual disruption of dispositions, learned in one institution and requiring modification in another. The deeply implanted habitus inculcated by the family faces different demands in the school, the workplace, the church. Even more salient are the clashes between habitus and field when people are upwardly or downwardly mobile or when they are in the cross-pressure of intersecting fields. The more entrenched is primary socialization and the more differentiated society, the greater the potential of societal transparency. That potentiality can be realized through the midwifery of the sociologist (socio-analysis) who can turn the disorientation (*allodoxia*) of the respondent into a sociological understanding. This is the conclusion I draw from the analysis of the interviews in *The Weight of the World*.

There appear to be two Bourdieus: the first is the Bourdieu of *Reproduction* and *Distinction* in which misrecognition is inherent to modern society as we get absorbed into structures that mask their underlying conditions of possibility. The working class cannot live with its crushing subordination and so makes virtue of necessity; it becomes inured to suffering. The middle classes distract themselves from their subjugation by imitating the dominant class, accepting its values, its patterns of consumption, hoping against hope to promote their children if not themselves into the dominant class. At the same time the dominant class reigns supreme, confident in its own superiority, its distinction, its giftedness. Their domination is seen not as a function of their class position that gives them the possibility of all sorts of leisure pursuits denied to the other classes but as a function of their inborn talents.

The empirical evidence for this theory is flimsy at best. Bourdieu tries to make it consistent with surveys of people's patterns of consumption. But there is no interrogation of individuals or observation of their practices—the sort of empirical research that his theory calls for. The critiques he applies to opinion polls—questions constructed from the standpoint of the dominant class and its intellectuals, asking questions removed from the concerns and interests of the working class—applies to the methodology of *Distinction* itself. The survey, the asking of questions about habits of consumption, is itself an act of symbolic violence, imposed on the working class and thereby representing it as passive and resigned, just as it gives rise to the opposite response from the middle classes, eager to emulate and thus legitimate the dominant class. The methodology of *Distinction*, its reliance on survey research, violates all the principles laid out in Bourdieu's essay titled "Understanding," where the interviewer must avoid imposing categories and prepackaged questions.

It is not surprising, therefore, that the very different methodology of *The Weight of the World* (in which sociologists intimately familiar with the experiences and life-world of their subjects conduct the interviews) elicits a very different picture—a picture of individuals battling to make ends meet, to uphold a certain dignity against all odds, projecting their frustration onto external forces. We don't find processes of naturalization, legitimation, and emulation, but painful struggles in a world they did not create—building a better life for their children, contesting images of the media, trying to keep schools working, keeping the fabric of society intact. The interviews get at the logic of practice, the daily transformations that make life livable, and curiously so many of the interviews revolve around the experience of work rather than consumption. Again there is a Marxist flavor to these renditions of daily life.

In *Distinction* (and in *Reproduction*) the sociologist is aloof, a godlike figure disclosing the truth behind symbolic violence—a truth accessible only to the sociologist. This is Bourdieu the traditional intellectual pursuing his own corporate interests. In *Weight of the World* (and his polemics against the media and the market), the sociologist has now joined the dominated, elevating them to a force against the devastation of modern-day capitalism. The sociologist has become an organic intellectual tied to the subaltern, has forged a collaboration with the subaltern. Paradoxically, after being so dismissive of the "myth of the organic intellectual," Bourdieu becomes one himself—of course, he may regard himself as special with his "cleft habitus" marking his lower-class origins, but an organic intellectual nonetheless.

The contradictory portraits of class structure as found in *Distinction* and *The Weight of the World* can be attributed to their divergent methodologies, but behind the different methodologies, could there be different political programs? What explains Bourdieu's moves between traditional and organic sociologist? Are they a function of Bourdieu's career in which he first has to make it as a scientist in the academic field and only then, when he becomes an established figure, can he project himself onto the political field as a spokesperson of the dominated? Undoubtedly there is truth to that, but the shift can perhaps also be attributed to changes in the social, political, and economic order. The 1960s and 1970s may have been politically turbulent, but even then the turbulence rested on a certain common understanding and acceptance of France, its hierarchies, and its distinctions. But the 1980s and 1990s—in France as elsewhere in advanced capitalism—brought the hammer blows of neoliberalism, and with them the securities of the previous era dissolved. We entered the age of precarity—a notion that Bourdieu himself popularized. For so many life lost its guarantees and uncertainty became ubiquitous. The disruption of the old order dissolved misrecognition, and social structure became transparent to itself. The old institutions of education, political parties, and trade unions lost their legitimacy, and people sought out alternative paths, not least the rising popularity of parties and movements, both of the Left and of the Right, that were detached from mainstream institutions. The disconnection of habitus and habitat, of expectation and opportunities, made France and other countries ripe for symbolic revolutions.

Bourdieu, you might say, is a prophet of the present, but in so being he became more rather than less Marxist, even as his hostility to Marxism intensified. His angry polemics against neoliberalism, however, lacked what Marxism has to offer, namely a theory of neoliberalism's origins, expansion, and crises. While Bourdieu adopted Marxian economic ideas, brilliantly turning them into an analysis of cultural production, he never managed to develop a political economy that would ground his political and social analysis; he never managed to grasp the totality of the modern era as a form of capitalism. In the end he remained a modernization theorist who had no explanations for the twists and turns of modernity.

THE LIMITS OF SYMBOLIC VIOLENCE

How should we engage our intellectual opponents? Ignore them? Demolish them? Absorb them? Within academia, where recognition is everything, denying recognition is often the most effective and least costly weapon. Refusing to recognize opponents only works, however, if they are not already in the limelight. When our opponents have won recognition, when they are powerful figures, what is to be done?

Within Marxism demolition has been a frequent practice, reducing opponents to intellectual rubble. Think of Lenin's withering criticism of opportunists, anarchists, social democrats. The only people worthy of such aggression, however, were competitors in the political field. There is a second tradition within Marxism: interrogating powerful opponents to assess their strength and then appropriating their ideas under an enlarged canvas. This is not vanquishing through demolition but domination through containment. Here the strategy is to critically appropriate the truth of the opponent by absorbing it within one's own expanded framework. This requires a certain appreciation of the opponent. Gramsci's critical appropriation of Croce, Marx's critical appropriation of Hegel or Ricardo, Lukács's critical appropriation of Weber, and Marcuse's critical appropriation of Freud come to mind.

Every strategy comes with risks. *Ignoring* the opponent leaves one unscathed, but it can also leave one out of touch with emerging intellectual currents. It can turn into a lost opportunity to expand one's own horizons through engaging others. *Demolition* can win one acclaim, and it can be accomplished without being accountable to an alternative perspective. But it can also bring free publicity and even support to the opponent. Distorting the opponent, or forcing them into a straitjacket, risks heaping disrepute onto the critic. It can also provoke a belligerent reaction. Finally, neutralizing the opponent by *absorption*, taking the enemy seriously, can so transform one's own thinking that allies may accuse one of betrayal. After all, the practice of critique, if carried out properly, shapes the critic as much as the criticized.

As I indicated in the prologue, in my encounters with the work of Bourdieu, I have followed all three strategies. I began by ignoring him, but that could not be sustained as he gathered steam in the last two decades of the twentieth century. I then attempted demolition but I was certainly not adequate to that task. The more I read the more impressed I became, leading me to a more complex process of absorption and critical appreciation. The result are the essays in this book that put Bourdieu into conversation with others.

Turning the spotlight back on Bourdieu, we see he is a past master at dealing with intellectual opponents, pursuing a combination of all three strategies: ignoring, demolishing, and absorbing. The title, if not the content, of Pierre Carles's 2001 film on Bourdieu, *La sociologie est un sport de combat*, captures Bourdieu's often combative approach toward others, for which he achieved some infamy, especially in France. Like any other major figure he was very selective about whom he engaged, ignoring vast swaths of contemporary sociology. Thus, much of this book is recovering conversations that never took place—conversations that Bourdieu refused. It is as if by showing the limitations of Marx's theory, it was not necessary to engage Marxism, even though Marxism had earlier made the same critiques of Marx as Bourdieu had. He followed the first principle of intellectual combat—to recognize, even critically, is to arm the enemy.[1]

Compared to Talcott Parsons or Jürgen Habermas, who built on the shoulders of giants, Bourdieu tends to bury the shoulders on which he stands, so that he becomes his own giant, the source of his own genius. He is well-known for appropriating the ideas of opponents without recognition. When the original author is well-known, he turns them into an enemy, distorts their ideas in order to facilitate their demolition, and thereby rises above them as a superior thinker. This is especially the case with regard to Marxism. Thus, he tries to hide the influence of Althusser and other structuralists with a two-pronged strategy: for the most part ignoring them while occasionally subjecting them to withering attacks. In ignoring or dismissing Gramsci (chapter 3), he deliberately overlooks the parallels between symbolic violence and hegemony. He claimed not to have read Gramsci, although that does not stop him from opportunistically citing Gramsci's critique of the sectarian tendencies of the Italian Communist Party. Similarly, he largely ignores his archenemy, Fanon, except for the occasional denunciation (chapter 4). This strategy reaches a climax in his dismissal of Simone de Beauvoir (chapter 6). He conceals the fact that *Masculine Domination* is a pale imitation of *The Second Sex* by ignoring Beauvoir except in a single footnote, where he dismisses her, and thus her work, as being in thrall to the symbolic violence of Sartre. It is ironic that, in a book devoted to exposing the way men silence women, Bourdieu should dismiss the author of the foundational work of second-wave feminism.

In this case Bourdieu deploys all three strategies—ignoring Beauvoir, appropriating Beauvoir (without recognition), and then belittling her by reducing her ideas to those of Sartre. What is Bourdieu up to? A Bourdieusian approach might focus on Bourdieu's place in the French academic field, which he enters with little inherited cultural capital, developing what he calls his cleft habitus, a psychic reaction to his own sense of estrangement and marginality. Analysis of habitus goes hand in hand with an examination of the distinctiveness of the academic field and, in particular, its rules of combat that make dismissal and demolition such an acceptable strategy in France but a dangerous game to play in the US. The logic of the scientific field, the practices it legitimates, and the corresponding habitus it cultivates vary across countries.

INTELLECTUALS ON THE ROAD TO CLASS POWER

As Bourdieu's field analysis defines struggle for domination through the accumulation of field-specific capital, so there is always the temptation to reduce ideas and projects to interests defined by position in the field. Indeed, Bourdieu's shift from being concerned with developing an inaccessible scientific sociology to being more focused on public engagement can be explained in terms of his ascendency to a dominant position within the academic field. However, his contradictory assessment of the character of working class struggles as between Algeria and France might be explained by the different contexts of the working class or different class habitus or by Bourdieu's shift from the Algerian political field to the French political field.

Looking at the field itself, individuals might adopt a strategy that maximizes resources through playing the game, but they may take a more risky strategy of trying to change the rules of the game, or even change the game altogether. Bourdieu had a political project that launched him from the academic field into public and political spheres—we can call it intellectuals on the road to class power.

The roots of this project were planted in Algeria, but the project really begins when he returns to France. Accordingly, I represent his career as having three stages: in the first stage, he reconstitutes sociology as a respectable academic discipline by changing the rules; in the second stage, he presents sociology as the vanguard of intellectuals by moving beyond the academic field into the public sphere; and in the third stage, the purely political phase, sociology comes to represent the interests of humanity.

In his early writings on France—*Reproduction* and *Distinction*—he seeks to establish the distinctive place of the sociologist as scientist. Here Bourdieu develops the unique science of sociology—at that time a moribund discipline in France—centering on the theory of symbolic violence, the cement that holds society together. This gives sociology privileged access to the hidden abodes of domination. As a science competing with other sciences and especially philosophy, its status is at least partly established through its *inaccessibility* to all but the initiated.

Once established as the theory of symbolic violence, sociology can presume to represent the interests of all intellectuals, defending cultural production in toto. The driving force for stasis and change is not class struggle but classification struggle—a struggle by and for intellectuals. This second phase of intellectuals on the road to class power coincides with Bourdieu's election to an exalted professorship in the Collège de France, allowing him to move from representing a single segment of the intellectual stratum to representing the stratum as a whole. From being the vanguard of sociologists Bourdieu seeks to make sociology the vanguard discipline of all intellectuals. His sociology embraces the work of artists, scientists, literary figures, journalists, lawyers, teachers. Few intellectuals are left out of account. He is now operating in the public sphere.

The third and final phase, the hegemonic phase, occurs when Bourdieu presents intellectuals as representing the interests of all—a move that calls for a far more sympathetic view of the dominated. He has to recognize them and support their collective action. He dignifies them with a rationality corresponding to their subjugation, rather than pejoratively describing them as blinded by their habitus, subject to misrecognition, and bereft of any positive cultural capital. Starting with *The Weight of the World*, the last ten years of Bourdieu's life were, indeed, devoted to intellectuals aspiring to power, standing at the head of social movements to combat a deepening neoliberalism. As he writes in *On Television* ([1996] 1999), the intellectual must pay not only an "entry fee" to acquire expertise in science or art that excludes the dilettante but also an "exit duty"—the obligation to speak to and for all. In his later years Bourdieu did gather around him a group of internationally distinguished intellectuals who defended social justice and human rights. This was his Internationale of intellectuals.

The idea of intellectuals on the road to class power derives from György Konrád and Iván Szelényi's (1979) classic work on state socialism. They claimed that in *state socialism* the dominant class performed the intellectual function of teleological redistributor, that is, the role of the planner who appropriates and then redistributes goods and services. The planners' job is to define the needs of society and who shall realize them—the function of an intellectual. Of course, it is one thing to say planners perform an intellectual *function* and another to claim that intellectuals, defined by their specialization in the production of ideas and techniques, actually *occupy* a dominant position. In the economic reforms of the 1970s across Eastern Europe, Konrád and Szelényi envisioned intellectuals arriving at their destiny, their true place in society.

But that was not to be.[2] Instead of intellectuals ascending into command positions, the entire order dissolved. The central appropriation and redistribution of surplus was overt and therefore only assured through some combination of force and legitimation that often followed each other in cyclical fashion. This proved to be a precarious way of sustaining domination—making legitimation claims for socialism encouraged dissent, which only intensified when force was applied.

The stability of advanced capitalism and the instability of state socialism cannot be attributed to processes of socialization, as this was as intensive and systematic in state socialism as in advanced capitalism.[3] In explaining the difference we might do better to consider the structure of these two societies and the social games they generate. Advanced capitalism possesses a relatively open and autonomous civil society that effectively absorbs and diverts practices into self-contained institutions (or fields, in Bourdieu's terms). Each institution organizes its own distinctive game or games—defined by taken-for-granted assumptions (*illusio*) and guiding principles (*nomos*). If advanced capitalism is distinguished by its civil society, it might follow that symbolic violence is a phenomenon of advanced capitalism, at least in regard to the game-metaphoric conception of social structure. In state socialism there is only a limited civil society and, moreover, one that superimposes a game-like structure defined by the party state. There's no concealing class domination. For Bourdieu, however, symbolic violence has a universal validity; it has no historical limits. It is a general theory of social order without a corresponding particular theory of particular societies.

Returning to the question of intellectuals, if they are on the road to class power under state socialism, what is their position under capitalism? Szelényi (1982) himself argued that, in contrast to state socialism, under capitalism where private property rules and markets distribute, intellectuals play a subsidiary role. They hold a contradictory class position, as Erik Wright (1978) once put it, divided in their allegiance between dominant and dominated classes. Once we introduce capitalism as the context for intellectuals, Bourdieu's project takes on an entirely different meaning. An Internationale of intellectuals, seemingly autonomous from and even critical of the dominant class, becomes a vehicle for the reproduction of capitalism by suppressing the very idea of capitalism and failing to project an alternative beyond capitalism. In failing to give capitalism its due place in history, Bourdieu exaggerates the importance of intellectuals and the state—overlooking the multiple institutions that conspire to reproduce symbolic violence as mystification, starting with the capitalist economy itself but extending to all the institutions of civil society. In misrecognizing capitalism Bourdieu is committing his own scholastic fallacy.

MISRECOGNIZING CAPITALISM

Like Marx, Weber, and Durkheim before him, the genius of Bourdieu lies in his theory of social reproduction, specifically his *theory of symbolic violence*—a still unexplored combination of a psychology of internalization and a sociology of games. As I have been at pains to suggest, there are two prongs to symbolic violence—a prereflexive unconscious element and a more reflexive, conscious game-playing element. What is left unresolved in Bourdieu's account is the relationship between the reflexive and the prereflexive, the conscious and the unconscious dimensions of the habitus. How does each influence the other? For that he needs a far richer psychology.[4]

Nonetheless, his theory of symbolic violence raises the question as to how it is that sociology can excavate a truth inaccessible to the agents it studies but also a truth more valid than that of neighboring disciplines. Here Bourdieu goes beyond the canon, subjecting sociology to the sociological eye. He develops a *reflexive sociology*—a sociology of the scientific field that is rooted in his theory of symbolic violence. The sociologist works in a competitive field that incentivizes the advance of science and that develops an interest in disinterestedness. This is the nature of all scientific fields, but sociology is special in that it does not commit the scholastic fallacy of mistaking the field of science for the world of the participant, the logic of theory for the logic of practice. Bourdieu asks how it is that everyday practices create a world which conforms to the social theory discovered in the "laboratory." Theory is incomplete if the sociologist does not understand how the practice of subjects makes sociology simultaneously true and obscure.

This is the third distinctive feature of Bourdieu's sociology—*engagement with the world of the participant.* Through such an engagement the participant observer can understand how agents simultaneously secure and obscure the relations of domination. Even so, it is not clear how this combination of theoretical reflection and practical engagement can transcend the deeply embedded and embodied habitus that occupies the sociologist like anyone else. Do sociologists have some privileged access to their own unconscious habitus?

Returning to the discursive realm, Bourdieu's challenge to Marxism lies in his intellectualist theory of knowledge—that truth is produced in artistic and scientific fields, each requiring a certain leisured existence, removed from material necessity. A Marxist theory of knowledge, by contrast, claims that truth is ultimately rooted in and validated by the experience of subjugation. Truth is the standpoint of the subaltern, even if it is produced elsewhere. In Gramsci's terms, for Bourdieu the common sense of the subaltern is entirely bad sense, whereas for Marxism the common sense of the subaltern contains a kernel of good sense, even if the outer layers are subject to the distortions of ideology. In the Gramscian view organic intellectuals exist to elaborate the good sense of the subaltern, while traditional intellectuals create ideologies that justify and elicit participation in and consent to capitalism. The counterpart to Bourdieu's classification struggle is a struggle between intellectuals representing different classes—not between ideologies but on the terrain of a dominant ideology. The more autonomous and critical traditional intellectuals appear to be, the more effective their representation of a universal interest, but it is a false universality as it obscures the fundamental structures and strictures of capitalism.[5]

The university, especially the elite university, is the home of Bourdieu's corporatism of the universal, from which the organic intellectual of humanity can project itself. Fearing the doxosophers—the pretenders to the scholarly throne—or the opportunistic allies of the doxosophers, Bourdieu defends the autonomy of the university. But the university is undergoing a major transformation.

In the past we could speak of the *university in capitalist society*, hemmed in by all sorts of constraints but still a self-governing knowledge workshop, designed to enhance the public good. It could be conceived of as a "subject" with its own agency or an "object" manipulated by outside forces, but, at its best, its internal structure was as close to a large-scale socialist co-operative as you'll find under capitalism. Today, however, we must conceive of the university as a set of social relations embedded in the wider society. More and more it is a *capitalist university* whose very structure mimics a capitalist corporation.

As public funding is withdrawn, the university—the world over—becomes a profit center, cutting costs and creating revenues. It cuts costs through a vast array of strategies: from new digital technology that makes possible distance learning, to the expansion of contingent faculty and the steady decline (in numbers and in power) of faculty with security of employment, to an array of outsourcing arrangements, whether to janitors or management consultants. On the other hand, it increases revenue by seeking funds from alumni interested in immortality by sponsoring new buildings or athletics, from industries such as pharmaceuticals seeking partnerships based on cheap graduate student research, and, most notably, by increasing student tuition and creating new degree programs that charge exorbitant fees. All this is accomplished by an expanding administration bent on the proletarianization of university labor and the degradation of education, all disguised with corporate-speak. As the university becomes less hospitable to Bourdieu's autonomous scientific field, as its capitalist structure becomes transparent, it becomes a terrain of struggle and its claims to autonomy becomes ever more illusory, not just from internal clash of interests but also from the invasion of outside forces.

In the US and elsewhere, the university is becoming a playground for the political Right as well as the political Left. The once-dominant liberal consensus is under assault from conservatives who no longer assume the university to be off-limits for their political projects. Small right-wing student cells with outside funding are abetting the invasion of campuses by extremist political forces. We can no longer imagine the university to be outside politics as Bourdieu seemed to believe—it is fast becoming a capitalist machine and a political battleground.

The university is still an arena for the production and reception of ideas, but the process of production has changed—faculty are losing control of their labor and of its products, while students are rapidly becoming indebted and desperate consumers. The class structure of the university is polarizing, and tenure-track academics have a choice: to collaborate with the administrative class or to side with dispossessed students, contingent lecturers, and beleaguered staff. In the short term their interests are to preserve the privileges of a labor aristocracy, but in the long term their common interests lie with the dispossessed because, with the exception of an ever-dwindling minority, they too will be dispossessed of their security and autonomy.

Structure and superstructure are becoming one. As the university moves from an ivory tower to a key battleground over ideas, the struggle against pro-capitalist ideologies assumes greater urgency and renewed vigor. The "autonomous" traditional intellectual is being squeezed out of existence, having now to take sides within as well as beyond the capitalist university—the claim of universality appears increasingly bogus. Anyone who examines the conditions of production of knowledge today cannot misrecognize capitalism.

If the followers of Bourdieu can no longer misrecognize capitalism and its pathologies, in grappling with the appeal of capitalism, Marxists have much to learn from Bourdieu's explorations of symbolic violence.

PROLOGUE

1. In the US, Paul DiMaggio (1979) was among the first, followed by Rogers Brubaker (1985) and Lamont and Lareau (1988). Then in the 1990s came more comprehensive assessments based on earlier articles: Swartz (1997), Robbins (1991), and the critical assessments in Calhoun, LiPuma, and Postone (1993). By far the most significant overview was written by Bourdieu and Wacquant (1992).

2. I still adhere to this view that Bourdieu has no theory of history or social change and his central contribution is to a theory of social reproduction. This is not to say that he does not undertake historical analysis. He certainly does, for example, when he studies the genesis of the literary field or the modern state, but this does not amount to a *theory* of social change; it is an *account* of social change. Thus, the essays in Gorski (2013) show how Bourdieu's ideas about social reproduction can be very useful in studying historical events, but they have no predictive power that would mark a theory of social change. There are germs of a theory of social change in his account of the self-destruction of the Béarn kinship system or French colonialism—how social reproduction is simultaneously social transformation. But these germs remain underdeveloped. Overall, if there is an implicit account of social change it is that of Durkheimian social differentiation.

3. David Swartz (2013, chaps. 6 and 7) offers an extended discussion of Bourdieu as public sociologist and how he fits with my own version.

1. SOCIOLOGY IS A COMBAT SPORT

Epigraph: Carles (2001).

1. See the responses of Anderson (2002), Duneier (2002), and Newman (2002) to Wacquant's (2002) attack on their work.

2. There is, of course, an element of combat in Parsons too, for example, in the way he deals with Marx at a time when Marxism was enjoying a certain renaissance in US sociology: "Judged by the standards of the best contemporary social-science theory, Marxian theory is obsolete" (1967, 132). Marx was a "social theorist whose work fell entirely within the nineteenth century. . . . He belongs to a phase of development which has been superseded" (135).

2. THE POVERTY OF PHILOSOPHY

This conversation is a revision of Burawoy (2018b). Epigraphs: Marx ([1847] 1963, 173); Bourdieu ([1984] 1991b, 251).

1. Note how different this is from Edward Thompson's (1963) classic, *The Making of the English Working Class*, according to which the working class makes history itself without the aid of a distinct body of intellectuals, especially Marxist intellectuals. In effect, Bourdieu is saying that Thompson commits the typical Marxist error of regarding the working class as making itself. Not surprisingly, many have accused Bourdieu of being a "Leninist" for his emphasis on the central role of intellectuals (Lane 2006).

2. Bourdieu often failed to specify the people he was attacking, leaving that to the reader's imagination and thereby leaving the enemy undefined and defenseless. This idea of class on paper might well be associated with Erik Wright's successive theorizations of class, although even his successive formulations were based on the analysis of survey research.

3. Indeed, some, such as Perry Anderson (1976) regarded the "idealism" of Western Marxism as a betrayal of a "true" Marxism. Ironically, what Anderson regards as the essential truth of Marxism, Bourdieu considers to be its essential flaw.

4. Throughout this conversation I will be referring to Marx except where he is a joint author with Engels. This is not to belittle the contribution of Engels but to reflect Bourdieu's focus on Marx whenever he is not making blanket statements about Marxism.

5. Here is how Marx and Engels berate Feuerbach: "Thus if millions of proletarians feel by no means contented with their living conditions, if their 'existence' does not in the least correspond to their 'essence' then . . . this is an unavoidable misfortune, which must be borne quietly. The millions of proletarians and communists, however, think differently and will prove this in time, when they bring their 'existence' into harmony with their 'essence' in a practical way, by means of revolution" (Marx and Engels [1845–46] 1978, 168).

6. As Jacques Bidet (2008) emphasizes, the dynamics of Bourdieu's fields relies on struggle and competition among its agents rather than an underlying structure equivalent to the interaction of the forces and relations of production.

7. While Talcott Parsons and Pierre Bourdieu share a commitment to a general theory of action, Parsons develops four analytical subsystems (analogous to fields) whose functions—adaptive, goal attainment, integrative, and latency—contribute to society as a whole and whose interdependence is orchestrated through universal media of interchange (money, power, influence, and value commitments) that are parallel to Bourdieu's capitals. From here Parsons develops a theory of history as differentiation, governed by evolutionary universals. Bourdieu makes no attempt to advance such a grand account of history and totality. Indeed, he recoils from any such project. He systematically refuses systematicity.

8. There is also a curious parallel between Bourdieu's concept of "habitus" and Marx's conception of "forces of production." Both are durable, transposable,

and irreversible—the one a measure of the development of the individual, the other of society. Both come into conflict with wider structures within which they develop. For Marx, however, those structures (relations of production) are transformed through revolutions that allow a new higher mode of production and that impel the expansion of the forces of production, whereas for Bourdieu, it is the opposite: habitus tends to give way to structures.

9. In the more abstract formulation of Bourdieu and Passeron ([1970] 1977), lower-class students accept the legitimacy of the school and exit quietly but later, following the reform of secondary education, the school becomes embroiled in rebellion. See Bourdieu et al. ([1993] 1999, 421–506).

10. In writing about Algeria, however, Bourdieu ([1963] 1979, 62–63) argues that it is the relative stability and the "privilege" of experiencing "permanent, rational exploitation" that gives the working class revolutionary potential, very different from the dispossessed peasantry and subproletariat, who live from hand to mouth and are, therefore, unable to plan for an alternative future. It is the distinction between a genuine "revolutionary force" and a spontaneous "force for revolution." This is a very different portrait than the one of the French working class weighed down by necessity, accepting the legitimacy of the dominant classes. While Bourdieu makes no effort to reconcile these opposed visions of the working class, he might argue that it revolves around the symbolic violence in France and the material violence of colonialism. Alternatively, these may be strategic positions that Bourdieu takes up in two different political fields: against the Front de Libération Nationale/National Liberation Front (FLN), which favored the peasantry as a revolutionary class in Algeria, and against the Marxists, who regarded the working class as inherently revolutionary in France.

11. They are what Alvin Gouldner (1979) calls a flawed universal class, only he was more realistic about the corporatism of intellectuals. Antonio Gramsci would see Bourdieu's intellectuals as "traditional intellectuals" who, in defending their autonomy, are able to present the interests of the dominant class as the interests of all, as the universal interests.

3. CULTURAL DOMINATION

Epigraphs: Bourdieu (1979) 1984, 386; Bourdieu (1987) 1990, 27–28; Bourdieu 1989, 109.

1. In another reference, Bourdieu (1991, chap. 8) opportunistically turns Gramsci's warnings about the dangers of the trade union oligarchy—"a banker of men in a monopoly situation"—and of the sectarian politics of the party apparatus, cut off from its followers, into a blanket denunciation of "organic intellectuals" as deceiving both themselves and the class they claim to represent. It is curious that Bourdieu here draws on Gramsci's more obscure political writings, while avoiding the *Prison Notebooks* and their key ideas of hegemony, civil society, intellectuals, and the state.

2. Reflecting their very different intellectual positions and dispositions, they diverge fundamentally in their relation to their class origins. In the film *La*

sociologie est un sport du combat, which is a portrait of Bourdieu's academic and political life, there is a scene in which Bourdieu describes his revulsion for the dialect of his home region in the Pyrenees, illustrating the class habitus he developed in the academic establishment, whereas Gramsci writes moving letters from prison to his sister imploring her to make sure that her children do not lose their familiarity with folk idioms and vernacular.

3. The obvious exceptions are Bourdieu's account of May 1968 in which there are temporary alliances between intellectuals and working classes, merging into general crisis, and his account of the Algerian "revolution within the revolution" when the colonized fuse into a struggle against colonialism.

4. Even Bourdieu is led to the appropriation of the idea of the organic intellectual: "All this means that the ethno-sociologist is a kind of organic intellectual of humanity, and as a collective agent, can contribute to de-naturalizing and de-fatalizing human existence by placing his skill at the service of a universalism rooted in the comprehension of different particularisms" (Bourdieu [2002] 2008b, 24). But it is an organic intellectual of an abstract entity (i.e., humanity)—the very antithesis of Gramsci's organic intellectual—indeed, the apotheosis of Gramsci's traditional intellectual.

4. COLONIALISM AND REVOLUTION

Epigraphs: Bourdieu ([1987] 1990, 7); Pierre Bourdieu, in Le Sueur (2001, 282).

1. The English versions to which I will refer are *The Algerians* ([1961] 1962); *Algeria, 1960* ([1963] 1979), which is an abridged version of the French *Work and Workers in Algeria* (1963); and *Algerian Sketches* (2013), which includes excerpts from *Le déracinement* (1964).

2. For an important set of essays on the contradictions and paradoxes of Bourdieu's Algerian writings, see Jane Goodman and Paul Silverstein (2009), especially the chapter by Fanny Colonna, who criticizes Bourdieu for his poor stylized fieldwork that misses the realities of daily life and for his unsubstantiated claim that the Kabyle misrecognize what they are up to.

3. First published in *Esprit* 1 (January 1961); English translation appeared in Bourdieu ([1961] 1962, chap. 7).

4. Bourdieu ([1997] 2000, 172) writes of the difficulty of changing the habitus, calling for "thoroughgoing process of countertraining." Fanon is saying the same: that the internalization of oppression is so deep that the colonized can only transform themselves through violence.

5. Writing with Sayad in 1964, Bourdieu analyzes the possibilities of socialism very much in terms familiar from Durkheim and Mauss. Bourdieu and Sayad cast doubt on the feasibility of self-organized, decentralized socialism based on autonomous peasant organization of the farms vacated by colonialists, just as they fear the possibility of a centralized authoritarian socialism imposed from above. Like Fanon, they hope for an educative leadership responsive to needs from below. They easily fall back, however, on the cultural legacies of tradition to explain economic and political regression.

6. We find this vision laid out in the earliest writings of Bourdieu ([1961] 1962)—a secondary account of the cultures of different ethnic groups—and then in the self-consciously theoretical works written in France, most notably *Outline of a Theory of Practice* ([1972] 1977).

7. Bourdieu does try to mark his distance from one of the modernization theorists of the day—Daniel Lerner (1958)—by criticizing his psychological characterization of modernity as the recognition of other, as the expression of empathy, and as a rationality freely chosen. As orientations to the world, "tradition" and "modernity" are not freely chosen, says Bourdieu, but spring from specific material contexts, the clash of unequal civilizations under colonialism (Bourdieu [1961] 1962, 117, 119–20). But the concepts of tradition and modernity are never called into question, simply redefined.

8. Bourdieu (2000) relies on the misinterpreted case of the Kabyle cook—a man who moves from one job to another. There is little evidence that this is a sign of anomie or that he is beholden to some traditional habitus. Instead, the cook shows great entrepreneurial adroitness in adapting to the exigencies of urban life under colonialism.

9. Gramsci seemed to think that the war of position either preceded the war of movement (in the West, where civil society was strong) or followed the war of movement (in the East, with its undeveloped civil society, where socialism would be built after the revolution). Fanon understood the dangers of postponing the struggle for socialism until after independence.

10. Interestingly, Fanon and Bourdieu held opposite views about the working class in advanced capitalism too: for Fanon, it was potentially revolutionary; for Bourdieu, it was not. Although there is no sign that Fanon had read Gramsci, he had a very Gramscian view of the West with a developed civil society and a bourgeoisie able to make concessions, all of which was absent in the periphery (Fanon [1961] 1963, 38, 108–9, 165, 175).

5. PEDAGOGY OF THE OPPRESSED

Epigraph: Bourdieu and Passeron (1977 [1970], 210).

1. Gramsci's use of the male pronoun throughout jars with contemporary sensibilities and leads him to miss the gender side of education, which is as important as the class dimension. Bourdieu and Passeron are more sensitive to contemporary usage, but they too are primarily focused on the significance of class.

6. THE ANTINOMIES OF FEMINISM

Epigraph: Bourdieu (1995, viii).

1. An obvious reference to *Memoirs of a Dutiful Daughter*, the first volume of Beauvoir's autobiography.

2. I will rely on the original English translation of *The Second Sex*, despite its known problems; see Moi (2002).

3. Toril Moi says as much herself. After referring to Françoise Armengaud's claim that Bourdieu stole the ideas of contemporary French feminists, Moi (1999,

283n21) goes on to write, "In the same way he [Bourdieu] completely fails to acknowledge that his own analysis of patriarchal domination echoes that of Simone de Beauvoir. . . . As I say repeatedly in the text, Bourdieu's general understanding of women's oppression is hardly original or new to anyone vaguely familiar with feminist thought in this century. My point, however, is that whatever we think about Bourdieu's own lack of feminist credentials, the concepts he develops (*habitus*, field, symbolic capital, distinction, and so on) remain deeply useful for certain kinds of feminist projects." This is also the general tenor of the collection *Feminism after Bourdieu* (Adkins and Skeggs 2004). Feminists too easily let Bourdieu off the hook by separating his concepts from his theory of symbolic violence—a theory pioneered by Beauvoir.

4. Beauvoir devotes a whole chapter to prostitution as an alternative to marriage. Just as lesbianism is a departure from normal sexualization, so prostitution is an alternative road to marriage whose significance and evaluation differ from society to society.

5. The same structure can also be found in Sartre's *Anti-Semite and Jew* ([1946] 1948), which appeared, probably not coincidentally, just as Beauvoir began work on *The Second Sex*.

6. This is what Patricia Hill Collins (1986) almost forty years later will call the perspective of "the outsider within," although she will trace its genealogy not to Beauvoir, but to George Simmel.

7. THE SOCIOLOGICAL IMAGINATION

Epigraphs: Mills (1959, 187); Bourdieu ([1977] 2008, 76–77); Bourdieu ([2000] 2008, 24).

1. Mills supported Norman Thomas's 1948 presidential bid as a candidate of the Socialist Party.

2. Exceptional, therefore, is Bourdieu's treatment of "love" and the gay and lesbian movements in *Masculine Domination* ([1998] 2001).

3. Obviously, Mills and Bourdieu are also affected by the styles of thinking and writing that prevail in their own national intellectual fields, manifested in the opposed styles of Continental and Anglo-American philosophy.

8. THE TWOFOLD TRUTH OF LABOR

An earlier version of this conversation was published in *Sociology* (Burawoy 2012). I am borrowing the term *Homo habitus* from correspondence with Bridget Kenny, who coined it to express Bourdieu's deeply pessimistic view of human nature. *Homo ludens* comes from the famous Dutch theorist Johan Huizinga ([1938] 2014). Epigraphs: Bourdieu ([1997] 2000, 202); Burawoy (1979, 30).

1. I would later call the internal state "the political and ideological apparatuses of production" or "the regime of production" (Burawoy 1985).

2. There is no shortage of studies that suggest the ubiquity of games. For some outstanding recent examples, see Ofer Sharone's (2004) study of software engineers, Jeffrey Sallaz's (2002) study of casino dealers, Rachel Sherman's (2007) study of

hotel workers, and Adam Reich's (2010) study of juvenile prisoners. With the development of the gig economy, the organization of work as a game has become an industry unto itself, employing consultants in "gamification." Digital platforms design incentives that exploit the human propensity to play games, especially when workers face coercive and boring regimens. See, for example, Sarah Mason's (2018) fascinating account of working for the ride-hailing company Lyft.

3. It was while working and teaching with Adam Przeworski at the University of Chicago that I developed the idea of social structure as a game. During this time he was developing his Gramscian theory of electoral politics: party competition could be thought of as an absorbing game in which the struggle was over the distribution of economic resources at the margin, thereby eclipsing the fundamental inequality upon which the game was based (Przeworski 1985).

4. Indeed, Przeworski (1985) has shown just how rational it is for socialist parties to fight for immediate material gains in order to attract the votes necessary to gain and then keep power.

5. This is more consistent with Bernard Lahire's (2011) view of individuals as carrying a plurality of selves, activated in different situations, than with Bourdieu's notion of a singular integrated and cumulative habitus.

6. Interestingly, the major Bourdieusian analysis of the transition in Eastern Europe—Eyal, Szelényi, and Townsley (1998)—is an analysis not of the collapse but of the post-socialist succession of elites in Hungary, Poland, and the Czech Republic. Again, it is an examination of the inheritance, fate, and distribution of different forms of socialist capital (economic, cultural, and political) in the post-socialist era.

7. This is most systematically elaborated in Bourdieu's ([1984] 1988) account of the crisis of May 1968, where he examines the consequences of the declining opportunities for expanding numbers of university graduates and the way the crisis in the university field dovetailed with the crisis in the wider political field.

8. Gil Eyal (2013) makes the point forcefully that, while Bourdieu is very concerned about internal relations *within* fields, he has little conception of the relations *among* fields. In a meticulous account of Bourdieu's treatment of the sociology of knowledge, Charles Camic (2013) also draws attention to the ambiguities in Bourdieu's understanding of the relations among fields and how his programmatic statements substitute macro forces—economic, political, and religious—for a constellation of fields.

9. "Knowledge and recognition have to be rooted in practical dispositions of acceptance and submission, which, because they do not pass through deliberation and decision, escape the dilemmas of consent or constraint" (Bourdieu [1997] 2000, 198).

9. THE WEIGHT OF THE WORLD

This chapter has been in gestation for many years. It was originally given at a conference on Bourdieu and Work in Paris at CNRS (Centre national de la recherche scientifique) in 2012. Since then it has been rewritten many times under the influence of comments from Erik Wright, Mike Levien, and Mark Gould. It is published here for the first time. Epigraphs: Bourdieu ([1997] 2000, 180); Bourdieu (*ww*, 614); Bourdieu ([1997] 2000, 163); Bourdieu ([1984] 1991a, 204, 206).

1. Hereafter, Bourdieu et al. (1993) 1999 will be cited as *ww*.
2. As we shall see, this is related but not reducible to the more conventional distinction between Bourdieu the professional sociologist and Bourdieu the public sociologist.
3. Inspired by *Weight of the World*, Javier Auyero (2015) and his students undertake a rare portrait of the underbelly of Austin (Texas) through extended interviews of carefully selected respondents. Unlike Bourdieu and his colleagues, the authors don't write introductions to excerpts from their interviews but instead use the interviews to create a mosaic of perspectives that pay attention to the broader forces creating the urban precariat. The overall impression is similarly bleak—individuals having to fend for themselves—except the "accidents" that befall the respondents have catastrophic consequences, in part because there is no safety net. Although Bourdieu is the guiding light behind these studies, there is no concern with issues of symbolic violence or misrecognition.

CONCLUSION

1. In developing his ideas in the lectures on the state at the Collège de France, Bourdieu ([2012] 2014) shows that he is quite aware of wide-ranging literature, including the Marxist literature. Their omission in the finished works is a strategy, not a sign of ignorance.
2. As Eyal, Szelényi, and Townsley (1998) write in *Making Capitalism without Capitalists*, it was only with the transition to capitalism that intellectuals finally ascended to power as managers of postsocialism. They describe this process using a Bourdieusian framework of the conversion of different forms of capital. But this, too, turned out to be a temporary aberration.
3. See chapter 8.
4. Perhaps the most interesting advances have been made by proponents of a "dual process" model borrowed from cognitive psychology (Lizardo 2004; Vaisey 2009; Lizardo et al. 2016), in which a distinction is made between reflexive action that requires slow, conceptual processes of symbolic mastery and the prereflexive spontaneous, impulsive action based on accumulated, embodied processes developing over a long period of time. Focusing on symbolic violence, I have sliced Bourdieu in a different way: an internalization process that is unconscious and a gamelike interaction that works at a more conscious level. Whichever approach one takes, the big question pertains to the dynamic interplay between the conscious and the unconscious, of the sort that psychoanalysis has explored.
5. See chapter 3.

REFERENCES

Adkins, Lisa, and Beverley Skeggs, eds. 2004. *Feminism after Bourdieu*. Cambridge: Blackwell.

Althusser, Louis. 1969. *For Marx*. London: Allen and Lane.

Anderson, Elijah. 2002. "The Ideologically Driven Critique." *American Journal of Sociology* 107 (6): 1533–50.

Anderson, Perry. 1976. *Considerations on Western Marxism*. London: New Left.

Auyero, Javier, ed. 2015. *Invisible in Austin*. Austin: University of Texas Press.

Balibar, Étienne. 1977. *On the Dictatorship of the Proletariat*. London: Verso.

Beauvoir, Simone de. (1949) 1989. *The Second Sex*. Translated by H. M. Parshley. New York: Vintage.

Beauvoir, Simone de. 1956. *The Mandarins*. New York: World Publishing.

Beauvoir, Simone de. (1963) 1964. *Force of Circumstance*. New York: Putnam.

Bernstein, Basil. 1975. *Class, Codes and Control*. London: Routledge.

Bidet, Jacques. 2008. "Bourdieu and Historical Materialism." In *Critical Companion to Contemporary Marxism*, edited by J. Bidet and S. Kouvelakis, 587–605. Leiden, Netherlands: Brill.

Bourdieu, Pierre. (1961) 1962. *The Algerians*. Boston: Beacon.

Bourdieu, Pierre. (1963) 1979. *Algeria, 1960*. Cambridge: Cambridge University Press.

Bourdieu, Pierre. (1972) 1976. "Marriage Strategies as Strategies of Social Reproduction." In *Family and Society: Selections from the Annales, Economies, Societies, Civilisations*, edited by Robert Forster and Orest Ranum, 117–44. Baltimore: Johns Hopkins University Press.

Bourdieu, Pierre. (1972) 1977. *Outline of a Theory of Practice*. Cambridge: Cambridge University Press.

Bourdieu, Pierre. 1975. "The Specificity of the Scientific Field and the Social Conditions of the Progress of Reason." *Social Science Information* 14 (6): 19–47.

Bourdieu, Pierre. (1977) 2008. "Giving Voice to the Voiceless." In *Political Interventions: Social Science and Political Action*, 70–77. London: Verso.

Bourdieu, Pierre. (1979) 1984. *Distinction: A Social Critique of the Judgment of Taste*. Cambridge, MA: Harvard University Press.

Bourdieu, Pierre. (1980) 1990. *The Logic of Practice*. Cambridge: Polity.

Bourdieu, Pierre. 1981. "Men and Machines." In *Advances in Social Theory and Methodology*, edited by K. Knorr-Cetina and A. Cicourel, 304–17. Boston: Routledge and Kegan Paul.

Bourdieu, Pierre. (1982) 1990. "The Uses of the 'People.'" In *In Other Words: Essays Towards a Reflexive Sociology*, 150–55. Stanford, CA: Stanford University Press.

Bourdieu, Pierre. (1984) 1988. *Homo Academicus.* Cambridge: Polity.

Bourdieu, Pierre. (1984) 1991a. "Delegation and Political Fetishism.'" In *Language and Symbolic Power*, 203–19. Cambridge, MA: Harvard University Press.

Bourdieu, Pierre. (1984) 1991b. "Social Space and the Genesis of 'Classes.'" In *Language and Symbolic Power*, 229–51. Cambridge, MA: Harvard University Press.

Bourdieu, Pierre. (1984) 1993a. "The Sociologist in Question." In *Sociology in Question*, 20–35. London: Sage.

Bourdieu, Pierre. (1984) 1993b. "Public Opinion Does Not Exist." In *Sociology in Question*, 149–57. London: Sage.

Bourdieu, Pierre. (1987) 1990. "Fieldwork in Philosophy." In *In Other Words: Essays Towards a Reflexive Sociology*, 3–33. Stanford, CA: Stanford University Press.

Bourdieu, Pierre. 1989. "The Corporatism of the Universal: The Role of Intellectuals in the Modern World." *Telos* 81: 99–110.

Bourdieu, Pierre. (1989) 1996. *State Nobility: Elite Schools in the Field of Power.* Stanford, CA: Stanford University Press.

Bourdieu, Pierre. (1989) 1998. "The Soviet Variant and Political Capital." In *Practical Reason: On the Theory of Action*, 14–18. Stanford, CA: Stanford University Press.

Bourdieu, Pierre. 1991. *Language and Symbolic Power.* Cambridge, MA: Harvard University Press.

Bourdieu, Pierre. (1992) 1996. *Rules of Art: Genesis and Structure of the Literary Field.* Stanford, CA: Stanford University Press.

Bourdieu, Pierre. 1995. "Apologie pour une femme rangée." Preface to *Simone de Beauvoir: Conflicts d'une intellectuelle*, by Toril Moi, vi–x, translated by Ana Villarreal. Paris: Diderot Éditeur.

Bourdieu, Pierre. (1996) 1999. *On Television.* New York: New Press.

Bourdieu, Pierre. (1997) 2000. *Pascalian Meditations.* Stanford, CA: Stanford University Press.

Bourdieu, Pierre. 1997. "Passport to Duke." *Metaphilosophy* 28 (4): 449–55.

Bourdieu, Pierre. 1998. *Acts of Resistance: Against the Tyranny of the Market.* New York: New Press.

Bourdieu, Pierre. (1998) 2001. *Masculine Domination.* Stanford, CA: Stanford University Press.

Bourdieu, Pierre. 2000. "Making the Economic Habitus: Algerian Workers Revisited." *Ethnography* 1 (1): 17–41.

Bourdieu, Pierre. (2000) 2003. "Participant Objectivation." *Journal of the Royal Anthropological Institute*, n.s., 9: 281–94.

Bourdieu, Pierre. (2000) 2008. "A Retrospective on the Algerian Experience." In *Political Interventions: Social Science and Political Action*, 20–24. London: Verso.

Bourdieu, Pierre. (2001) 2003. *Firing Back: Against the Tyranny of the Market.* New York: New Press.

Bourdieu, Pierre. (2002) 2008a. *The Bachelors' Ball*. Chicago: University of Chicago Press.

Bourdieu, Pierre. (2002) 2008b. *Political Interventions: Social Science and Political Action*. London: Verso.

Bourdieu, Pierre. (2004) 2007. *Sketch for a Self-Analysis*. Chicago: University of Chicago Press.

Bourdieu, Pierre. 2005. *The Social Structures of the Economy*. Cambridge: Polity.

Bourdieu, Pierre. (2012) 2014. *On the State*. Cambridge: Polity.

Bourdieu, Pierre. 2013. *Algerian Sketches*. Cambridge: Polity.

Bourdieu, Pierre et al. (1993) 1999. *The Weight of the World: Social Suffering in Contemporary Society*. Stanford, CA: Stanford University Press.

Bourdieu, Pierre, Alain Darbel, Jean-Pierre Rivet, and Claude Seibel. 1963. *Travail et travailleurs en Algérie*. Paris: Mouton.

Bourdieu, Pierre, and Jean-Claude Passeron. (1964) 1979. *The Inheritors: French Students and Their Relation to Culture*. Chicago: University of Chicago Press.

Bourdieu, Pierre, and Jean-Claude Passeron. (1970) 1977. *Reproduction in Education, Society and Culture*. London: Sage.

Bourdieu, Pierre, Jean-Claude Passeron, and Jean-Claude Chamboredon. (1968) 1991. *The Craft of Sociology: Epistemological Preliminaries*. New York: Aldine de Gruyter.

Bourdieu, Pierre, and Abdelmalek Sayad. 1964. *Le déracinement: La crise de l'agriculture traditionnelle en Algérie*. Paris: Editions de Minuit.

Bourdieu, Pierre, and Loïc Wacquant. 1992. *An Invitation to Reflexive Sociology*. Chicago: University of Chicago Press.

Bowles, Samuel, and Herbert Gintis. 1976. *Schooling in Capitalist America*. New York: Basic.

Brubaker, Rogers. 1985. "Rethinking Classical Sociology: The Sociological Vision of Pierre Bourdieu." *Theory and Society* 14 (6): 745–75.

Burawoy, Michael. 1979. *Manufacturing Consent: Changes in the Labor Process under Monopoly Capitalism*. Chicago: University of Chicago Press.

Burawoy, Michael. 1985. *The Politics of Production: Factory Regimes under Capitalism and Socialism*. London: Verso.

Burawoy, Michael. 2010. *O marxismo encontra Bourdieu*. Campinas: Unicamp Press.

Burawoy, Michael. 2012. "The Roots of Domination: Beyond Bourdieu and Gramsci." *Sociology* 46 (2): 187–206.

Burawoy, Michael. 2017. "On Desmond: The Limits of Spontaneous Sociology." *Theory and Society* 46: 261–84.

Burawoy, Michael. 2018a. "Making Sense of Bourdieu." *Catalyst* 2 (1): 51–87.

Burawoy, Michael. 2018b. "The Poverty of Philosophy: Marx Meets Bourdieu." In *The Oxford Handbook of Pierre Bourdieu*, edited by Thomas Medvetz and Jeffrey J. Sallaz, 375–97. New York: Oxford University Press.

Burawoy, Michael, and János Lukács. 1992. *The Radiant Past: Ideology and Reality in Hungary's Road to Capitalism*. Chicago: University of Chicago Press.

Burawoy, Michael, and Karl von Holdt. 2012. *Conversations with Bourdieu: The Johannesburg Moment*. Johannesburg: Wits University Press.

Calhoun, Craig, Edward LiPuma, and Moishe Postone, eds. 1993. *Bourdieu: Critical Perspectives*. Chicago: University of Chicago Press.

Camic, Charles. 2013. "Bourdieu's Two Sociologies of Knowledge." In *Bourdieu and Historical Analysis*, edited by Philip Gorski, 183–214. Durham, NC: Duke University Press.

Carles, Pierre, dir. 2001. *La sociologie est un sport de combat*. C. P. Productions. Film.

Chodorow, Nancy. 1978. *The Reproduction of Mothering: Psychoanalysis and the Sociology of Gender*. Berkeley: University of California Press.

Collins, Patricia Hill. 1986. "Learning from the Outsider Within: The Sociological Significance of Black Feminist Thought." *Social Problems* 33 (6): 14–32.

Collins, Patricia Hill. 1990. *Black Feminist Thought: Knowledge, Consciousness, and the Politics of Empowerment*. Boston: Unwin Hyman.

Collins, Patricia Hill. 2005. "Black Public Intellectuals: From Du Bois to the Present." *Contexts* 4 (4): 22–27.

Colonna, Fanny. 2009. "The Phantom of Dispossessions: From *The Uprooting* to *The Weight of the World*." In *Bourdieu in Algeria*, edited by Jane Goodman and Paul Silverstein, 63–93. Lincoln: University of Nebraska Press.

Desan, Mathieu Hikaru. 2013. "Bourdieu, Marx, and Capital: A Critique of the Extension Model." *Sociological Theory* 31 (4): 318–42.

Desmond, Matthew. 2007. *On the Fireline: Living and Dying with Wildland Firefighters*. Chicago: University of Chicago Press.

DiMaggio, Paul. 1979. "Review Essay on Pierre Bourdieu." *American Journal of Sociology* 84 (6): 1460–74.

Duneier, Mitchell. 2002. "What Kind of Combat Sport Is Sociology?" *American Journal of Sociology* 107 (6): 1551–75.

Durkheim, Émile. (1893) 1984. *The Division of Labor in Society*. New York: Free Press.

Durkheim, Émile. (1912) 1965. *The Elementary Forms of Religious Life*. New York: Free Press.

Eyal, Gil. 2013. "Spaces between Fields." In *Bourdieu and Historical Analysis*, edited by Philip Gorski, 158–82. Durham, NC: Duke University Press.

Eyal, Gil, Iván Szelényi, and Eleanor Townsley. 1998. *Making Capitalism without Capitalists: The New Ruling Elites in Eastern Europe*. London: Verso.

Fanon, Frantz. (1952) 1967. *Black Skin, White Masks*. New York: Grove.

Fanon, Frantz. (1961) 1963. *The Wretched of the Earth*. New York: Grove.

Fligstein, Neil. 2002. *The Architecture of Markets*. Princeton, NJ: Princeton University Press.

Freire, Paulo. 1970. *Pedagogy of the Oppressed*. New York: Continuum.

Friedan, Betty. 1963. *The Feminine Mystique*. New York: Norton.

Gerth, Hans, and Charles Wright Mills, eds. 1946. *From Max Weber: Essays in Sociology*. New York: Oxford University Press.

Gerth, Hans, and Charles Wright Mills, eds. 1954. *Character and Social Structure: The Psychology of Social Institutions*. London: Routledge and Kegan Paul.

Godelier, Maurice. 1972. *Rationality and Irrationality in Economics*. New York: Monthly Review Press.

Goodman, Jane, and Paul Silverstein, eds. 2009. *Bourdieu in Algeria*. Lincoln: University of Nebraska Press.

Gorski, Philip, ed. 2013. *Bourdieu and Historical Analysis*. Durham, NC: Duke University Press.

Gouldner, Alvin. 1979. *The Future of the Intellectuals and the Rise of the New Class*. New York: Seabury.

Gramsci, Antonio. 1971. *Selections from the Prison Notebooks*. New York: International Publishers.

Habermas, Jürgen. 1984. *The Theory of Communicative Action*. Boston: Beacon.

Hochschild, Arlie. 1983. *The Managed Heart*. Berkeley: University of California Press.

Huizinga, Johan (1938) 2014. *Homo Ludens: A Study of the Play Element in Culture*. Boston: Beacon Press.

Kahn, Shamus. 2011. *Privilege: The Making of an Adolescent Elite at St. Paul's School*. Princeton, NJ: Princeton University Press.

Konrád, György, and Iván Szelényi. 1979. *Intellectuals on the Road to Class Power*. New York: Harcourt Brace Jovanovich.

Lahire, Bernard. 2011. *The Plural Actor*. Cambridge: Polity.

Lamont, Michèle. 1994. *Money, Morals, and Manners*. Chicago: University of Chicago Press.

Lamont, Michèle. 2009. *How Professors Think: Inside the Curious World of Academic Judgment*. Cambridge: Cambridge University Press.

Lamont, Michèle, and Annette Lareau. 1988. "Cultural Capital: Allusions, Gaps and Glissandos in Recent Theoretical Developments." *Sociological Theory* 6 (2): 153–68.

Lane, Jeremy. 2006. *Bourdieu's Politics: Problems and Possibilities*. Milton Park, UK: Routledge.

Lareau, Annette. 1989. *Home Advantage: Social Class and Parental Intervention in Elementary Education*. New York: Falmer.

Lareau, Annette. 2003. *Unequal Childhoods*. Berkeley: University of California Press.

Lenin, Vladimir. (1902) 1975. *What Is to Be Done?* In *The Lenin Anthology*, edited by Robert Tucker, 12–114 New York: Norton.

Lenin, Vladimir. (1917) 1975. *State and Revolution*. In *The Lenin Anthology*, edited by Robert Tucker, 311–398. New York: Norton.

Lerner, Daniel. 1958. *The Passing of Traditional Society: Modernizing the Middle East*. Glencoe, IL: Free Press.

Le Sueur, James. 2001. *Uncivil War: Intellectuals and Identity Politics during the Decolonization of Algeria*. Philadelphia: University of Pennsylvania Press.

Lizardo, Omar. 2004. "The Cognitive Origins of Bourdieu's *Habitus*." *Journal for the Theory of Social Behavior* 34 (4): 375–401.

Lizardo, Omar, Robert Mowry, Brandon Sepulvado, Dustin S. Stoltz, Marshall A. Taylor, Justin Van Ness, and Michael Wood. 2016. "What Are Dual Process Models? Implications for Cultural Analysis in Sociology." *Sociological Theory* 34 (4): 287–310.

Macey, David. 2000. *Frantz Fanon: A Biography*. New York: Picador.

Marcus, George. 1998. *Ethnography through Thick and Thin*. Princeton, NJ: Princeton University Press.

Marcuse, Herbert. 1955. *Eros and Civilization*. Boston: Beacon.

Marx, Karl. (1845) 1978. *The Holy Family: A Critique of Critical Reason*. In *The Marx-Engels Reader*, edited by Robert Tucker, 133–35. New York: Norton.

Marx, Karl. (1845) 1978. "Theses on Feuerbach." In *The Marx-Engels Reader*, edited by Robert Tucker, 143–5. New York: Norton.

Marx, Karl. (1847) 1963. *The Poverty of Philosophy*. New York: International Publishers.

Marx, Karl. (1850) 1964. *Class Struggles in France, 1848–1850*. New York: International Publishers.

Marx, Karl. (1852) 1978. *The Eighteenth Brumaire of Louis Bonaparte*. In *The Marx-Engels Reader*, edited by Robert Tucker, 594–617. New York: Norton.

Marx, Karl. (1859) 1978. "Preface to *A Contribution to the Critique of Political Economy*." In *The Marx-Engels Reader*, edited by Robert Tucker, 3–6. New York: Norton.

Marx, Karl, and Friedrich Engels. (1845–46) 1978. *The German Ideology*. In *The Marx-Engels Reader*, edited by Robert Tucker, 146–200. New York: Norton.

Marx, Karl, and Friedrich Engels. (1848) 1978. *The Manifesto of the Communist Party*. In *The Marx-Engels Reader*, edited by Robert Tucker, 469–511. New York: Norton.

Mason, Sarah. 2018. "Chasing the Pink." *Logic Magazine* 6: 17–32.

Medvetz, Thomas. 2012. *Think Tanks in America*. Chicago: University of Chicago Press.

Merton, Robert. (1942) 1973. "The Normative Structure of Science." In *The Sociology of Science*, 267–78. Chicago: University of Chicago Press.

Mills, Charles Wright. 1948. *New Men of Power: America's Labor Leaders*. New York: Harcourt.

Mills, Charles Wright. 1951. *White Collar: The American Middle Classes*. New York: Oxford University Press.

Mills, Charles Wright. 1956. *The Power Elite*. New York: Oxford University Press.

Mills, Charles Wright. 1958. *The Causes of World War Three*. New York: Ballantine.

Mills, Charles Wright. 1959. *The Sociological Imagination*. New York: Oxford University Press.

Mills, Charles Wright. 1960. *Listen, Yankee*. New York: Ballantine.

Moi, Toril. 1994. *Simone de Beauvoir: The Making of an Intellectual Woman*. Cambridge: Blackwell.

Moi, Toril. 1999. "Appropriating Bourdieu: Feminist Theory and Pierre Bourdieu's Sociology of Culture." In *What Is a Woman? and Other Essays*, 264–99. Oxford: Oxford University Press.

Moi, Toril. 2002. "While We Wait: The English Translation of *The Second Sex*." *Signs* 27 (4): 1005–35.

Newman, Katherine. 2002. "No Shame: The View from the Left Bank." *American Journal of Sociology* 107 (6): 1576–98.

Parsons, Talcott. 1937. *The Structure of Social Action*. New York: McGraw-Hill.

Parsons, Talcott. 1951. *The Social System*. New York: Free Press.

Parsons, Talcott. 1967. *Sociological Theory and Modern Society*. New York: Free Press.

Poulantzas, Nicos. 1973. *Political Power and Social Classes*. London: New Left.

Przeworski, Adam. 1985. *Capitalism and Social Democracy*. Cambridge: Cambridge University Press.

Przeworski, Adam, and John Sprague. 1986. *Paper Stones: A History of Electoral Socialism*. Chicago: University of Chicago Press.

Reich, Adam. 2010. *Hidden Truth: Young Men Navigating Lives In and Out of Juvenile Prison*. Berkeley: University of California Press.

Riley, Dylan. 2017. "Bourdieu's Class Theory." *Catalyst* 1 (2). https://catalyst-journal.com/vol1/no2/bourdieu-class-theory-riley.

Robbins, Derek. 1991. *The Work of Pierre Bourdieu*. Boulder, CO: Westview.

Rubin, Gayle. 1975. "The Traffic in Women: Notes on the 'Political Economy' of Sex." In *Toward an Anthropology of Women*, edited by Rayna Reiter, 157–210. New York: Monthly Review.

Sallaz, Jeffrey. 2002. "The House Rules: Autonomy and Interests among Contemporary Casino Croupiers." *Work and Occupations* 29 (4): 394–427.

Sallaz, Jeffrey. 2009. *The Labor of Luck: Casino Capitalism in the United States and South Africa*. Berkeley: University of California Press.

Sallaz, Jeffrey, and Jane Zavisca. 2007. "Bourdieu in American Sociology, 1980–2004." *Annual Review of Sociology* 33: 21–41.

Sartre, Jean-Paul. (1946) 1948. *Anti-Semite and Jew*. New York: Schocken.

Schwarzer, Alice. 1984. *Simone de Beauvoir Today: Conversations, 1972–1982*. London: Hogarth.

Sharone, Ofer. 2004. "Engineering Overwork: Bell-Curve Management at a High-Tech Firm." In *Fighting for Time: Shifting Boundaries of Work and Social Life*, edited by Cynthia Fuchs Epstein and Arne L. Kalleberg, 191–208. New York: Russell Sage Foundation.

Sharone, Ofer. 2014. *Flawed System/Flawed Self*. Chicago: University of Chicago Press.

Sherman, Rachel. 2007. *Class Acts: Service and Inequality in Luxury Hotels*. Berkeley: University of California Press.

Silverstein, Paul. 2004. "Of Rooting and Uprooting: Kabyle Habitus, Domesticity and Structural Nostalgia." *Ethnography* 5 (4): 553–78.

Swartz, David. 1997. *Culture and Power: The Sociology of Pierre Bourdieu*. Chicago: University of Chicago Press.

Swartz, David. 2013. *Symbolic Power, Politics and Intellectuals*. Chicago: University of Chicago Press.

Szelenyi, Ivan. 1982. "The Intelligentsia in the Class Structure of State-Socialist Societies." In *Marxist Inquiries: Studies of Labor, Class and States*, edited by Michael Burawoy and Theda Skocpol, 287–326. Supplement to *American Journal of Sociology* 88.

Thompson, Edward P. 1963. *The Making of the English Working Class*. London: Victor Gollancz.

Vaisey, Stephen. 2009. "Motivation and Justification: A Dual-Process Model of Culture in Action." *American Journal of Sociology* 114 (6): 1675–1715.

van Velsen, Jaap. 1960. "Labour Migration as a Positive Factor in the Continuity of Tonga Tribal Society." *Economic Development and Cultural Change* 8: 265–78.

van Velsen, Jaap. 1964. *The Politics of Kinship*. Manchester: Manchester University Press for the Rhodes-Livingstone Institute.

van Velsen, Jaap. 1967. "The Extended Case Method and Situational Analysis." In *The Craft of Urban Anthropology*, edited by A. L. Epstein, 29–53. London: Tavistock.

Wacquant, Loïc. 2002. "Scrutinizing the Street: Poverty, Morality, and the Pitfalls of Urban Ethnography." *American Journal of Sociology* 107 (6): 1468–1532.

Wacquant, Loïc. 2004. *Body and Soul: Notebooks of an Apprentice Boxer*. New York: Oxford University Press.

Weber, Max. 1970. *The Protestant Ethic and the Spirit of Capitalism*. London: Allen and Unwin.

Willis, Paul. 1977. *Learning to Labour: How Working Class Kids Get Working Class Jobs*. Westmead: Saxon House.

Woolf, Virginia. 1927. *To the Lighthouse*. London: Hogarth.

Wright, Erik Olin. 1978. "Intellectuals and the Class Structure of Capitalist Society." In *Between Labor and Capital*, edited by Pat Walker, 191–212. Montreal: Black Rose.

University of Algiers, 79
Uprooting, The (Bourdieu and Sayad), 77, 82–83, 89, 186

value consensus, 15–16, 21, 30–31
van Velsen, Jaap, 5–6
voluntaristic theory of action, 21

Wacquant, Loïc, 7–9, 20
war of movement, 67, 88, 107, 205n9
war of position, 67–68, 88, 107–8, 170, 205n9
Weber, Max, 10, 21–22, 43, 68, 87, 134, 136, 191, 196
Weight of the World, The (Bourdieu), 9, 16, 26, 30, 139, 144, 172–90, 194–95

White Collar (Mills), 137, 139–40, 142
Willis, Paul, 4, 98–99
women. *See* Beauvoir, Simone de; feminism; gender
Woolf, Virginia, 19, 115–16, 122
working class, 34–35, 49–50, 57, 98–99, 137–41, 149–51
Wretched of the Earth, The (Fanon), 13, 77, 80–81, 128, 146
Wright, Erik, 12, 196, 202n2

Young Hegelians, 36–37, 39

Zambia, 162
Zola, Émile, 140–41